Desktop Conferencing

Desktop Conferencing

A complete guide to its applications and technology

Dr Barry K. Aldred

McGRAW-HILL BOOK COMPANY

London · New York · St Louis · San Francisco · Auckland · Bogotá · Caracas · Lisbon · Madrid · Mexico · Milan · Montreal · New Delhi · Panama · Paris · San Juan · São Paulo · Singapore · Sydney · Tokyo · Toronto

Published by

McGRAW-HILL BOOK COMPANY EUROPE
Shoppenhangers Road, Maidenhead, Berkshire, SL6 2QL, England
Telephone 01628 23432
Facsimile 01628 770224

British Library Cataloguing in Publication Data

Aldred, B. K.
Desktop Conferencing: Guide to Its Applications and Technology.
– (IBM McGraw-Hill Series)
I. Title II. Series
004.6

ISBN 0-07-707642-7

Library of Congress Cataloging-in-publication Data

Aldred, Barry K. (Barry Keith)
Desktop conferencing: a guide to its applications and technology/Barry K. Aldred.
p. cm.
Includes bibliographical references and index.
ISBN 0-07-707642-7 (pbk.)
1. Computer conferencing. 2. Business communication–Interactive multimedia. I. Title.
HF5734.7.A43
651.7–dc20 95–35252 CIP

McGraw-Hill
A Division of The ***McGraw-Hill*** *Companies*

1234 CUP 9876

Typeset and printed and bound in Great Britain at the University Press, Cambridge.
Printed on permanent paper in compliance with ISO Standard 9706.

Contents

About this book

Desktop conferencing is a rapidly emerging technology that will transform the desktop computer into the primary business tool for spontaneous personal communication. Recent developments in networking, multi-media and collaborative computing have brought costs and usability within reach of a mass market. Major investments are being made by the computer and telecommunications industries to realise its potential. New generations of application software and value-added network services are under development.

This book gives the essential overview to the desktop conferencing technologies and standards. It describes in detail the ITU-T H.320 and T.120 recommendations and compares and contrasts this with the IBM real-time multimedia communications architecture. It is aimed at the computing professional who wishes to stay abreast of recent developments, the programmer writing multimedia collaborative applications, and the information technology manager considering the introduction of desktop conferencing.

Acknowledgements

The author wishes to thank his colleagues at IBM United Kingdom Laboratories for the discussions and ideas which form the substance of this book. In particular, the comradeship, help and support given by Gordon Bonsall, Howard Lambert, and Dave Mitchell have made the book possible and the task of writing it bearable.

ITU-T Recommendations

Disclaimer

The views expressed in this book are those of the author alone and do not represent those of any company or organization.

Trademarks

Apple Macintosh
AT&T: Global Business Video Services
AT&T: Personal Conferencing Services
AT&T: Vistium
AT&T: WorldWorx
CoLAB
DataBeam
Ethernet: EtherTalk
FarSite
Fujitsi: DTC
Future Labs : TalkShow
HP
IBM
IBM/Motorola/Apple: Power PC RISC
IBM: Person-to-Person
InSoft: Communique!
Intel: 286, 386, 486, Pentium; Indeo
Intel: ProShare
Lakes: API, SDI, RLI
LapD
LocalTalk
Lotus Notes
Microsoft
MovieTalk
MPC Multimedia PC Marketing Council
Northern Telecom: Visit
Novell
Nuts: Connect 918
Picture Tel: PCS 100
QuickTime
Sun MicroSystems
TeamFocus/EMS (IBM & University of Arizona)
TokenTalk
VideoServer
Vistium
Xerox
Xerox Parc

Trademarks

CHAPTER 1

An introduction to desktop conferencing

1.1 Origins

Desktop conferencing at its most basic level provides the ability to participate in a meeting with one or more people at remote locations, without leaving the normal office environment. Participation includes both seeing and hearing the other parties to the conference, as well as being seen and heard. At the time of writing desktop conferencing is not in widespread use, in fact on the contrary, examples of its use are rare. The importance of desktop conferencing lies in its potential, both in benefits to future users and in services and product sales for the telecommunications and computer industries. Its supporters argue that it is one of the few pervasive applications yet to be developed and is set to join word processing, spreadsheets, and data bases as essential tools of business and commerce.

Tools for spontaneous communication between people separated by distance are remarkably few. Only the telephone is in common use and readily available. However, this instrument is somewhat restricted in its capabilities, although familiarity with its functions blinds us to its deficiencies. Usually the telephone is limited to audio conversations; thus users cannot normally see each other or exchange information such as documents, data, pictures and files. It is possible to send such information over telephone lines but the ordinary telephone instrument can neither send nor receive them. In contrast, the specialized machines that can transmit and receive such data do not normally allow audio conversations at the same time. The importance of a video exchange between telephone users—to have the ability to see as well as hear the remote party—has been recognized for a long time. Many products aimed at the mass market have appeared over the years to add this capability, but have not proved popular. The reasons are not well understood but the explanations put forward include: price, picture quality and a desire for privacy. Another contributor to failure must be that two video phones are needed to make a video call; thus there is a critical market penetration that needs to be reached in order that new purchasers of video phones have a good chance of finding others they need to call who are suitably equipped.

The telephone has many other limitations as a communication tool. Although it is very easy to call one other party, it is difficult if not sometimes impossible to call two or more such parties. Not only is the capability not available for most phone users—although this is rapidly changing with the re-equipment of public networks—but it also involves complicated keying sequences with little or no feedback available to the user. Additionally, there is limited flexibility in allocating the cost of a call so that, generally, the person who makes the call pays for the call. When a multi-party conference call is a prospect, a choice of algorithms for allocating the cost would seem to be desirable. Operational difficulties exist when a multi-party call is in progress because it is very difficult to control the interactions between the people, or even, in some cases, to understand them. In a physical meeting of a group of people, a combination of body language and formal procedural control exists, visible to all. In a telephone conference call even the identity of who is speaking may not be obvious; it is very difficult to signal an intention to speak; and when many people speak at the same time most of the speech is lost. Only in the simple, person-to-person call is there a natural exchange that resembles the human interaction of those same people meeting face to face.

Although it is easy to criticize the telephone as a substitute for a conventional meeting, it is also necessary to appreciate the achievements of the telephone companies. In particular, the ease of connection is striking; it is rapidly becoming true that any telephone in the world can be connected to any other, with a user requiring only knowledge of the destination telephone number. Quite remarkably, this works in a transparent way which is both independent of the nature of the telephones involved and of the networks which connect them. To emphasize this point, the telephones can be pulse dial or tone dial, can be connected to the analogue public switched telephone network or the integrated services digital network, can use the audio coding system common in Europe or the different one used in North America, can have answering machines attached or not, and can be connected to sophisticated private exchanges or can be attached to the local exchange. The magnitude of this achievement, which fails to amaze us only because it is now so pervasive, can be more appreciated through contrast with the parallel world of the computer industry. Here almost the converse is true; even when everything is known about a remote computer and the networks it is attached to, establishing useful connection is frequently difficult or impossible and is a province reserved for the computer expert.

The move towards desktop conferencing has two distinct origins. The first is a combination of factors, one of which has been mentioned already, namely that the telephone—the tool in use today—is very limited in function and usability. Added to this is the indication that the desktop computer appears to offer the rudiments of an alternative solution. This is becoming increasingly true as desktop computers become linked together for other, more easily justified, business solutions and as they expand their role from word data processing devices to multi-media communications devices, with the capability to handle audio and video.

The second origin is video conferencing. This is a technology that arose out of a desire to avoid the time and expense of travel and was once justified only at a senior executive level. Developments in video compression and high bandwidth communications in the 1980s meant that it became possible for executives in remote locations to interact without physically meeting. The technology was expensive but so were the conventional alternatives; and the users were discriminating and required high standards. The solution was the deployment of video conferencing suites in large international companies, where both high quality pictures and sound of their remote counterparts were available. Typically, each suite was set up as an executive boardroom with fine furniture and a large display showed the corresponding connected suites. The sound system was equally sophisticated so that simultaneous conversation between any of the participants, wherever located, was possible. The early systems did not support continuous motion for the video stream and freeze frames were used instead; later developments in video compression technology removed this restriction. In all cases facilities were available to exchange documents, either by scanning them from one location and printing at another, or by scanning them and displaying the scanned image on the display. Of particular note was that the control of the equipment during the conference was normally undertaken by the participants themselves and, therefore, usability was important, although the establishment of the conference call could be left to the technical experts.

Over time, the advancement of technology has reduced the cost of video conferencing equipment although it still remains a premium product. Also others, below the rank of senior executive, now wish to exploit the same benefits but the boardroom approach cannot be justified for most of these applications and ever lower-cost solutions are required. In the early 1990s the video conferencing cart appeared—a trolley containing conferencing equipment which could be moved from meeting room to meeting room and used wherever the service was required. The purpose-built suite still remains for the senior executive but that market is no longer dominant. The next development is dispense with the trolley and allow existing equipment on the office desktop to provide the service.

Thus desktop conferencing is the convergence of two trends, an offshoot of the continuing evolution of the telephone merging with the cost reduction in video conferencing equipment. In order to succeed, the technology needs to be affordable as a mass market offering and to fulfil a genuine market need. Affordability is a question of time alone, the market need is more debatable but relies upon the ever growing demand for more immediate exchange of increasingly varied information.

1.2 The nature of desktop conferencing

Desktop conferencing is not to be regarded as a substitute for the precursor technologies that have led to its conception. The traditional telephone will continue to exist and will evolve to suit its major applications; likewise the executive conferencing suite, with its emphasis on high quality video and sound and its attempt to simulate a traditional meeting around a conference table, will also continue. Desktop conferencing is destined to become a unique form of exchange to be judged on the benefits and the costs it brings to its own area of application, and not against the standards set by the telephone and the video conferencing suite. The potential of desktop conferencing lies in its promise to deliver a multi-media experience to its participants: an expansion of the audio telephone call to one enriched with data from the desktop computer, and possibly further enhanced with video.

The benefits of data exchange complementing voice interactions are well accepted. The data requirements are twofold. Data exchange should be spontaneous, no pre-planning should be necessary, so that users can exchange information as needs arise. This is in contrast to conventional phone calls involving data, that oblige the parties to ensure that all documents have been sent ahead. The second requirement is that all of the data on the workstation should be available in the desktop conference; this is a broad requirement and includes not just files of various types, but data entered via the keyboard or graphics input device and, indeed, all the application information displayed to a user. This pervasive data requirement is not easily satisfied because it must be assumed that the applications present on one workstation are not present on another. Given the plurality of workstation operating systems, it cannot even be assumed that the parties to a call use the same operating system.

There are differing views on the value of video in a desktop conference, that is the ability of the parties to see each other. While the precursor video conferencing products would seem to mandate video, this is not a simple matter. A video capability brings a need for cameras and, since video data is voluminous, a requirement for additional workstation hardware to compress and then decompress the image. Moreover workstations designed to display graphics cannot display video with acceptable performance without additional video windowing hardware. The consequence is that a video capability brings with it considerable additional cost, unlike audio or data support where the hardware costs are small or non-existent. Furthermore, the video picture requires a window on the display and screen real estate is in short supply for most users. The conventional wisdom on video is as follows: a video window capability in a desktop conferencing product is essential; products without video, and not capable of being upgraded, look dull and dated. However, the extra cost of video means that it must be a feature and not intrinsic. Observations on casual desktop conferencing participants have revealed that the video window is used extensively at the beginning of a call, as the participants introduce themselves to each other; this is also true at the end of the call when the participants leave. The use of video is especially pronounced in those cases where the parties have never previously met. However, in calls where the discussion centres on interacting with data displayed in windows, the video assumes much less importance during the call, and if screen space is insufficient, then the video window becomes covered by data windows. Some user trials have even concluded that video calls last longer on average than just audio/data calls and produce less of value.

Other studies have investigated varying qualities of video and have unearthed a variety of results. Unsurprisingly, it has been shown that video pictures that are not lip-synchronized with the relevant voice are found to be very disconcerting to users. Very low quality video is not appreciated and users have indicated that they prefer occasional high quality still images to low quality moving pictures. Very high quality video, however, brings its own problems. Where the video quality was so high that facial blemishes and make-up could be accurately distinguished and evaluated, there was an observable reluctance to use video without careful preparation. This has been likened to the perceptions and use of fax—the general low quality of fax has led to an attitude that anything can be faxed to anybody without poor quality reflecting on the sender. Thus, users are willing to fax a rough sketch, a crumpled piece of paper, or a scribbled note; they are certainly willing to fax material of a much lower quality than they would be prepared to mail above their signature. A similar effect seems to be observable with video and too high a quality may detract from the frequent casual use that is required of the technology.

The most important uses of video, however, may not be to show the participants in the conference. The video camera can be used to display pictures of the subject of the discussion; for example, a design meeting may use the camera to display different aspects of the object being designed, or video may be used to review television commercials in an advertising campaign. Such alternative uses for a video capability bring their own unique requirements, for example detachability, field of view and light sensitivity requirements for cameras, or the ability to substitute a video recorder for the camera and enable it to be remotely controlled within the conference.

Expectations for desktop conferencing are, however, set by the price/performance of what customers view as apparently similar, or at least related, products. For example, there is an audio quality standard set by the telephone that is familiar to everybody. Judged by the standards of a television, telephone audio is not very good; judged by the more demanding standards of a hi-fi system, telephone audio quality is very bad. Given the very low consumer price of telephone handsets and the trivial cost of short local phone calls, the general public expectation is that this audio quality is the minimum that should be available. It would be difficult to market a desktop conferencing system that failed to achieve even this low audio quality, irrespective of price. However, as will be discussed later, the audio quality of the telephone network can be very difficult to achieve over conventional data networks.

Another domestic technology that sets standards is the ordinary television, again freely available to most consumers at an affordable price. Televisions display a colour picture; moreover the picture retains its quality independent of the nature of the programme being displayed, thus in a fast action game the picture does not become jerky or blurry. This seems an almost foolish observation and yet there are technologies which result in products—vastly more expensive than televisions—that offer a picture quality worse than the average television, a picture quality which, moreover, degrades as the degree of movement in the picture increases. Considerable customer resistance can be expected.

Another challenge faced by desktop conferencing relates to connectivity and ubiquity. The typical business desktop includes, among other things, a personal workstation and a telephone. The computer is generally attached to a local area network (LAN) and frequently onwards to a wide area network (WAN). On the other hand, the telephone is attached to the private telephone network and then onwards to the public switched telephone network (PSTN). In principle, either of these networks can be expanded in capability to meet the requirements of desktop conferencing. Certainly from the user's perspective, a single wire to the desktop would be more attractive than installing and maintaining separate voice and data networks. Previously there has been little requirement seriously to contemplate the convergence of these networks at a desktop level. Even where public voice networks have been used for data, they have tended to be used where there was no associated audio traffic, for example for messaging or for file transfer. There are other examples where there is a data and associated audio requirement but these have been handled by coarse synchronization of activities on the two networks. Such an example is the call centre, where operators may be taking orders from customers. The state of the art is to determine the identity of the caller from the caller's telephone number, itself supplied automatically by the telephone network and obtained before the telephone call is answered. This identity is passed by the telephone switch to the computer system which then uses it to retrieve the caller's file from the computer data base, displaying the contents on the operator's console. The operator sees the information and uses it to give a personalized response when answering the call. All this can be performed so quickly that the originator of the telephone call experiences no unusual delay.

This example shows audio and data integration at the desktop but is characterized by the audio and data networks remaining independent, with the synchronization between their traffic being infrequent and relatively coarse. The requirements of desktop conferencing are often for a much more continuous form of synchronization with much tighter tolerances. An example will highlight the differences. In a conversation with a remote party it may be necessary to point to items on a displayed list and to make comments, for example: 'Buy this share, but sell that one'. This degree of data and audio synchronization is only likely to be achieved if the audio and data travel over the same network in a carefully controlled manner. It is this unacceptability of independent voice and data networks that has brought the computer industry and the telephone companies into direct conflict over control of connectivity to the desktop.

1.3 Interaction styles

Desktop conferencing was described earlier in this chapter as a unique form of exchange. Perhaps it is better regarded as a spectrum of forms of exchange, for there are many different ways in which people may wish to collaborate remotely. In tracing the antecedents of desktop conferencing previously, the telephone call and the video conference were cited as key contributors. Expressed differently, the antecedents can be described as the casual interaction between two or more people, and the formal, highly structured meeting. However, there are many ways in which people may wish to interact and these are just two familiar examples.

The telephone call is a common but arbitrary style of interaction, governed by a set of rules which are well understood. For example, the conventional rules of telephony insist that a telephone call must have at least two participants and should the number drop below this, the call is terminated. As stated earlier, the person making the call normally pays the cost. The parties to a call have the ability to add further members to a call—there is no concept of being able to break into an existing call. Similarly there is no concept of being able to split a multi-party call into two or more smaller calls. All members of a call can speak whenever they like. There are many more such aspects of a phone call which we take for granted. The rules, or policies, have arisen partly through customer requirements and partly through technological limitations as the telephone system has evolved. They have proved their value for casual interaction, especially between two parties, but there is nothing to suggest that they represent the most appropriate set of policies for other kinds of human interaction.

Video conferencing has developed to support the formal meeting. With these systems participants are expected to be grouped around the equipment; each group of participants has a leader who normally controls the equipment. This controlling person can decide who speaks, what documents are transmitted, and when the group joins and leaves the conference. Again, this set of procedures has proved its value and mirrors, to some extent, the formal chaired meeting but there is nothing to suggest that this is a preferred set of rules for a much broader range of interactions. Desktop conferencing, being a multi-media exchange between multiple participants each with their own equipment, need not follow the rules established for other technologies, but can develop others more suited to the tasks at hand. It can be expected that there will be many sets of policies needed, each slanted towards a different style of interaction. The need for originality may be illustrated by the requirements of data; for example, consider a desktop conference where there is audio and data exchange between the participants. The data exchange takes the form of a shared whiteboard; like its conventional counterpart, all participants can draw on a common area and the results are visible to all. Imagine that the conference has been under way for some time and then an additional party is added in. For the audio interaction, the normal rules of telephony are applied, that is any new party can hear the other parties from the moment they join the call. Since the new member will be unlikely to understand all that is said, it is likely that the other members will be asked to explain where they have got to in the conference and why they have asked the new party to contribute. Note that, unsurprisingly, there is no automatic transmission of all the previous audio interactions to the new member. However, for the shared drawing area, a different policy is applied. From the instant of joining it would seem helpful to show the new party the result of all the previous whiteboard operations. In this example it can be seen that data and audio have been treated differently, even though it may have been easier to treat them the same. When other uses of desktop conferencing technologies are considered, such as a remote teacher instructing a scattered class of students, it will be seen that other policies are more appropriate than those developed for casual interactions or structured meetings.

1.4 Application content

Desktop conferencing is not an easily isolated application but merges into many other familiar applications. For example, desktop conferencing is closely identified with spontaneous and immediate interactions with other people, as typified by the telephone call. However, it is frequently the case that the called party is not present at the time of calling and then the desktop conferencing application merges into mail, messaging and transaction processing applications, designed for the situations when communicating parties are not simultaneously available. The primary tools of desktop conferencing, such as the shared whiteboard briefly mentioned earlier, are expected to be used during the conference; however, such tools also need to be designed so they can be used in advance of the conference in order to prepare material. In this situation, the whiteboard is being used in a standalone, unshared situation, and is hard to distinguish from a conventional graphics editor. Finally, there are bespoke software systems designed for specific distributed interactions; for example the salesperson in the field entering orders and querying the stock situation or the current discounts and prices; or the insurance agent getting a complex quotation from the expert at head office. The line between the general purpose tools of desktop conferencing and the custom features of a tailored system is impossible to draw.

Of particular interest are the nature and sources of desktop conferencing applications. A number of functions have become standard, in the sense that versions of the same applications exist in most commercial products. They have not yet become standard if this is defined as meaning that different implementations can inter-operate. Such standard features are file transfer, shared whiteboard, message exchange facility or chat line, audio and video capabilities, and the ability to see copies of application windows on one machine remotely on another. Becoming more common are various forms of remote control, where a user on one machine can remotely operate an application elsewhere. There is great value in tools that enable existing, traditional, installed applications to be used in a collaborative way.

Ultimately the development of desktop conferencing applications will become divorced from the provision of the desktop conferencing environment, in a similar manner to the way in which conventional application development is distinct from operating system development. The existing, successful application software developers will extend their current products, where appropriate, to make them collaborative and thereby exploit their customer base. An example of such development would be a cooperative word processor which enabled multiple users to edit a single document at the time; such a tool could be useful for lawyers at different companies agreeing the terms of a contract. In contrast, new applications can be envisaged which are not natural evolutions of existing products. Perhaps an example of this type of application would be software for remote shopping which enables the user to browse through a catalogue; see a particular product in their chosen colour, size and style, possibly even modelled to a stored image of themselves; allows a discussion with a salesperson on some aspect of product; and finally takes the order.

The development of collaborative applications is difficult and even more complex than the development of distributed applications. The configurations to be supported are diverse, with each participant likely to be operating in a different hardware and software environment. This complexity is a direct consequence of desktop conferencing being just one of the many uses of a personal workstation, and probably not the dominant use. This means that the hardware, operating system, associated applications and, possibly, even the connectivity options will have been chosen for reasons unique to that user. Moreover, the spontaneous use of desktop conferencing means that it must accommodate people joining and leaving calls dynamically; there is no constant environment that can be guaranteed to last during the call. Further factors include the variety and complexity of the network options and the requirement to accommodate with devices as such as telephones and video telephones. Users come with an expectation that the desktop conferencing functions should exist as a natural extension of their own environment, well integrated into the operating systems and applications that they have uniquely selected.

Considerations such as these, coupled with the need for inter-operability between products, have focused attention on the need for common development tools, i.e. programming interfaces that hide the networking and systems complexity and enable the application developer to concentrate on the application aspects alone. Such an approach would, for example, take call set-up and tear-down out of the individual collaborative applications and either integrate it into the operating system or leave it as a standard shared utility. This partitioning also contributes to usability since the user is given a single consistent way of making calls, independent of the specific application function. Agreement on industry standards in this development area does not yet exist, although proprietary candidates have been proposed.

1.5 Inter-operability

An essential characteristic of desktop conferencing is the ability to inter-operate with a diverse and widespread population of other users. The telephone system presents the ideal, which is probably unattainable for this more complex technology. There are many aspects to inter-operability. The first is simply awareness of the other users and there has been no attempt to date to solve this problem. The situation is akin to that existing for fax machines; just as there is no generally available directory of fax machines ordered along the lines of the conventional phone book, likewise there is no equivalent index for the users of desktop conferencing equipment. The result has been the emergence of closed user groups, generally within companies or restricted to groups of cooperating companies. One reason for the reluctance to publish directories, is that lists of users are regarded as commercially valuable and would enable a rival supplier to mount a competitive sales campaign.

Another aspect of inter-operability is standards which, if followed, would enable one machine to communicate with another machine without both having been designed by the same supplier. There is a strong move towards standards and this has been driven primarily by the telephone companies through the ITU-T (formerly the CCITT). The telephone companies tend to regard desktop conferencing equipment as simply another device that can be connected to the telephone network and, in this light, see it as a something that should inter-operate, where possible, with existing end user telephone equipment. As an example, if an ordinary telephone makes a call to a desktop conferencing unit, then a normal audio telephone call should take place because this is the only common capability that exists. Similarly, if a call is made from a video phone, then the desktop conferencing unit should behave as a video phone. Only if a desktop conferencing unit is called by another desktop conferencing unit should the richer multi-media exchange of information take place. This philosophy has other implications. Traditionally in telephony, end user equipment is connected on a point-to-network basis, each user having a single connection to the telephone network. Multi-point operation is a service, which can be charged for, and is provided by the network. Thus a multi-party telephone call is provided through a device known as a multi-point control unit (MCU) within the telephony network. An MCU for desktop conferencing is a much more complex device than an MCU for ordinary audio calls, and requires an understanding of the detailed data formats and protocols being used. This approach has led to a movement to standardize desktop conferencing at a very detailed level, down to the subtleties, features and functions of all the component applications.

Such an approach is alien to the computing industry which is already familiar with distributed computing, remote data base access, transaction processing, electronic mail and messaging, and work group computing. Such uses are characterized by their diversity and volatility. In almost all examples, the networks that connect the participants together do not understand the significance of the data they carry, except insofar as is needed for delivery. Real control is at the end point, at the workstations and computers attached to the networks. Indeed, there has been a general decline in customer interest in networks which are controlled by a single central processor and a rapid growth in peer-to-peer networking where the physical and logical network changes dynamically. Another major difference in approach is that the point-to-network connection model does not generally apply; all possible connection models co-exist, from the simple point-to-network case, through the gateway approach, to the random connectivity approach where multiple links exist between apparently random points across the network. From this viewpoint, desktop conferencing is seen as just another networked application and its technical challenges are more associated with the demands of multi-media communications, than with standards for inter-working.

1.6 Usability

Perhaps the hardest requirements for desktop conferencing relate to ease of use. If the challenge is initially to persuade business users, and later a broader population, that desktop conferencing is the preferred means of remote real-time interaction with people, then it needs to be as easy to use as the telephone, at least for an equivalent function. For a simple audio call this is not difficult to achieve, since the workstation is comparatively richly endowed with a display, useful input devices, and much storage and processing power. For a multi-party call, the desktop conferencing system has the potential to make operation much easier, since status information can be displayed and prompts can be supplied. Thus on straight telephony the task is easy, but even here there are other considerations. As an example, the telephone in the office is not just a device for business telephone calls; it also doubles as an emergency device to summon help if the building is on fire. If the telephone were to be replaced by a computer, this aspect would be in question. If the computer needed both an electricity supply and its operating system fully initialized before contact could be made with the outside world, it would not be a viable replacement for the telephone.

Usability problems arise in desktop conferencing because of the enormous functional scope that is possible: starting with simple audio and video services; extending to audio, video and data; then all of these compounded by multi-party operation; and finally complicated by the option of simultaneous, multiple, concurrent calls. Some of the basic problems are evident in the traditional multi-point telephone call, such as the inability to know who is speaking, to signal an intention to speak, and generally to control the flow of events. With audio, video and data the problems are made much worse and the availability of the visual display does little to help. In fact, the display itself is frequently a source of further problems since it is unable to show all of the information and windows of interest are hidden behind other windows. The user not only has to follow the interactions, but may need to shuffle the displayed data at times in order to keep track. Many trials have been done on multi-point desktop conferencing for casual unstructured uses, and the results have been disappointing, with usability dropping alarmingly in proportion to the increase in the number of participants. There is much scope for invention needed in this area. More promising are bespoke systems suited to particular kinds of use, with functions and modes of operation optimized to the specific nature of the interaction—such as a casual conversation, a chaired meeting, a student class, and so on.

1.7 Use in the local area

The conventional view is that desktop conferencing is only of real benefit in the wide area. However, there is also a local area opportunity which can be most easily appreciated by first considering audio telephony. Few would suggest that a PBX (private branch exchange) is not required in a building because the distances are short and can easily be walked. Other examples illustrate the same point. Language laboratories are accepted as essential tools in education; they allow a teacher to intercept the interactions of a student with the teaching material and can monitor multiple students in turn, interrupt their work, and give individual attention where needed. The justification for the technology has nothing to do with travel avoidance and, indeed, the teaching usually takes place in a single room. Computers and local area networks would be an analogous facility, but where students are learning to use a computer program; a collaborative tool would allow the teacher to talk to the whole class, monitor individual students, and share results among class members. Clearly the call policies that would be needed in such a system would not be those provided in conventional telephony, but a different set of rules could govern the interactions among the students themselves, and between individual students and the teacher.

There are other examples involving local collaboration. Enhancement of the normal office telephone call to include the data on the workstation, optionally supplemented by video, may prove a more effective means of local communication than the audio-only standard. Similarly, an open audio capability between cooperating offices, again possibly supplemented by video, may enhance interactions between departments. An ability for a senior manager to broadcast important messages to employees; a help-desk facility for advice to employees on procedures, personnel issues, information technology, etc.—these are all examples of local collaboration that may be justifiable without a long-distance element being involved. The justification is aided by a desire to take advantage of any unused local area bandwidth.

Exploitation of the local area network characteristics facilitates some of these examples. A broadband capability enables both high volume data applications, and that subset of multimedia where buffering can be used to overcome unpredictable delivery. Thus video broadcast is easily accomplished in a local area network situation because the end-to-end delay is not significant, with the recipient generally being unaware of small delays between the video being started remotely and it being received—provided it is displayed smoothly once begun. This contrasts with person-to-person interactions where buffering delays are unacceptable because they inhibit the natural interactions necessary between people. The free nature of the transport enables establishment of the open office scenario, which might be difficult to justify over a wide area network where the connect time incurs real cost. The ready availability of multi-point communications enables group discussions, electronic brainstorming, and broadcast applications which are almost impossible over the wide area.

Other features of the local area that can sometimes be exploited are the existence of the parallel phone network and the ability to send out-band analogue data over the digital network. The parallel phone network enables the local switch to be used for the audio, and possibly even the video, while the data network is used for the related high volume, digital traffic. As long as the end user is not required independently to establish these dual connections, the service available meets many application requirements, with the major functional omission being an ability to synchronize information tightly across the two independent networks. The out-band analogue approach is closely related; this exploits a capability, for example on token ring local area networks, to send multiple analogue streams (e.g. of audio and video) across the physical data network, with the streams being selected by a tuner at the receiving station. In this way multiple audio and video streams can co-exist with the normal LAN traffic, and can be used to implement very high quality, lip-synchronized, audio video conferencing simultaneously with high bandwidth data interchange.

1.8 Cost benefits

The success of desktop conferencing will ultimately depend upon the customer benefits delivered for the system cost. Such costs vary widely, depending upon the functions available and the quality delivered. Moreover, costs will change through time and what is difficult to justify today may not be so next year. The most favourable view of falling costs is reached by considering the executive desktop conferencing suite as the precursor product, in which case costs have fallen by several orders of magnitude in the past 10 years. However, as was observed earlier, desktop conferencing is not an equivalent substitute for such systems. The most gloomy view of costs starts from the regular telephone and observes that the capital costs of the equipment involved is frequently between 100 and 500 times more expensive and is likely to remain so. Again, the functions available are not the same although they may be valid alternatives to the customer. If it is assumed that the desktop computer is already cost justified for some other reasons (an increasingly likely assumption), and if it is also assumed that this equipment is connected to some existing network that can be successfully used (a less likely assumption), then the costs involved are the delta costs to upgrade the workstation.

The unique software required is typically a few hundred pounds but this is likely to fall. If other previous workstation applications are used as indicators of what may happen, such as word processors, a likely outcome is that a basic capability will be supplied free with the operating system, with more elaborate implementations being available at a range of prices comparable with other medium function pervasive applications, such as spreadsheets, data bases, word processors and graphics editors.

The hardware costs vary much more widely. The data component, on the same assumptions as above, typically requires no extra cost. An audio capability is relatively inexpensive since sound boards have found a volume marketplace through the growth in computer games, and the only additional device required is a microphone/speaker handset or headset. Indeed, it is likely that the pervasive nature of sound boards will result in this function migrating to the planar and being available as standard. The video situation is very different. Video requires a camera on each workstation that is to transmit pictures and it is necessary that these cameras be small and unobtrusive. Given the lack of demand elsewhere, these devices are expensive, although the basic technology costs are low through cost reductions driven by the home video market. There are applications where each participant does not need to transmit pictures, for example, a system used for a daily briefing of company employees needs the briefing executive to transmit, all other participants need only receive.

Video transmission requires an analogue to digital converter and a compression board, or codec, to reduce the data transmission requirements. Similarly at the receiving end, a decompression board is required and an associated device to display the resultant image. The cost of these hardware components is decreasing rapidly, and the fridge size units of the late 1980s have become the single adapter cards of the mid-1990s. While this function is not likely to migrate to the planar over the next few years, a promising trend is the development of software decompression algorithms that use the main PC processor. This eliminates the costs associated with video receipt.

While the costs are relatively easy to determine and extrapolate, the same is not true of the benefits, which necessarily vary widely depending upon the application scenario. The most frequently quoted benefit is the elimination of travel—both the direct costs of the travel itself and the indirect costs associated with time spent travelling. There is a lot of evidence that executive video conferencing can replace some travel and the rapid growth in video conferencing when travel was avoided during the Gulf War in 1991 lends further support. Whether, in practice, people actually make less trips because of video conferencing, or simply intersperse richer interactions between those trips is not clear. There are many other attractions of travel that are not replaced by video conferencing and many discussions too important to be prejudiced by the deficiencies of the technology. A question that has been asked of the enthusiasts is: 'Would you play poker for high stakes over a conferencing system?' Desktop conferencing is much less likely than video conferencing to be a substitute for travel; the justification depends much more upon productivity benefits and improved decision making from its use, rather than any direct cost elimination.

1.9 Collaborative computing

Desktop conferencing is closely related to the area of study known as collaborative computing, CSCW (computer supported cooperative work) or groupware. This has attracted the attention of computer scientists, social scientists and developers over a number of years and there is a large body of accumulated knowledge. The most significant conferences have been the biennial meetings sponsored by the ACM which began in Austin in 1986 and there have been many others, for example the series of European CSCW conferences starting in 1992. References to these and others are given in the Bibliography.

Allied to the groupware computing activity is much other research into, for instance, high bandwidth communications (exploring such technologies as ATM (asynchronous transfer mode), isochronous Ethernet and Priority Token Ring); multimedia hardware (i.e. video and audio capture, and playback adapters), and associated software techniques (e.g. compression algorithms for voice, video and image, data encryption and user authentication).

Other topics also lie at the boundaries, such as the research being undertaken into active agents. Here there is a concept of launching surrogates into a computer network to carry out tasks on behalf of users. Such a request entrusted to an agent might be to find a particular item of information; the surrogate would then look for data bases that could contain such an item and attempt to retrieve it. Such surrogates may launch other agents that can keep in touch both with each other and with the originator. Although CSCW is primarily concerned with direct person-to-person interactions, such agents can provide indirect personal interactions that can extend the applicability of collaborative technology.

Active badge technology is an attempt to make the process through which electronic meetings happen more akin to the realities of human interaction. Thus, a badge worn by potential participants enables their whereabouts to be tracked electronically and ad hoc meetings between people can be achieved over a network. Communications can be routed to the nearest telephone or terminal; intrusive telephone calls can be reduced by sensing the presence of others in the vicinity, i.e it is apparent when someone is either alone and potentially available, or with someone and possibly busy.

Another area just on the edge of CSCW is virtual reality research where the objective is to create realistic or futuristic environments in which people can interact either with each other or with inventions. Virtual reality meetings have been staged where the participants assumed a personality and an appearance which is not their own; likewise such meetings have taken place in environments which are not real but imaginary. The same technology can be applied to simulated real interactions, where an electronic environment is substituted for the real physical meeting environment and the remote attendees.

Cooperative working is also a key area in social science research where investigations have addressed the related human issues, such as organizational change in large companies, and the increased focus on cooperation and collaboration between groups of people versus competition and conflict.

Although many of the CSCW issues are technical and these are discussed in later chapters in some detail, even at a product implementation level there are many complex human factors aspects of considerable importance. These include determining:

- who is in control. Who can do what and when can they do it? How is control established? What is needed to give up control?
- what is private and what is shared. How can you tell the difference? How do you change from one to another?
- how the actions of remote users are displayed and identified.

Evaluation of CSCW software is thus very difficult and subjective, partly because its success depends so much on the expectations and experiences of the users but also because the benefits are specific to the details of the tasks attempted.

Computer supported cooperative work takes many forms but can be broadly categorized in terms of the time and place of the interactions. The boundaries between these are not rigid and particular interactions may span categories. For instance, a telephone call intended to be between two people separated only in space, may become a message left on an answering machine and thus a transaction between two people separated both in time and space.

Computer research, and indeed products, exist for all the quadrants of the time/place matrix (see Fig. 1.1).

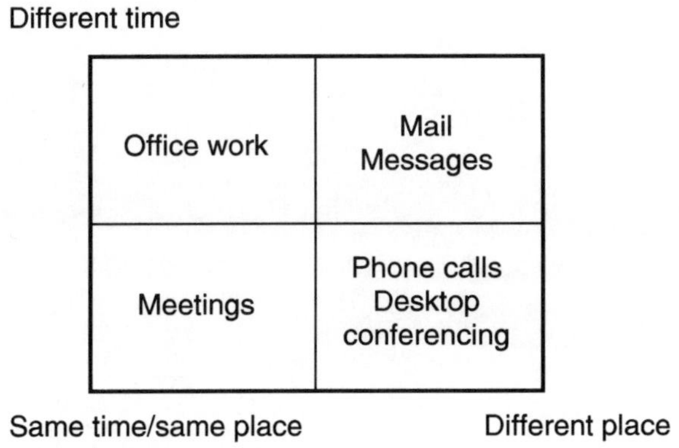

Figure 1.1 The different forms of collaboration

Office work dominates the 'same time-different place' quadrant. Some systems support notions of requests, promises, actions and responses; others attempt to capture the decision-making process through concepts such as issues, positions and arguments. The best known product providing information sharing facilities for use within this quadrant is Lotus Notes. This also provides extensive facilities for the mail or 'different place-different time' quadrant. Very many other mail products exist, as do asynchronous conferencing tools, and standards have been evolved to allow inter-operability. The products and technology are fully described elsewhere.

The computer assisted meeting has proved beneficial in some instances. The simplest arrangement is where the users sit round a table, each having access to a workstation allowing them anonymously to enter comments and suggestions. One of the earliest was CoLAB from Xerox Parc; one of the most successful commercially is TeamFocus/EMS from IBM and the University of Arizona. Results suggest that such systems result in shorter, more productive meetings, with greater participation and stimulated idea generation.

CHAPTER 2

Casual desktop conferencing

2.1 General requirements

Casual desktop conferencing needs to be ubiquitous and, therefore, available independent of hardware, operation system or communication link and protocol selection. The equipment supported should extend beyond desktop computers, even if these can reasonably be expected to be the dominant choice of users. Thus public network attached and video telephones are significant in the connectivity story, even though the function that can be offered to their users is necessarily limited. Portable equipment important in the requirements list extends to the more advanced devices such as notepads, laptops and personal data assistants (PDAs) that are becoming available. These mobile computers either communicate through modems or are linked through wireless connections. The primary design point remains the conventional desktop unit but it is necessary that software is also available that takes into account the fact that though some participants will have restricted capabilities, their users can nevertheless benefit from desktop conferencing technology.

Similar assessments apply to communications; while it is easy to design attractive systems that exploit high bandwidth networks, the reality remains that many users are likely only to have access to slow speed links. The pervasive implementations are likely to be those that take advantage of high bandwidth when available, but exploit the more traditional links when necessary. One of the challenges of desktop conferencing system design is that in general, each of the participants in any one conference is likely to have equipment which varies considerably in capability. It is probably unacceptable simply to subset the facilities in a call down to the lowest common dominator. An example illustrates the point. Imagine two users with sophisticated audio, video and data capability in a desktop conference; at some later time a colleague is required to join the call but, unfortunately, this valued contributor is travelling in his car and only has a mobile phone. After joining the conference for a few minutes, the third party leaves and the two original users continue. It does not seem appropriate for the conference to degrade to a low quality, audio-only exchange for all parties while the third party is present.

An almost essential prerequisite for the workstation users is that they are running a window-based operating system, since it allows the necessary functions to be provided in an easy to use manner. While the comments on subsetting the function for PDAs (personal digital assistant) might seem to apply here for those users with non-windowing-based operating systems as well, there are several arguments against this approach. Such operating systems represent a declining market, the equipment involved is liable to have other restrictions besides that imposed by its operating system, and the likely participants in the technology are biased towards those who would naturally be expected to have higher function workstations where windowing systems are more prevalent.

2.2 Software requirements

The functional requirements for general purpose, casual desktop conferencing can be grouped together under the following categories:

- user interface issues
- call set-up and tear-down
- basic facilities provided
- support for existing non-collaborative applications
- new collaborative applications

2.2.1 User interface issues

Interface style

There are two basic approaches to user interface design for a multi-platform product. One is to ensure that the interface is consistent across all the implementations, such that users can find an identical user interface wherever they find the product. The other approach is to ensure that the implementation of the product fits naturally into its local environment; if this results in the varying platform implementations having a different look and feel, this is regrettable but necessary. Both alternatives have been adopted by different products in the marketplace that offer multi-platform implementations. A consideration here is to recognize that desktop conferencing is probably not best regarded as an independent application, such as word processing and spreadsheet; it is much closer to being an enabling set of tools or capabilities that allows existing applications and data to be used collaboratively. The essential information does not primarily exist in unique desktop conferencing software, but in those other existing applications. Taking this approach, it is important that desktop conferencing support should be presented as a natural extension to the user's choice of environment and not as a possibly alien alternative. The choice may also be approached from the perspective of the individual user. If the potential users are expected in the main to be using their normal personal computing equipment, such as their office desktop systems, their notebooks and so on, then it can be assumed that they are familiar with those environments and will appreciate software support which is designed with each of those unique environments taken into account, albeit each may be different. If, however, the expected target user population is expected to repeatedly use other people's equipment with which they cannot be expected to be familiar, then a consistent desktop conferencing user interface is more likely to appeal.

Since desktop conferencing is intended to be used in conjunction with other applications software, an important interface design issue is that it does not itself monopolize or make excessive use of the screen area, since this is always a precious resource. Many consequences flow from this consideration, such as a minimal use of multiple windows to present supervisory and other information, a facility to simply remove all the windows associated with a call and easily restore them, care to ensure that windows can themselves be shrunk to only present the minimum basic function, and a general regard to economy in this area as a whole.

Some providers have taken desktop conferencing as a unique set of software that provides the necessary collaborative function in a fixed and generally non-extensible format, while others have viewed the requirement as a need for a general framework for application sharing. This latter approach is more attractive because it leaves the choice of individual application selection open. The collaborative framework is primarily concerned with call management, application installation and application launching; the individual applications supply their unique collaborative function but do not themselves get involved in call set-up or call tear-down. This split of function has usability advantages because the call management can be centralized and provided consistently by a call manager service, independent of the user's choice of collaborative applications.

Simplicity and migration

One measure of the suitability of the user interface is the ease with which a simple call can be made. The benchmark in this regard is the telephone and a straightforward audio call should be possible with little more interaction than is normal with a telephone handset. Similar simplicity tests apply to two-way audio and data calls; or audio, data and video calls. Special user interface provision should be expected for a repeat of a relatively recent call or a standard type of call to a stable list of other users. The creation of customized call types to suit the user can also simplify call set-up. Another ease of use test of commercial products is the extent to which they support fast access to a previously unknown party through direct entry of the telephone number, or its electronic equivalent. It is unhelpful if all contacts need to be enrolled as members of a desktop conferencing community, since this precludes easy interaction and is at variance with the phone system. Enrolment should only be absolutely necessary if they are to be provided with services for which they will subsequently be billed; enrolment may be sensible in other cases because it simplifies the process of making repeated calls to that party. The essence of usability is that those operations that the user wishes to perform most often, or which the user perceives as simple, should involve a minimum of user interactions with the system. Complexity should only be apparent when the situation itself appears complex to the users—perhaps when a multi-way call is being established, or when multiple concurrent calls exist.

Another user interface issue arises from the need for desktop conferencing to co-exist with conventional telephony since even the most enthusiastic user is unlikely to entirely abandon use of the telephone. The relevance of this is that a conventional telephone call may be established by either the local or remote party and, subsequently, it may be desired to extend this call into a desktop conferencing session in order to include information stored at one or both of the workstations. Such a possibility should be included in the design of the user interface in order to avoid a need for the existing telephone call to be dropped and a subsequent desktop conferencing call initiated.

The existing telephone system gives rise to another user interface requirement: a need to preserve its immediacy of access at all times. If the telephone and the desktop conferencing support are integrated into a single implementation in the office, it is highly desirable that internal or external audio calls to other telephones should still be able to be made without requiring the computer operating system software to be operational. This applies to PSTN (public switched telephone network) and PABX (private automatic branch exchange) calls. Some manufacturers have recognized the importance of this requirement, which also has important safety implications.

Customer migration raises other requirements. For those potential users who are unused to desktop computing, and yet who must be persuaded to migrate from the familiar telephone, it may be appropriate to offer that familiar metaphor as a screen image. Such a call set-up option becomes a helpful transitional aid. As the range of users extends from those simply accessible over the PSTN or ISDN (integrated services digital network) networks to those identified by complex network addresses, then this metaphor loses its value and call set-up from electronic phone books becomes a more suitable mechanism.

Synchronization and serialization

Desktop conferencing is frequently a multimedia experience for the user and it is to be expected that concurrent multiple information streams may need to be supported between the participants. The time-dependent and distributed nature of the interactions requires that they be synchronized together in time. Ideally, the requirements can be simply expressed as a need for all the participants in a call to see and hear the same things at the same time. This is generally difficult to achieve in practice because, not only are the users connected together in a variety of different ways with the links having different performance characteristics, but also the workstation equipment used by the various parties itself varies in capability. An acceptable, and more modest restatement of the objective is to require that, first, all users be given the same information in the same sequence, and second, any items of information that must be presented at the same time, because not to do so would change their significance, are indeed presented together.

The identical sequencing requirement is typically necessary in situations where each party in the call is independently maintaining data, yet all parties must produce the same result. An example is assigning a name to a shared document; if the last name received is the one actually used, then everybody in the call must get all the names supplied in the same sequence. Similarly, if a group of users are each independently storing a shared picture, and all the users are constantly changing it by adding and deleting items, then the result of these independent updates will only remain consistent if the updates are identically sequenced. This sequencing process between a group of users is known as data serialization.

The second information synchronization requirement arises because several of the streams of information may have time-critical dependencies. The lip-synchronization of audio and video is one such case, although failures here in maintaining synchronization give rise to annoyance rather than error. Synchronization is a much more widespread requirement than just audio with video, and other examples are more critical. Consider a surgeon discussing an image of a brain scan with a view to subsequent surgery; while moving a pointer over the picture, the surgeon may indicate which part should be removed during the operation. Clearly, the synchronization of the pointer with the voice is fundamental to this use of the desktop conferencing technology. Another synchronization example, albeit of a slightly different type, is seen when attempting to rubber-band a box by dragging an edge with a mouse. The brain expects the movement of the mouse by the hand to be reflected in the image seen by the eye. While a small degree of delay is tolerable, a significant delay in updating the image causes the user to move the mouse too far to achieve the desired result, making it very difficult to perform the operation. Desktop conferencing contributes to this problem by adding networking delays; if, in addition, the response times are different for picture updates and mouse movements, then usability is severely impaired.

2.2.2 Call set-up and tear-down

Set-up

The basic requirement is simply to be able to establish a call to another party. Typically the party to be called will be selected from a list of those available to be called, i.e. from a phone book. More usually, additional alternative ways of identifying the party required are also provided, such as a list of those most recently and/or those most frequently called, thereby giving fast access to important subsets of the phone book. Other phone book searches can be simplified if structure can be imposed on the information, for example through identifying groups of related entries, such as the members of a department. Allowing grouping to be hierarchically nested provides for departments within departments and so on. Simple access by matching name fields is not normally sufficient to allow easy identification of the desired entries and more advanced searches on related information need to be provided. Hence, the phone book needs to store ancillary information to aid identification and retrieval, for example fields with data such as department, manager, secretary, external phone number, home phone number, fax number, and details of last contact. Given the considerable variety of information that may be considered relevant, a useful general purpose system must allow this information to be tailored both by the installation and by individual users. The search criteria on fields needs to support partial matching, phonetic matching and support for search criteria involving combinations of conditions on multiple fields.

Besides the retrieval functions, products need to provide update functions such as the ability to add, delete or modify entries and their associated data. It is also particularly helpful if some degree of automatic data capture is available so that when a previously unknown party makes an incoming call, the local system captures the details of that party automatically and stores the essential data, such as name and electronic address. This then allows the called party to make a subsequent outgoing return call without the user having to acquire this information and update the phone book manually. In a large installation it is impractical for all of the phone book information to be regarded as personal to individual users, stored separately on their own workstations and updated by each user; on the other hand it is unacceptable for individual users to be able to update a centralized phone book and affect other users. Typically, the requirements can be satisfied by a phone book that is logically split—where local additions or modifications are personal to the individual user and stored locally, but where the common elements of the phone book are available to all, stored on a server and updated centrally. It is most often the case that the phone book data for desktop conferencing is a subset of an already existing data base and duplication of this information is unnecessary and undesirable. The customer requirement is frequently, therefore, that the desktop conferencing system be interfaced to already existing data bases which are centrally or otherwise independently maintained, with the option of user-owned supplements.

Call set-up should provide for two or more parties to the conference, although experience to date shows that the majority of casual interactions involve only two parties. Of the remaining calls, those involving more than four parties are relatively infrequent, in part no doubt due to the fact that existing desktop products do not handle multi-way calls very successfully. Other applications beyond casual desktop conferencing have very different requirements for call set-up; a good example is that of a teacher involved in remote education. In this case the total participants may be in double figures, and the call may be set-up very differently, with students arriving and departing at their convenience. Where more than two parties are to participate in a casual desktop conference, facilities are needed not only for all the parties to be identified at the outset, but also for extra parties to be added later.

Simple systems may only allow a single call to be in progress at any one time; more sophisticated systems allow several simultaneous calls. Multiple concurrent calls present unique difficulties, both in implementation and in ease of use. Typically, extra control facilities are needed to allow the user to manage multiple calls, such as the ability to bring a selected call into focus and hide the others, or an ability to tile windows so that all calls are visible but the various windows are arranged in such a way that the user can easily associate windows with calls.

Audio and video support requires special consideration in call set-up. While an operator can allow several data application windows belonging to different calls to be updated independently and viewed simultaneously, the same is not true for the audio being delivered by the remote parties. For audio, it is sensible to mix the streams being sent by the remote participants in a single call; however, it is not sensible to mix the streams being sent across calls. Likewise, audio input from the user can be sent to all the remote members of a single call, but normally it cannot sensibly be sent simultaneously to all the other members of all the calls in progress.

Video display hardware frequently imposes restrictions that affect call behaviour. Typically only one video source can be displayed to a user at any one time, therefore, within a call a user may have to select between remote parties. When multiple video calls are in progress, this selection process is additionally complicated. The outgoing video scenario is similar to that described for audio; however, there are more occasions when it is sensible for the output to be sent to all parties in all calls.

Call set-up is more complicated than just the selection of the parties to a call because, except in most basic systems, the applications and any other facilities relevant to the call must also be specified. This can be done through a simple default mechanism, i.e. where certain basic capabilities are always available without further user specification. Such basic facilities may include a simple text message exchange facility, or chat line, which has minimum hardware requirements and can, therefore, be almost guaranteed to be available. Defaults on call facilities can be associated with classes of call and, through such a mechanism, flexibility can be offered to the user without excessively complicating the user interface. Thus, the user can set up a 'casual' call and this might make available a chat line with audio, video and simple data exchange, while a 'conference' call might result in audio, video, remote presentation and minute-taking applications. Given the wide range of possibilities, such decisions on appropriate combinations of applications are best left to the users to specify directly. For the less common call requirements, provision must be made for selected applications to be launched into a call at the start, with additional applications able to be added later. In general it is helpful if any of the parties to the call have the capability to launch additional applications, and not just the person who set up the call.

Applications, beyond the basic audio and video capabilities, are the source of considerable complexity. In the simple case, all participants can be assumed to be running an identical copy of the conferencing software and, therefore, all of the applications are available to all parties. For example, if the 'chat' application is launched into the call, it is likely to be running on all the machines, available to all participants. However, even this cannot be guaranteed; for example, the facilities may not exist at every workstation to run even the basic application set. Supported devices may not be attached, or even more mundane resources such as memory or fonts may not be available, thus preventing the application from running. Therefore, in all but the most simple and highly constrained systems, provision must be made in the conferencing software for the call to include users in different states, with not all applications in the call being available at all workstations.

As desktop conferencing becomes more pervasive and the choice of desktop conferencing products and associated applications increases, the probability increases of different users having different collaborating applications in the call. Thus, a 'chat' application may be present at each workstation, but the implementations of the application are different and offer their users different facilities. This complication will be considered later, but adherence to standards provides the only way in which this situation can be tolerated.

The complexity introduced by independent applications goes further than just the selection, availability and inter-working difficulties. Restricting the discussion just to one of the workstations in a call, it is not sufficient to consider an instance of an application as being associated only with a single call. If that were the case, then an instance of an application would need to be started for a particular call and remain executing while the call is in progress, then disappearing either before or at call termination. While this is simple, understandable and therefore appealing, it does not reflect the reality of the requirements. For example, an application may need to be launched before the call itself commences, as illustrated by a lawyer preparing a report before making contact with a client. When the report is in an appropriate state, the call is initiated. It is likely that the lawyer does not want a new instance of the shared text editor created; instead the lawyer wants the existing running editor to be launched into call, with a corresponding instance of a text editor launched remotely. If the client happens to have a text editor already running, then neither of them wants that editor to become associated with the call.

Conversely, different behaviour is sometimes desirable. Video offers a good example; a workstation user may have a video application which is already in use, even though the user is not yet in a call. This local application may be being used to display a local image, a common procedure which allows users to check their own picture prior to subsequent transmission. Since most affordable video hardware is restricted to the display of a single image, it is necessary that the already-running video application is shared into any new call, with the video source being switched from the local camera to the remote camera. Thus, in this example, a remote user has caused an existing local application instance to become involved in a call.

The ability to set-up multiple concurrent calls can give rise to even more complex application considerations. It is possible, and sometimes desirable, for a single application instance to participate in multiple calls. The text example above can be used to illustrate this situation. The lawyer in the call with the client may wish to consult a colleague, unbeknown to the client. In order to do so the lawyer initiates a second call, this time to the colleague, and shares the existing instance of the text editor into that call as well. The lawyer then participates in two calls simultaneously, with the text application being shared between both calls. While it is relatively easy to identify such user scenarios, it is not a simple task to design a user interface that presents these capabilities in a way which is easily used and understood. An alternative solution to the lawyer/client/colleague example is to have a single, common document which is shared between two instances of the text application; each text application instance is in a single call and is independent of the other instance. While this is not necessarily an ideal solution, it does make what is going on easier to control; however, there are other examples where the shared application instance across calls is the only acceptable approach. The need for this can be seen in the above example if we make the assumption that the colleague needs to see the interactions between the lawyer and his client. This requires that in the lawyer/colleague call the document is automatically scrolled to the same place as it is in the lawyer/client call; moreover the colleague sees the cursor in use in the other call.

Tear-down

Call tear-down has important implications for applications. The end of a call does not necessarily mean the termination of all applications in that call. For some applications, such as the audio and video applications being used for live communication, this may be the case since there is no useful task to be performed outside the context of the call. For other applications the situation is different. Taking the example of the lawyer and the client used earlier, it is likely that the lawyer will wish to continue work on the document when the call has finished, just as work was started on the document before the call was placed. This means that facilities must be provided in desktop conferencing products that allow users to set call tear-down options for individual applications. In some cases the applications should be terminated, in other cases the user will need to be involved in the decision process. Relevant actions may be either to close the application and optionally save the data, or to allow the application to continue execution but in an unshared state.

In casual desktop conferencing, call tear-down may take one of two forms. Calls may be torn-down in such a way that all the parties leave at the same time; alternatively the call may gradually lose attendees until the call can no longer exist. Conventional telephony provides both of these modes, but restricts the availability of some of the tear-down functions to certain members of the call. The party that set up the call, and is therefore paying the cost, forces the termination of inter-communications for everybody by leaving the call. This is justified on the sensible grounds that since nobody is now paying, all parties must be disconnected. On the other hand in telephony, those parties that did not establish the call have the right to leave the call whenever they choose. In desktop conferencing the same rules can be enforced but need not be. Once a system is established whereby the billing rules are not necessarily determined by who makes the call, many more possibilities emerge. Thus there is no need for the call to be terminated when the originator leaves and, in many cases, this is very desirable. If billing considerations are ignored completely, as they may be when communication is over private cabling, then a simple policy can be adopted whereby casual calls are terminated when only one party is left.

Gradual call tear-down can affect shared application behaviour in ways which users may find disconcerting. Since it is possible for particular shared applications to be present for only a subset of the parties, it is possible that when a party leaves—although the call is still intact—an application that was previously shared for someone else in the call now becomes unshared. If, as was suggested earlier, applications reaching this state should then make appropriate termination options available to the user, some users will find themselves presented with these options during an ongoing conferencing session. This application behaviour could be deferred to the moment when the application owner actually leaves the call, but this is not without its problems since it is curious and difficult to maintain the pretence of an application being shared when it is not actually in this state.

This brief discussion on application considerations highlights some of the complexities of providing an open desktop conferencing system where applications run independently and are selected by users. The user interface and control considerations are massively more difficult than those faced in a simple telephone call; on the other hand, the functions possible and opportunities that can be addressed, are similarly broader in scope. Commercially-available products have targeted the unsophisticated user and have attempted to achieve simplicity by imposing inflexibility. If the product capabilities are reduced to a single call at a time, then one dimension of complexity is removed. If that single call is then reduced to two parties only, as is often the case with ISDN conferencing software, then another dimension of complexity is removed. If, further to this, the applications that can be used are predetermined and required to be available in all such calls, the result is a very simple facility which ought to be easy to use if well designed. However, such an approach discards the tremendous potential of desktop conferencing and reduces it to a relatively trivial extension to existing telephony. The future is more likely to lie with those products which exploit the full potential of the technology while addressing the difficult usability issues.

Call logging

Call set-up and tear-down needs an associated call logging capability so that users have a record of calls made and can search or analyse call-related information. Typically, such a log will contain details of the call start and end times, the names of the parties called, details on other parties who joined and left the call, supplemented by user-provided information on the reason for the call, any messages exchanged, and so on. The log is also often accessed by applications used in the call and, through this means, can also contain information on files and/or other data both transmitted and received. If the desktop conferencing system is linked to a billing system, then call cost information can be added and used to validate subsequent charges. Any product should store the log in such a way that it is amenable to computer display, search and analysis by other programs.

Another form of logging not associated with the call log just described allows the conference to be recorded as it happens. This recording normally stores the interactions that take place rather than the results themselves; the interaction sequence when replayed re-creates the original conference. Such a recording may optionally include not only any audio and video, but also any application interactions. This recording can then be used in a future desktop conference as it is, or can be edited before use. An example of the value of a recording facility is the management meeting, where an executive decision is being passed down the management chain. The exact words, diagrams and illustrations could be a powerful tool, saving both time and misunderstanding. Editing of the recording might be necessary to remove sensitive data, similarly inserts and changes could allow the material to be made relevant to the intended audience. An extension of this facility leads to computer-assisted minute taking, selected portions of the conference exchanges being identified as items to be added to the conference minutes.

Options and preferences

There are many ways in which the call management facilities of a desktop conferencing system can be tailored to suit an individual user. One way is that the applications to be automatically launched into a call of a particular type, are set on a per user basis. Similarly logging options can be specified, ringing tones customized, and all the usual functions provided that are normally associated with application personalization.

Apart from these general facilities, there are some desktop conferencing specific customizations to be considered. An example is answering machine behaviour—the actions to be taken by the system when the user is not present but the workstation is still active. There is considerable scope for intelligent responses, far removed from the simple 'please leave a message after the tone' approach of telephone answering machines. It is possible to provide user facilities that are easily programmable and take specific action depending upon the identity of the caller. For example, such a system could transfer incoming calls to a colleague, make available certain data that has previously been promised, run a specific application, or transfer operation of the entire user's system to another operator. While these facilities are not generally available at the time of writing, they are under investigation as candidates for future product releases.

Another desktop conferencing-specific facility is related to auto-answering, but is active even when the user is present. Such an intelligent agent may reject calls from unwanted parties, interrupt with calls from priority parties, and otherwise automate the call process through automatically accepting, rejecting or diverting incoming calls, and re-trying failed outgoing calls.

Non-workstation devices

Call set-up considerations are not complete without mentioning the needs of non-workstation devices. Participation should be possible from simple fixed function devices such as telephones and video phones. This is another example of a customer requirement that can only be satisfied if calls may be unsymmetrical, that is, where the users in a call have equipment with different capabilities. In order to preserve the consistency of the call model to the other users, the participant with just a telephone can be presented as a member running only a basic audio application. In a similar manner, the video telephone user appears to others as a party in the call with audio and video applications. The ability of people using these simple devices to participate in call control or other advanced features is minimal but, by providing just basic functions, the availability and utility of desktop conferencing is considerably increased. For some advanced devices such as the video telephone, unique support can be included which exploits the peculiar features of the device; for example, the video screen can be used as a monitor for the display of text, image, graphics and status information.

2.2.3 Basic facilities

Messaging

The simplest facility that can be provided in a desktop conferencing system is a basic text messaging capability that allows text entered by one party to be received by the other parties. This function is sometimes conveniently combined with the system call logging facilities so that the messages are interspersed with the call set-up and tear-down details. This text facility can be used to illustrate some of the problems involved in providing a system suitable for casual users. One basic design decision for text messaging is to choose whether the characters should be transmitted immediately as typed, or gathered together into larger blocks before transmission. If the design objective is taken to be the emulation of a person writing on a physical whiteboard, then here characters are visible to the audience as written and, therefore, this would seem the natural way to proceed. However, another factor needs to be considered: many of the users will be inexperienced at operating a keyboard and, if the characters are sent exactly as typed, then all of the user's mistakes will also be sent and any fumbling attempts to correct these errors will also be highly visible. Indeed, since the remote participants will have little else to do while they watch the message appearing, mistakes are likely to be more conspicuous than might normally be the case for keystroke entry. Alternatively, if complete lines are built by the user and then transmitted, the correspondent has an opportunity to scan the line and correct it before it is visible to others. Such line-by-line transmission also provides a more efficient use of the communication network, which provides a second reason for adopting this approach.

The text messaging application in a multi-party conference illustrates another design consideration. As messaging data is entered into the system log, it is important that the log both remains readable and provides easy access to messages. This is most conveniently achieved if an entire message from one user is kept together, but a problem arises when more than one party to the conference is messaging at the same time. Ease of use requires that the data should therefore be displayed not exactly in the order in which it was created, but in coherent contributions from each user, interspersed to reflect the time of creation. There are two distinct problems here: one is that the order in which items are received is not normally a good indication of the order in which they were created, and second, the interspersing of the complete messages does not give a real indication of what previous correspondence is being replied to by any particular message. Thus a reply may have been started to some earlier message but a message shown later in the log may have been finished before the reply was completed. Such a log will subsequently be read as a correct transcript of the conversations between the participants, which it clearly is not; all it records is what was sent but it provides no precise information on how the various entries relate to each other. Time stamping each line with a creation time from a universal master clock does not fully resolve the problem either, it still provides no information on what was visible to the author when a line was sent. Closely allied to the above discussion is the issue of whether the messaging logs should be the same on all the participating machines. While the answer may seem to be 'yes', this requirement might force the log to be even further removed from reality because a process needs to be introduced that will guarantee all messages are received in the same order by all users. Such a process will increase messaging delays in an unpredictable manner.

One solution is to allow a very stilted form of messaging that restricts messages to only one user at a time, with users bidding for permission to speak. Additionally, new contributions must be prohibited until the previous contribution has been delivered to all the parties in the conference. Whilst this approach is superficially attractive, it is tiresome to use because it only provides for a very unnatural conversation between the participants.

Audio and video

Software audio requirements depend upon how the audio is being provided. If, as is sometimes the case, the audio is simply provided by the normal telephone system, the most that can be expected is for the phone call set-up to be integrated with the data conferencing call set-up. This special case apart, a fully-integrated audio system should allow multiple participants to converse both clearly and simultaneously, with each party having individual privacy and volume controls. Although the requirements are easily expressed, achieving a satisfactory audio quality is difficult in practice. The time delay, or latency, for the audio stream to reach its destination should not exceed 150 ms. if natural conversation is to be enjoyed. Furthermore, if full duplex operation is allowed, considerable processing of the audio signal is usually necessary to suppress echoes and provide clear sound.

The principal video requirement is that the picture should be of a satisfactory quality, be synchronized with the corresponding audio, and that the usual television-type controls for brightness, colour and contrast be available. Video quality is an important subject and many trade-offs are involved; this topic is considered in Chapter 6. Like audio, video requires a privacy control to allow the user to prevent pictures being transmitted to other members of the call.

Less obvious video requirements must also be supported. Facilities are needed so that the local picture from the camera can be displayed, optionally flipped into its mirror image. Such a flipped view is the one that we recognize of ourselves and it allows the user to adjust their appearance—it is very difficult to brush your hair in front of a normal video image of yourself. Multi-party calls bring requirements to allow the selection of the particular remote picture to view; automatic systems that select on the basis of who is thought to be speaking at any time are unsuccessful and are too restrictive. For example, they do not allow participants to focus on other parties when they are not speaking, which may be important. Picture-in-picture technology can be exploited to display the user's own picture as a window in the remote user's picture.

Video support in a multi-party call is usually somewhat unsatisfactory because video hardware capabilities rarely enable all the participants to be seen simultaneously, either each in their own video window or all tiled as a composite video image in a single window.

File transfer

Perhaps the most basic capability that can be provided in desktop conferencing is an ability to exchange files. In order for this to be useful the recipient must have an installed application capable of dealing with the format and content of the files being sent, but in the case of the leading applications, such as word processors and spreadsheets, this is likely to be the case. File transfer between certain operating systems is not straightforward and can involve problems caused by different abilities to handle basic characteristics, such as the lengths of file names.

More interesting than file format conversions, are some of the other issues raised by such a simple function as file transfer. If the approach is that file transfer is just one of several operations that may take place within the context of a call, then a party wishing to send a file should, for consistency, send it to all the members of that call. Given that files can be large and that the various parties are likely to be differently connected, this has the consequence that the operation will probably complete at different times for different people—indeed, for some users it may take a very long time indeed. It is clearly sensible that the other facilities of the call should not be held up while this operation continues and, therefore, file transfer should be implemented as a background activity. A direct consequence is that not everybody can be expected to be in exactly the same state at any particular time. Moreover, some users may wish to use the data immediately on receipt, while others will prefer to wait. This raises the general point that it is not possible, or even desirable, to hide these differences from the participants and the system behaviour may only be readily understandable in a simple two-way call. The problems of file transfer also point to a preferred implementation where the file is not actually sent by the party that wishes to distribute the file; instead it is simply made available to the other participants. Those who wish to receive the file request the desk conferencing system to make it available; this approach allows those participants on slow links to opt out of an operation that could prove very tedious.

File transfer considerations raise another more general problem: that of naming and the use of a consistent set of names for entities within a call. In the case of files, it is unlikely that the name given to a file by its original owner will always be acceptable to its recipient; trivially, the recipient may wish to rename it to one more relevant to the local environment, more seriously the name may clash with that of an existing file. If the possibility of the transferred file containing a computer virus is also considered, it seems desirable that files imported through a desktop conference are placed in some limbo state on receipt for processing before being fully accepted into the local environment.

2.2.4 Existing non-collaborative applications

Window sharing

Perhaps the most important function that can be provided in a call is to allow existing application software to be used collaboratively. Although by definition these applications were not designed to be used in this way, it is likely that most workstation information is available through these applications and their participation is, therefore, highly desirable. The most basic method is to enable the windows that the application normally presents, to be made available remotely in a display-only mode. Along with the displayed information, pointer support is needed so that all parties can identify areas or items of interest themselves and see those identified by others. Using a window-based operating system, it is relatively straightforward to provide snapshots of application windows displayed in this way. This snapshot level of support represents the lowest level of function but is useful. In order to use snapshots, the application owner gets the application into a desired state and then shares that state with colleagues. In principle the user can then further interact with the application privately until it is in the next state for a snapshot to be shared. If the conferencing software operates in this way, a snapshot window for the application must be created on the sending station as well as on the receiving stations so that all parties have a common shared window. If further snapshots are to be sent after the first, an option is required to control whether the new snapshot replaces the previous one or is to be displayed in addition.

The creation of windows on a remote workstation, by an application owned and operated by someone else, brings other considerations. It is possible that the source and destination screens are different in terms of resolution and/or size. Without question they will have different windows displayed from local applications outside the call, and any common windows will probably be in different positions. Given these variations, the remote user must be given some control over the snapshot window so that it can be scrolled, sized and possibly scaled independently of the source. As a consequence, the local user cannot be certain that a remote party is able to see things visible on the local machine, which means that the shared pointer support needs to give users feedback when the intended position is outside the displayed area. Automatic scrolling of a snapshot window could be provided, but this has been found to be disconcerting and sometimes prevents users from viewing portions of the window away from those being remotely identified.

Identification of interesting features in a snapshot window is needed by all parties and, therefore, a mechanism is required through which control of the pointer can be requested by other parties and relinquished by the holder. An alternative approach is to allow multiple remote pointers, so that each party to the call controls their own pointer and all are visible at the same time. While this can be an effective approach for a two-way call, it does not scale well for the multi-party call and the proliferation of pointers can be confusing.

Shared windows are also affected by differences in the availability of resources. The simplest example is provided by colour support: if the source window has more or different colours in use than are available at the destination, then a colour mapping algorithm must be implemented. In some cases this is possible with little loss of information content; in other cases, most obviously when a coloured window shares with a remote monochrome display, then there may be a very significant loss of information. More alarmingly, the colour mapping may lead beyond just visual difficulties in interpretation where the parties are aware of the problems, to misleading data caused by it being colour mapped into another valid category and with none of the parties being aware of the substitution and its significance.

While colour provides the best example of the difficulties of the remote mapping of windows, other resource differences may lead to problems. For instance, the unavailability of a font on a remote workstation may result in that system substituting a replacement font that does not have identical properties. Ignoring the possibility of this substitution causing confusion simply because text in that font may now not be distinguished, there is still the problem that the visual representation may be completely different from that intended. This may be caused because differences in font metrics result in words appearing in unintended places; it may also mean that the displayed symbols are totally different—for example, a Greek character may be replaced by a Roman character, or a flow-charting symbol may transmute into an alphabetic character. A solution to the font resource problem is to rely on the exchange of bitmaps rather than coded characters, but this can have both performance and visual quality problems.

Snapshots fulfil a clear requirement but more advanced levels of function are also needed. For some uses it is important that the remote parties see constantly updated copies of the application window on their workstations, with any changes in the local application window being immediately reflected as changes in the remote windows. In this way the local users can manipulate their application window with the confidence that all remote parties are seeing exactly the same contents without any need to initiate refresh operations. Such a facility would be useful, for example, if the local user was instructing a remote party on the operation of a workstation application because all the local user's manipulations and their results would be visible remotely.

Such continuous mirroring is more complicated than might at first appear. Normally a user is not unduly concerned with the precise ownership of the windows, options and menus presented on the display. It is sufficient that they are presented as appropriate and can be used or not as the need arises. When an application is being shared in this way, and especially when the application is one that was not written with collaboration in mind, such ownership issues take on greater importance. For example, an application might own several windows on the screen and the user may have chosen, unconsciously, to share only one of these. Should they all be automatically shared, as the local user is not able to see what is appearing remotely and, therefore, has no idea of the problems that may have inadvertently been created for the other participants in the call? On the other hand, the selection of one window, from many, may have been a deliberate act which should be respected by the conferencing software. More subtly, there are menus and panels that are displayed in windows that are not owned by the application but are nevertheless a consequence of application activity. These should probably be displayed remotely, but it is frequently very difficult for the collaborative conferencing software to determine, from all the screen activity that exists, what visual effects logically belong to any individual application.

Remote control

Exploitation of non-collaborative application software can be extended, beyond continuous mirroring, into remote operation. This provides for application control to be passed to someone else in the call, i.e. it is that person's mouse movements and keystrokes that now direct the application. This does not turn a non-collaborative application into a fully distributed or shared application, because only one person can use the application at a time and the application still runs on the original machine where it was installed. However, a person other than the owner of that machine can operate it, with the owner and potentially others in the call, being able to see the results of its execution.

The value of the various levels of remote application sharing can be appreciated by considering the example of a remote software help-desk service. Initially, the user with a software problem calls the help-desk and explains the software problem. This could perhaps be achieved in a very basic way through the sending of a snapshot of the application window in some error situation, accompanied by pointing in that window to aid discussion of the problem. Stage two in the scenario could involve instructions from the help-desk; the user may wish the results of following those instructions to be immediately visible to the help-desk and thus continuous mirroring would seem to be required. Stage three assumes that the user is unable to overcome the problem despite following instructions and, therefore, a more detailed investigation is initiated; this involves the remote control of the application by the help-desk. The user now watches his or her application being operated by the help-desk while the problem is resolved.

Remote control in a windowing systems environment generally imposes very significant performance requirements if the system is to be usable. Normally very close coordination is required between the hand and eye for application operation, and the interpositioning of a remote machine must not significantly degrade this close coupling. Text-based applications are much less susceptible to these problems than graphics applications.

An ability to control individual applications, with the owner's concurrence, is a highly desirable feature of a desktop conferencing system, although the implementation can be difficult in a cross-platform environment. An extension of this approach, and in practice rather easier to implement, is to allow the control of the entire workstation to be transferred. In this mode the remote party has the ability to initiate new applications and, in extreme implementations, even to remotely reload the operating system. An essential function that must be provided is one which enables the workstation owner to regain control at any time.

Remote operation, either at the application level or at the desktop level, requires decisions on which system's parameters are to be used; for example, are the mouse timings for the double click speed to be taken from the local or the remote workstation settings? Generally it is desirable to try and use the settings familiar to the person actually controlling the software, whether the owner or not. In the help-desk scenario described above, there are grounds for requiring an option to use the owner's settings instead of the help-desk's, since it may be that the source of the problem lies in the way that the system has been configured.

Application data interchange

Use of non-collaborative applications in desktop conferencing is not limited to mechanisms associated with window sharing. The normal facilities that exist for local cut and paste of application data can be extended to the other members of the call through the provision of a shared clipboard. This allows one user to make application data easily available to other users through a familiar mechanism. Along similar lines, the dynamic data exchange facilities (DDE) provided for inter-application communication, often manifested to users as 'paste special' functions, can also be made to operate within a call. In this way modifications made by one user can appear automatically in another user's application. An extension of this approach is the use of object linking and embedding (OLE) across users in a call; thus an object generated by one user can be embedded in data owned by another application elsewhere and can be made to reflect updates in the source.

2.2.5 Collaborative applications

Collaborative applications are distinguished by being designed to operate in a shared multi-user environment and where the actions of one user may have an immediate impact upon the actions of another. Typically, collaborative applications are designed to operate in a distributed way and usually an identical copy of the application runs at each participating workstation. The multiple executing instances exchange information to keep themselves synchronized and provide collaborative functions to their individual users. An alternative implementation approach is for a single, central executing instance of the application to provide the function to all the users, but this implementation strategy is not well suited to desktop conferencing where the individual parties can join and leave at will and there is no obvious central computing facility.

An almost infinite variety of collaborative applications can be developed, each with a bias to a specific task and/or a bias to a particular group of users. In the casual desktop conferencing environment the following collaborative applications have become recognized as important:

- Shared whiteboard
- Shared text editor

although the list is liable to change in the future as the user population grows and their requirements are better understood.

Shared whiteboard

The shared electronic whiteboard was originally selected as an essential collaborative tool through a desire to emulate the familiar physical drawing tools such as flip charts, whiteboards, blackboards, chalkboards, overheads, etc. normally available in conference and other meeting rooms. The key feature is that two or more users can draw on the electronic board, with their combined results visible to all. The metaphor has commonly been adapted to exploit the computer medium by the provision of a layered model in which users draw over a static background image. This background may be blank, or more usually, may be pre-loaded with electronic images from other applications. An almost essential feature is that one such background can be a snapshot of an existing application window. Most implementations provide facilities to allow this background to be easily updated in order to show the current contents of the selected application window. In this way the whiteboard facility overlaps with the capabilities of the window mirroring facility described earlier.

Although the basic function of the shared whiteboard is easily described, it is instructive to observe that even this simple application has not been standardized in current products, although the ITU-T standards body has now made a draft recommendation. One design point takes the view that users are to be treated as independently as possible and, therefore, no user should be able to modify the work of another, i.e. each user should have total control over their input and be certain that it remains unchanged. Adopting this philosophy, the whiteboard model presented is one of a background plane, which may be pre-loaded, with a number of superimposed transparent planes. Each user in the call owns one of these transparent planes, which are visually distinguished from each other by being associated with a single colour. In this way the contribution from each participant is both independent and obvious. Moreover, facilities can be provided to separate out these contributions later, if desired. While these advantages are important, there are also significant disadvantages with the model. Limiting each user to a single preselected colour may be unduly restrictive, and one user being unable to modify the work of another is also a handicap in some situations. Thus, in a scenario where one user makes a proposal and a second user would like to make a small change to that same proposal, the participants will find the model disappointing.

Other products adopt a free-for-all approach, more akin to the original physical metaphor. With this model there is only a single transparent plane above the background, and all users have access to all colours and can freely modify anything drawn by anybody else. This approach addresses the limitations described earlier but, as a consequence, fails to deliver that solution's unique benefits. There is an interesting implementation problem associated with this second approach, which arises because the state of the whiteboard depends upon the sequence in which the individual changes are made. Since it is necessary to implement the function as a distributed application, the corollary is that the drawing orders must be transmitted in an identical sequence to all the participants, which means that they must be serialized. This is not trivial and early implementations avoid the problems by requiring users to press a 'synchronization' button if they want to be sure that all the users in the call have the same whiteboard contents. This clumsy approach suspends the individual user interactions and causes all the whiteboards in the call to exchange a common version of the current contents. If this is significantly different to the current view for a particular user, the result of synchronization is somewhat disturbing.

There are other design approaches to whiteboards that also make the different implementations essentially incompatible. However, it is worth while observing that even those that take a very similar conceptual approach, and offer almost identical functions, are also incompatible due to proprietary implementations—although this is rapidly changing. Whiteboards can be implemented either as image editors or as graphic object editors. The image approach takes the user's drawing as a statement of which picture elements, or pels, are to change colour; the individual elements of the drawing have no other significance. Thus, if the whiteboard has a line-drawing facility, it is simply presenting the user with an easy way to change the colour of certain parts of the picture that happen to lie visually in a straight line. Once drawn, the line does not exist as such; thus an eraser can be used to remove parts of that line, just as it could be used to remove any other part of the picture. This mode of operation is simple to understand and closely parallels the original physical metaphor. A consequence of this approach is that the resultant drawing is expensive in both computer memory and in subsequent physical storage. The image is not well suited to transmission down slow communication links; moreover, it is difficult to provide 'undo' or other editing operations. For example, if a line has been drawn in the wrong place it is impossible to pick up one end of it and move it to the correct location; the line has to be erased by the user, pel by pel, and a new line drawn. Anything that had been under the original line, except in the background plane, would also need to be redrawn.

These disadvantages are overcome with an object-based graphics editor. In this case, the user draws objects which are saved by the system and rendered onto the display. The object can be easily modified and persists in that object form. Moreover, the object representation is compact, making it well suited to slow communication links. The disadvantage is that the objects do not easily transmute from one form to another; for example, if a user draws a line and wishes to erase selected portions of it, the system would be required to implement this by changing the original line to a series of disconnected lines. Moreover, the user would have to understand this possibly confusing behaviour. A likely solution in this case is only to support deletion of the line object and require the user to draw the replacement in its entirety.

There are many excellent painting, imaging and drawing packages available for workstation users, but so far these have been developed for standalone individual use. The current whiteboard software applications in desktop conferencing suites have evolved independently to meet a different user requirement, but it cannot be long before these product streams merge into a new generation of editors that meet both sets of requirements in a consistent manner. An obstacle to this convergence would arise if the conferencing community were independently to adopt standards for shared whiteboard function and behaviour that ignore the accumulated experience of the personal computer community. Such a development would cause marketplace confusion and delay the evolution of an essential technology. The current standards body approach is to provide a rich set of functions that allow all options to be implemented. While this is good in that sophisticated products can be created, it does cause interesting difficulties when simple systems (offering few functions to their users) interact with complex systems. Although both sets of software will be able to understand the data streams exchanged, it is not clear that the users at either end will always be able to understand the interaction.

Shared text editor

The whiteboard is designed for the exchange of ideas through simple drawings; it is not a suitable vehicle for the sharing of primarily text-based information. Given the scarcity of alternatives, however, whiteboards are frequently used for this task, with the basic text document being rendered onto the background plane and annotations drawn over the text using the transparent overlay capability. Such annotations do not modify the base text and any permanent changes must be subsequently copied into the text source by hand, using a conventional word processor.

An alternative approach to interacting with text is to use shared windows, possibly coupled with remote application control. The word processor executes on one machine and the owner can mirror the text application window so that it is visible to the other members of the call. If the discussion is more substantial than simply pointing at areas of interest, then remote application control can be used sequentially to allow participants to modify the document contents, with the remaining parties being able to see the changes as they happen.

A shared text editor goes beyond this level of function by allowing multiple parties to work on the same document simultaneously, and in a coordinated manner. There is still a single source document but now all the parties have facilities independently to scroll around the document to find portions of interest. Moreover, the content remains consistent; thus, if a section is being updated by one user, those changes will be visible to any other user viewing that portion of the document. Depending upon the implementation, multiple users may be allowed simultaneously to update all or part of the document. Thus portions of the document can be locked to one user—with that individual alone being allowed to make changes—and this locking may be on a paragraph or section basis, or a free-for-all can be permitted. The free-for-all approach brings with it the serialization problems discussed earlier for the whiteboard.

Shared text editors are most acceptable if they are extensions to existing common workstation applications, because this collaborative use is simply an addition to existing uses of a conventional word processor, not a substantially different application requiring a different product. It is important to build consistently on what has gone before, rather than create a new document format, function set and user interface metaphor.

Somewhat simpler are shared editors for modifying simple ASCII files. These are natural extensions of the existing notepad style of editor, and collaborative variants are now appearing in desktop conferencing products where they are useful adjuncts to the whiteboard applications.

2.3 Hardware considerations

2.3.1 System unit and display

Desktop conferencing to some extent, should be possible from the typical workstation that already has a communications capability and should not necessitate additional hardware. However, the market segment interested in the technology has so far not been the everyday workstation user, but specific groups such as senior executives, health care professionals, consultants, the computer industry itself, and so on. As a result, less attention has been paid to providing a minimum capability for everyone and more on supporting a fairly rich set of conferencing services, independent of hardware requirements.

Commercial desktop conferencing products generally require that the workstation run a windowing-based operating system, this itself imposing a minimum system configuration. Ideally the display should be capable of displaying a page from a document on the screen such that an 8-point type is legible, as well as leaving room for the document application control menus. This requires approximately 1600 x 1200 pels of screen resolution, with a physical screen size measured by the diagonal, of about 17". Such screens are available but not typical; those in common use range from 640 x 480, through 800 x 600, and up to 1024 x 768 pels, generally on a 14" screen. A direct consequence is that individual pages of documents must be scrolled in order to make all of the content visible; this degrades usability but is regarded as acceptable. It is unlikely that this situation will improve rapidly because high resolution cathode ray tubes with the right characteristics are expensive to manufacture and are likely to remain so. Progress in display technology is increasingly directed towards flat panel devices, driven by the demand for highly portable computers. These are very difficult to manufacture in large sizes and, to date, have not been produced economically in resolutions greater than 640 x 480 pels.

2.3.2 Pointing devices

The typical workstation control device is the mouse. While this has proved its value for menu and option selection, program control, and other general computing aspects, its unsuitability for freehand drawing is a major disadvantage in desktop conferencing. A frequent requirement is to mark an area of interest in a document or picture, write comments, add a signature, and so on. Writing with a mouse is difficult for several reasons, one of which is the lack of visual feedback associated with pencil on paper. Most mouse drivers implement a non-proportional displacement algorithm which means that the distance covered by the cursor on the screen is not simply related to the distance moved by the mouse, but is also a function of its speed. While this does allow the mouse to be 'thrown' across the screen by rapid hand movement, it also destroys any possibility of use for writing. Another problem is caused by the mouse being a relative device, meaning that the cursor does not move when the mouse is picked up and repositioned; instead its movements are always relative. This is in contrast to the familiar pencil, which can be picked up and placed where it is to be used and does not require dragging into position. The stylus input device overcomes these deficiencies and emulates a pencil well but is relatively uncommon. Also, the characteristics of the stylus that make it good for annotation unfortunately make it difficult to use as a mouse substitute for normal control and selection operations. As a consequence both input devices need to be available for a full function system with good usability but, typically, the stylus is omitted.

2.3.3 Audio

Given the basic need for audio support, some form of input/output device is required. Generally, audio capabilities are provided in one of two ways: the first is through an association with the conventional telephone network, in which case the normal range of telephone equipment is available for use. Alternatively, the audio stream is multiplexed with the computer data, requiring the audio device to be attached to an adapter card within the computer. For wide area conferencing using ISDN, the audio connection is directly to the ISDN adapter card; for other communications protocols, the audio connection may be to a unique adapter card or to the communications card itself. In almost all cases the audio connection is such that conventional telephone equipment cannot be used, which has many disadvantages. Not least of these drawbacks is that the wide range of low cost devices available in the mass telephony marketplace is unusable; another that new equipment must be purchased when an office is upgraded from telephony to desktop conferencing.

Audio requires decisions to be made on the style of the equipment. Most successful, in terms of pure technical performance, is headset equipment which provides ear pieces with an attached microphone. Despite being visually obtrusive and cutting off the user from normal office activity, it has several advantages: there is no extraneous noise received by the microphone which gives clarity to the other parties in the call; the ear pieces enable the wearer to concentrate on the conference; and it provides hands-free operation so that the user can operate the keyboard and mouse in a normal unhindered fashion. For many people the aesthetics outweigh the benefits and it is unlikely to be universally adopted.

The next option is something akin to the conventional handset which provides as good audio quality as the headset, but restricts the user's freedom of movement. This makes using the keyboard almost impossible for most ordinary people, but the mouse and/or stylus are easily manipulated.

The third option available is the loudspeaker telephone, similar to that used in teleconferencing. While this is splendid in a room dedicated to the conference, it is a nuisance to others in a desktop environment. Furthermore, it has a technical deficiency resulting from the phenomenon known as echoing. This occurs because the microphone in the equipment picks up general background noise, including the conference itself. This audio feedback gives rise to distortion which must be dealt with, usually in one of two ways. The low cost solution is to suppress the loudspeaker output when the microphone picks up local sound, thereby preventing multiple parties speaking at the same time and affecting free conversation between the participants. Alternatively, more expensive equipment incorporates sophisticated echo cancellation signal processors which remove the audio feedback before transmission.

All of the available audio options are to some extent less than ideal and selection is a compromise between usability, cost and obtrusiveness.

2.3.4 Video

Selection of video hardware also involves compromises. Video is very much an optional feature of a system, with the curious property that the provider derives no personal benefit. A camera allows a remote user to see the local user; a local camera is not necessary for the remote user to be seen. This aspect may have a significant influence on the purchase decision.

A video camera should be mounted in a position which allows the user to face it directly; if the camera is too high, the user presents a 'shifty' image—that is, the user appears downcast and seems to be avoiding eye contact. Similarly, the camera mounted in too low a position presents an odd perspective which prevents natural behaviour. Practically, of course, the camera cannot be mounted in the ideal position because that is where the screen is, and a compromise has to be reached. One of two compromises are generally accepted; either the camera is mounted on top of the monitor or it is mounted on a stand to the side. There is something disconcerting about a camera being obviously visible to the terminal operator, especially in the early days of system use. This inhibition can be reduced by choosing a very small camera but the problem here is that camera prices increase as size decreases. One compromise is to use a unit where the camera head is separated from the main electronics, which can then be stacked away out of sight. More desirable is to hide the camera in the bezel of the monitor and this has been demonstrated in product prototypes, but is not yet an option available to the general public. Only when desktop conferencing develops as a mass market will a range of such multimedia monitors become available.

The camera is not just of value for showing the head and shoulders of the speaker; it may have a more important role in displaying objects to the remote parties. For this use the camera head needs to be detachable and/or alternative cameras should easily be attachable. These other uses of the camera have implications for focal length and light sensitivity. In some cases the desktop system is occasionally used for mini-video conferences and the camera is then required to view a significant portion of the office. Easy adjustment between these various uses is important.

The quality of the camera lens and electronics has a significant impact upon the quality of the transmitted video image, which is perhaps unexpected. Because there is so much degradation of video quality due to the compression necessary to transmit the picture at affordable data rates, a high quality input would seem to be unnecessary; however, experiments show that the compression algorithms used are particularly sensitive to original video quality and poor cameras are not recommended.

The audio/video subsystem should not be restricted to just camera and microphone input. In many applications alternate audio and video sources are useful; for example, for the review of video commercials in the advertising industry. The subsystem should allow switching between a variety of both separate and combined audio and video streams.

2.3.5 Products

The products commercially available typically provide a packaged solution, with all the necessary components supplied as a bundle. While this has the advantage that the components are matched together, it does take away the element of personal choice and an ability to mix-and-match to meet particular requirements. As the market matures and standards are recognized between components, this situation will undoubtedly change.

CHAPTER 3

Call management

Call management is a misleading term that conjures up an image exclusively based on telephony. Whilst this is where the term originated, it is now used to cover the much broader range of interactions that are possible between users exchanging multimedia information. However, it is useful to examine the original telephony concepts of call management, as available to ordinary users, in order to appreciate how restrictive these policies are and how they can be extended to allow many other styles of user interaction.

3.1 Telephony call management

The policies implemented by most telephone companies can be summarized as follows:

- A call comprises at least two parties (when the penultimate party leaves the call is terminated).
- Only parties within a call can invite additional parties to join (third parties cannot normally break into an existing call).
- All parties within a call have equivalent facilities available when a call is set up (for example, calls cannot be set up that allow some parties to listen but not speak).
- A party that sets up a call pays for that call (unless unusual arrangements have been made).
- On joining an existing call, no previously exchanged data will be automatically sent to the new party (for example, there is no option for replay of the conversation to date).
- The existence of a call is private to the parties in that call.
- Multiple independent calls cannot be combined into a composite call.
- A call cannot be split into multiple calls.
- A party cannot be in more than one call simultaneously (although membership of a call can be suspended to allow activity in another call).
- A party in a call can be substituted by another party (using a transfer option).
- One party in a call cannot exercise control over another party in that call (for example, by enabling or disabling options during the call).
- Status information on other parties in a call is not available (for example, one party cannot tell if a remote party has held down the mute button).

If a telephone is considered as a personal computer, it can be described as having:

- launch and cancel buttons for a single application (lifting and lowering the hand set begins and ends calls)
- a set of menu buttons for that application (the dial pad)
- application input and output devices (microphone and speaker)
- application status device (feedback tones via the speaker)

Seen in these terms, the standard telephony policies have a very arbitrary feel about them—and to view a telephone as a computer is at least a plausible, if unusual, exercise. It is therefore not surprising that, when much broader human interaction possibilities are considered using the high function, multimedia device that is the personal computer, the existing telephony model appears to be an unlikely solution. The role of call management is to impose order on the interactions between people, with the intent of avoiding chaos. The telephony call management model was designed for very simple devices, collaborating over slow networks with a rigid topology, and has been extremely successful. The challenge is to replace it with something, or several things, more suited to extremely complex devices collaborating over a wide range of networks with dynamic topologies.

3.2 The varieties of calls

There are many variations on the theme of a call that are far removed from the model provided in normal telephony. Some examples are listed below, with a brief description of their distinguishing characteristics:

- *Teacher and students* (e.g. remote networked education) The minimum number of participants is one, for example the teacher starts on time even if all the students are late. The class finishes if the teacher leaves, but may not finish if all the students leave. The teacher is aware of all the students but the students may or may not be aware of each other. The facilities available to the teacher are different from those available to the students. It may be reasonable for others outside the class to be able to find out what classes are running. Enrolling new people into the class may be reserved to the teacher or to a third party outside the class.
- *Live broadcast* (e.g. a speech) All the information flows from the speaker to the audience; there is no return flow. There may be no control on who can join the broadcast. One member of the audience has no knowledge of other members of the audience.
- *Seminar* All the participants can communicate both with each other and with the guest speaker. The speaker has privileges other members do not have, for example the speaker needs to be able to stop discussions if necessary. The call can exist before the guest speaker has arrived and continue after the speaker has left.
- *Formal meeting* (e.g. a board meeting) The chairperson is in control. and decides who attends, when the meeting starts and finishes, who speaks and when, and what documents and other aids are brought into the meeting.
- *Consultant* (e.g. a lawyer advising a client) The meeting is private and all parties must agree before a new member can be admitted.
- *Brainstorming session* Only one person can speak at a time but everyone can hear. The organizer decides who speaks next but individuals can flag their intention to speak. Everything said is logged in a document and immediately available to all present; the document is frequently rearranged by the organizer.
- *Electronic gaming* Almost any exotic combination of rules of behaviour and multimedia information exchange can be described under this heading.

With this broad scope in mind, the role of a call manager can be defined as:

- the means by which connections, between users and between applications, are established, monitored and controlled.
- the enforcement of a set of policies through which the interactions, both among and between users and applications, are managed.

This combination of roles gives a collaborative system its personality, as perceived by its users. There is no concept intended here of a right or a wrong set of policies; just an infinite set of choices which are more or less suited to a specific collaborative task.

3.3 A framework for call management

Given the complexity and choices available, it is perhaps not surprising that existing implementations of desktop conferencing systems have taken a very arbitrary and inflexible approach to call management. With few exceptions, each product has defined a set of rules, close to those of telephony, and produced an environment with an open style of behaviour, suited to casual conferencing. The openness tends to be such that willing participants can discipline themselves to behave in a manner appropriate to a formal meeting, but the system does not assist, it simply tries not to get in the way.

As desktop conferencing increases in acceptance, some trends are certain. Inter-operability between different user communities will become more important, thereby requiring certain call management styles to be architected and agreed as standards adhered to by the various product suppliers. One such attempt is the T.120 recommendation being set by the ITU-T, the implications of which are discussed in Chapter 7. The single concept of making a desktop conferencing call will, in time, need to be replaced by making a chosen form of call, such as a casual conversational call, a formal meeting, a class and so on. Likewise, an incoming call will also be distinguished in this way and systems will need to be capable of simultaneously implementing different call styles, to allow a user to be in multiple calls. The advent of these standard call models will also bring a demand for user modifications of such standards, so that customized interactions can be established for particular purposes, or to suit user idiosyncrasies.

The user interface of the call manager should be independent of the call management model, there being no reason why flexibility in user interface design cannot co-exist with a particular call management style.

3.3.1 Call manager policy topics

The call manager is concerned with the management of three kinds of resources:

- calls (which contain users and applications)
- users (or parties to a call)
- applications (available or executing in a call)

The assumption here is an application-oriented programming model, where the applications own data or control access to data. An alternative view, which is gaining prominence but is not yet pervasive, is an object-oriented paradigm where the distinction between applications and data no longer exists. Assuming the application model, the major policy questions that define a type of call are:

- *Call and user related:*
  - Which users are allowed into a call?
  - How does a call get established?
  - How does a call get terminated?
  - How does a call member leave?

  - How do new users get added into a call?
  - How do calls get combined?
  - How do calls get broken up into other calls?
  - Who can determine what information about a call?
- *Application related:*
  - Which applications are allowed into a call?
  - How does an application get launched?
  - How does an application get terminated?
  - How are application resources managed within a call?
  - For systems that permit multiple simultaneous calls, there are additional policy questions:
- *Cross call related:*
  - How are resource conflicts between calls managed?
  - Can applications and/or users be in multiple calls of the same/different type?

3.3.2 Call manager policy example

Consider two parties A and B, in a call AB, sharing a single application, for example exchanging graphical information through a shared whiteboard. A third party C is to be involved. Some of the behaviour options that may be appropriate are:

- either A or B can invite C to join
- either A or B can invite C to join, but the other must agree
- only one of A and B can invite C to join
- the invitation rules are dependent upon conditions to be satisfied by C
- the rules applying to A and B are different
- C invites himself without consulting A or B
- C invites himself with the agreement of both A and B
- C invites himself with the agreement of either A or B
- C invites himself with the agreement of a specified one of A or B
- C needs to get the agreement of some fourth party in order to join

The possible rules concerning the extension of the two-way call to a three-way call are almost endless, even in this very simple example; yet there are very plausible user scenarios associated with each of the above cases, and indeed with some of those not listed, where a particular rule describes the natural behaviour that would be expected.

Assuming the call is extended to C, there are now decisions to be made about the state of the whiteboard application. For example:

- the application is automatically launched at C
- the application is launched at C with the concurrence of C
- the application is not launched at C

If C already had an instance of the whiteboard application running, some of the possibilities available are:

- the existing instance is shared with those of A and B
- a new instance is launched and shared
- C is asked to decide what should happen

Assuming that the whiteboard execution decision is satisfactorily resolved, then there are still further decisions to resolve:

- the whiteboard of C is made to match those of A and B
- the whiteboard of C is left alone
- the three whiteboards include all the contents of the contributing boards

Finally, there is the question of how to end the call:

- only the person who started the call can end it
- only A or B can end the call
- anybody in the call can end the call
- those in the call, plus selected parties outside, can end the call
- anybody can leave; the call ends when only one party is left
- anybody can leave; the call ends when nobody is left

The concept of a call manager is based on the premise that applications should not normally include consideration of these issues; instead these decisions should be resolved in some common component. Indeed, if applications are heavily involved in call issues, then an impossibly complex situation will arise when multiple applications—all with differing views on call policy issues—find themselves shared and collectively managing the call.

3.3.3 Advanced call management

Despite the large number of options available in the almost trivial example above of a two-way call with a single application being extended to a third party, all options are in some aspect similar. There are many other ways in which call managers can add value to collaborating applications. For example, consider the simple case of a user A who wishes to make a call to B, in order to run a single application—the shared whiteboard. User A makes a call to B, but now there are many other kinds of call development options that deserve consideration and which may be considered to fall within the scope of call management:

- B is available to accept the call
- A is not allowed to contact B
- B will only accept calls if certain criteria are met (time, priority, identity, etc.)
- B is not available
- B is not available but C is handling B's calls
- B is not available but has left a message for A
- B is not available but A can leave a message for B

Assuming A and B make a call, there are still further options that concern application sharing:

- A's whiteboard is shared with a new instance of B's whiteboard
- A's whiteboard is shared with a different application owned by B
- B does not have a whiteboard but wants C's to be used instead
- B has a whiteboard but does not want it to be used

A further dimension to call management is brought about by the realization that there are finer distinctions to be made about a call than just establishing collaboration between the required users through identifying the necessary applications, or their surrogates. For example, a video conferencing call between three parties, A, B and C, may be initiated by A. A has a fully capable system and would like to use both audio and video facilities; accordingly A attempts to establish a call where audio and video applications are automatically launched at B and C. If the remote parties can launch these applications, there is no problem. However, it is likely that one or both of them will not have all the same facilities; let us assume C is similarly equipped to A but that B can do audio exchanges but has no video capability whatsoever. In this case the following options exist:

- the call should not go ahead
- the call should go ahead with audio only
- the call should go ahead with audio for A, B and C, and audio and video for A and C

This complexity is not just associated with call set-up. If, continuing the example above, the audio capability fails because of network problems, is it then correct to terminate the call, or should it proceed with video only, as a two-way call between A and C? Alternatively, if the video capability fails, should the call be terminated or should it now be an audio-only call; assuming it carries on as an audio-only call and later the network is able to resume video traffic, should the video capability between A and C be restarted?

In a complex interaction there may be many facilities that are regarded as fundamental to a call and others that are regarded as optional. Moreover, some of these facilities may be differently regarded depending upon who is affected. Thus, a conference call should go ahead if all the principal participants are available and have the necessary tools; others may be regarded as lesser participants and it is sufficient that they can at least hear and speak; while yet others may be regarded as observers of little consequence.

Call management has to cope with all of these problems, though the present state of the art in commercial products is to be very authoritarian and rigidly define the rules of behaviour and the preconditions for a call. Given that most products only support two-way calls with little or no flexibility on the applications available, this has not yet surfaced as a major issue.

A promising approach is to define a set of call policies that address the most common requirements and allow these to be customizable, with these custom options able to be saved by users as new policies, in effect.

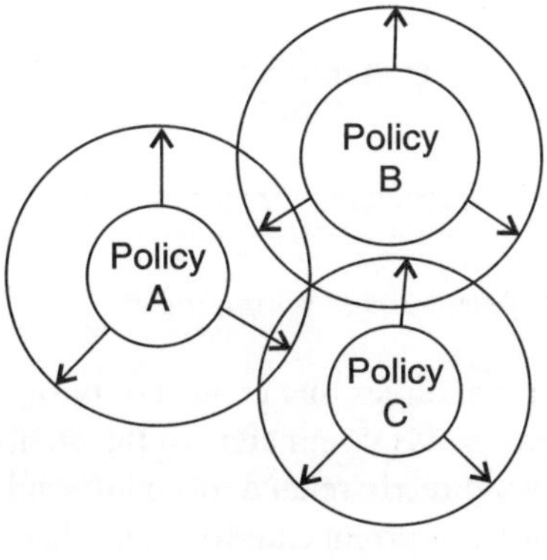

Figure 3.1 Customizable call policies

As the technology becomes more mature certain policies will attain the tried, tested and well-understood nature of the existing telephone call, and will be generally recognized and understood by desktop conferencing systems. To cope with the special cases, ways must be found to enable the degree of customization to be extended so that the broad scope of customer requirements can be accommodated. The diversity of these requirements is evidenced by considering the number of common words in the English language associated with group behaviour: calls, meetings, seminars, chats, conferences, talks, presentations, discussions, brainstorms, classes, debates, hearings, consultancies, referrals, speeches, shows, etc. These styles of behaviour are affected by the use, or presence, of: deputies, secretaries, answering machines, assistants, projectors, whiteboards, documents, minute takers, etc.

The status of a meeting, human interaction, or participant can be described as: open, available, in conference, closed, priority interrupts only, bookable, busy, on holiday, sick, working from home, on temporary assignment elsewhere, available in a different location, pending, finished, late, early, on time, in progress, etc.

3.3.4 Call manager user interface functions

The user interface function can be divorced from the particular call management styles being implemented. Logically, the call manager can be regarded as a call manager engine, which implements one or more call manager policies, and a call manager user interface, which presents that functionality to the user. The way that it is presented, and indeed how much of it is presented, depends upon the target user population. Customization facilities allow the user some degree of personalization without changing the basic policies. Figure 3.2 illustrates the approach.

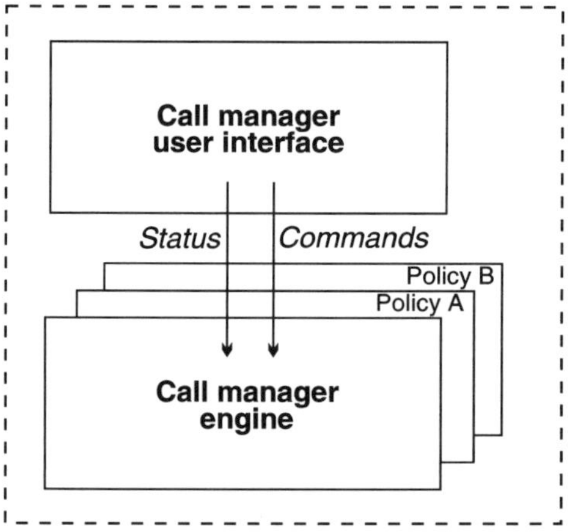

Figure 3.2 Call manager engine, policies and user interface

This model is simplified in that it assumes that control of the call manager engine comes only from the user. The user interface sends commands to the engine and receives status back; it may also receive status that is not directly related to a command but informs the user interface of something that has happened on a current call, for example that a participant in that call has hung up.

While this model is useful in simple cases, it is unduly restricting. For example, it may be desirable that an application itself has the ability to control the call manager, so there is a sense in which the call manager controls the application and the application may control the call manager. Although this appears complex, the need is real; thus if an application wanted to offer, embedded in its own user interface, an option for the user to terminate both the application itself and the call that it was a part of, it would be necessary for the application to issue a command to the call manager engine. This can be illustrated as in Fig. 3.3.

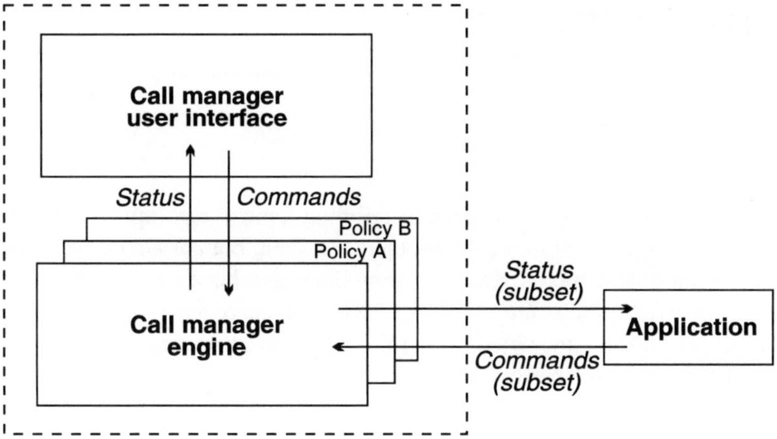

Figure 3.3 Application control of a call

To avoid possible conflict between the instructions sent by the now multiple controllers of the call manager engine, applications are limited to a subset of both commands and status. It must always be clear which controller is to take action on information reported back by the call manager engine.

Depending upon the sophistication of the system, the tasks the user interface has to present to the user are:

- *Call set-up and tear-down*
  - selection of parties
  - selection of existing applications instances
  - selection of new applications to launch into the call
  - tearing down a call
- *Call management*
  - adding or removing users from a call
  - adding or removing applications from a call
  - combining/splitting calls
  - displaying and/or logging call status (selected call or all calls)
- *Incoming call management*
  - joining or declining a call request
- *Customisation*
  - default behaviour
  - determining application name mapping and application behaviour
  - setting system values such as messages, time-outs, etc.

CHAPTER 4

Local and wide area communication

Data communications technology is an extremely broad topic, the complexities of which are in part justified by the difficult nature of the problems tackled, but are also a consequence of the long history of development and the diversity of products that have resulted. The result is now a bewildering set of overlapping options and a technical language which makes this a field reserved to the expert. It is not the objective of this chapter to summarize the technology on offer but rather the intent is to describe some basic criteria that must be satisfied in order to meet the requirements of desktop conferencing. Necessarily, this results in broad approximations and the omission of much that is important. The reader is referred to the many excellent books on communication technology that take a particular communications medium and the associated protocols, and describe the performance and related characteristics (see Bibliography).

Some contribution to the complexity arises from the development of many alternative physical media: from simple copper wiring through to coaxial cables; wireless transmission technologies such as infrared, radio and satellite; and onwards to optical fibre. Remarkably, the more humble physical links, such as the twisted pair used in the local telephone network, have been revisited many times and dramatic improvements continue to be made on old—what many have thought to be obsolete—networks.

In the early days, data communication was associated with limited capacity and error prone links. Prior to the early 1960s, the US telephone network was an integrated analogue network designed solely for voice communication. As a consequence, early work sought both to maximize the useful data capacity of telephone links and to hide the occurrence of errors in the links from users. Thus, session-oriented communications were important, the establishment of a session allowed all the routing information to be specified once, independently of the data. The link was then set up to carry data from source to destination until the session was concluded; errors were handled by increasingly sophisticated combinations of error detection and correction protocols. Later technological development, exemplified by optical fibre, changed the situation dramatically. Capacity was no longer a precious resource—instead the notion that 'bandwidth was free' was propounded. Simultaneously, error rates fell dramatically. The need to minimize processing of the data during transmission became much more important because computer cycles became relatively much more expensive than transmitted bits, and processing became a bottleneck in communication. In this environment, therefore, a very different set of optimizations became important. More recently, mobile communications have become important and these media have characteristics reminiscent of the early fixed link systems: error rates are very high and capacity is at a premium. Recent developments in communications have concentrated where possible on the exploitation of existing infrastructure rather than replacement, and on extensions to current architectures rather than incompatible new protocols.

A very crude approximation is to identify historical computer networks with efficient data transmission; thus high bandwidth and high utilization are important criteria. Error recovery is another characteristic of such networks. On the minus side is a tendency to relatively long end-to-end delays and unpredictability of the exact moment of arrival. Using the same crude approximation, telephony-based networks until relatively recently were associated with low bandwidth, due to their history of voice traffic. On the positive side is unrivalled coverage, superb reliability and a smooth flow of information delivered with very small end-to-end delays.

All of these approximations are rapidly becoming out of date. The same new technologies such as optical fibre and ATM are bringing high bandwidth, low latency networks at affordable prices. In parallel is an increasing trend away from proprietary systems to open systems, multiple suppliers and a high degree of inter-working. The movement dates from the early 1970s with the development of the reference model for Open Systems Interconnection (OSI) by the International Organization for Standardization (ISO).

A more recent driving force has been the increasing importance of multimedia communications and its requirements for low latency and isochronous transmission. While this was always important for voice networks, the integration of audio and video with more traditional forms of data communications has given rise to yet more standards.

4.1 Protocol stacks and standards

An understanding of protocols and protocol stacks is necessary to appreciate the diversity of communication options and the drive towards standardization and inter-operability. Application programs do not now normally communicate directly with the physical communications adapter. The reason for this is there is great similarity in the requirements of many different applications, for example many communications applications need routes established, communication errors corrected, buffering schemes to cope with network traffic, and so on. The approach that has evolved is, conceptually, a layered approach, where each layer of software above the adapter, adds function to what is already present. These layers have become standardized, although many different versions of each layer exist and, therefore, there is much choice in the standards that can be adopted. Thus, the standards form a hierarchy—standards being built upon standards, with each additional layer adding higher level functions and taking advantage of previous capabilities. For inter-operability, however, compatibility is required at all levels in the hierarchy.

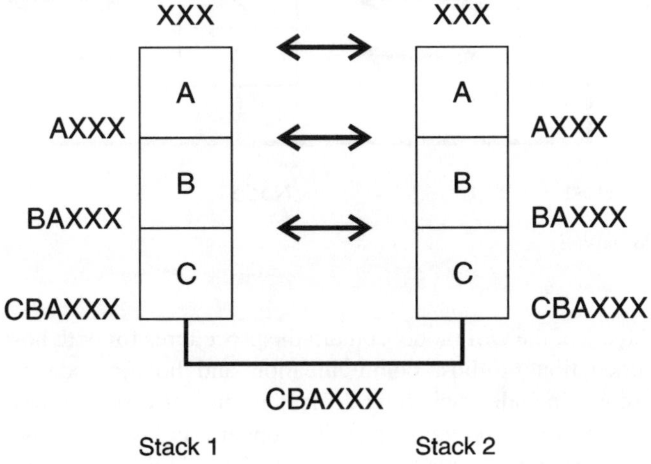

Figure 4.1 Two communicating stacks

Figure 4.1 shows two identical protocol stacks, one representing a transmitting terminal and the other a receiving terminal. Each level in the protocol stack adds value; thus the lowest level C may be concerned with effecting basic delivery; level B may add error-free transmission capabilities, i.e. if the data sent to level C did not get delivered or was delivered with error, the B levels will detect the problems and cause a retransmission to occur. Level A may add ease of use characteristics for an application; thus level A might detect the kind of data being sent and use different techniques that are available to it through level B as appropriate. Generally each layer finds it necessary to add something to the data being transmitted, which is picked up and understood by the corresponding layer. Thus if XXX is what the application really wants to send, CBAXXX may actually be sent over the network, with CBA representing a series of headers added by the various layers in the protocol stacks. The need for identical stacks at both transmitting and receiving terminals is now apparent. In this example, the application receiving the data expects to see XXX; any other headers left on due to absent protocol layers will make the delivered data unintelligible.

In the late 1970s the International Organization for Standardization (ISO) developed the reference model for Open Systems Interconnection (OSI). The model is a seven-layer architecture, intended to be the basis of open network systems allowing different manufacturers' systems to inter-operate. The layering of the OSI model provides transparency, in the sense that the operation of each layer is independent of each other layer. Figure 4.2 shows the seven layers of the model.

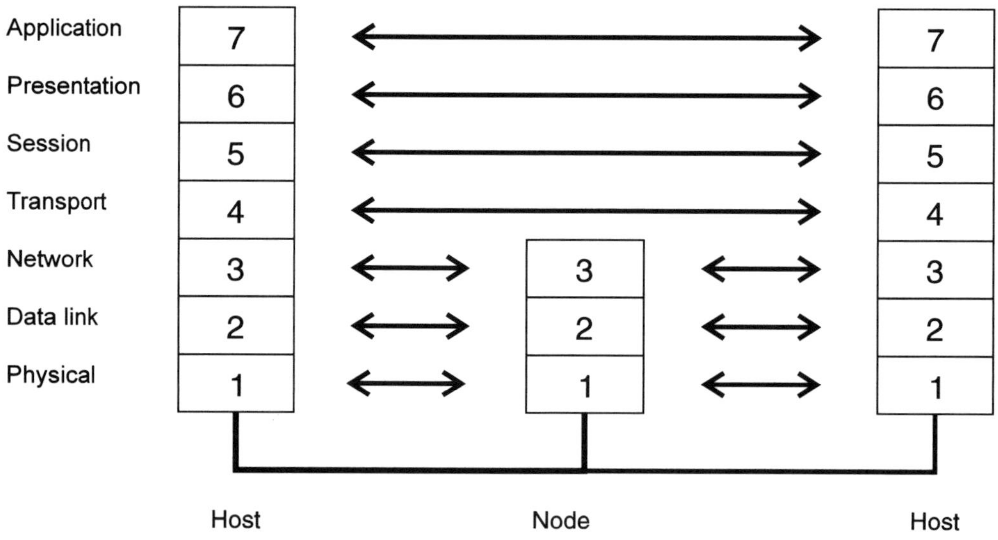

Figure 4.2 The OSI model

The three lowest layers of the OSI model contain the procedures for both host (which includes terminals and workstations)-to-host communication and host-to-node communication. A node, in the OSI sense, includes switching devices in the network and they have no need to unwrap the higher levels of the protocol stack. The upper four layers are known as the end-to-end layers since they are implemented only in hosts. The significance of the seven layers of the OSI model is:

1 *Physical layer:* specifies the electrical and mechanical characteristics of the protocol used to transfer bits, e.g. RS-232C and RS-449 for modems.
2 *Data link layer:* specifies the protocol for error-free communication across the physical link including encoding and framing, e.g. SDLC, HDLC, NDIS, LapD, LapF.
3 *Network layer:* specifies the protocol for routeing, congestion control, accounting, call set-up and termination, and user-network communications, e.g. IP, X.25, IPX.
4 *Transport layer:* specifies the higher level protocols for error-free communication between hosts across the sub-network including quality of service and security, e.g. TCP, UDP, SPX, NetBIOS.
5 *Session layer:* specifies the process-to-process communication.
6 *Presentation layer:* specifies a set of general, non-application specific user services such as encryption, compression and character set conversion.
7 *Application layer:* specifies the user interface to the network and a set of specific applications such as file transfer, transaction processing, network management, electronic mail, etc.

In practice, the functions of many of the layers in protocol stacks are not simply described and, depending upon the stack selected, some layers are combined or omitted. Many different protocol stacks exist—some for historical reasons, some to support proprietary networks and equipment, and others as an implementation of international standards intended to further the cause of inter-operability.

4.2 Requirements

It is difficult to give absolute requirements for desktop conferencing systems because the applications are so diverse and the networks which attach them so varied. The intent here is not to classify individual communication links as suitable or not, because desktop conferencing is not amenable to that approach. More useful is simply to understand what can be achieved over a link with particular characteristics; at the time, the user will decide whether the limitations associated with that link make a potential call pointless, or whether useful business can be transacted. Desktop conferencing is more about exploiting what already exists, rather than demanding high speed links capable of the full range of possible multimedia interactions. As users continually bump up against the limits of what is possible with their existing installed networks, their traffic and business requirements will provide the cost justification for network upgrades.

4.2.1 Throughput

The requirement for communications throughput, or bandwidth, depends upon the nature of the applications and data being used in the desktop conference. In particular, bandwidth requirements can be understood by considering the combination of data objects involved and the frequency at which the objects must be updated. This topic has been studied by James Russell and the numeric data in this section are based substantially on his work (James D. Russell, Multimedia Networking Performance Requirements, TRICOM 93 Conference (1993)). Table 4.1 summarizes typical bandwidth requirements for different kinds of data.

Table 4.1 Bandwidth requirements for multi-media communications

Information type	*Size of a unit of data*	*Units/s.*	*Bandwidth (kbits/s.)*
Alphanumeric coded data	1,000 bytes/page	0.01–1.0	0.1–10
Graphics (e.g. CAD/CAM)	35,000 bytes/page	0.01–1.0	3.5–350
Office image	60,000 bytes/page	0.01–1.0	6.0–600
Medical image	600,000 bytes/page	0.01–1.0	60–6,000
Audio (15 Hz–20 kHz)	n/a		2.4–1,410 (depending upon compression ratio and audio quality)
Video (moving pictures)	n/a		64–2,000 (depending upon compression ratio and video quality)

The audio and video requirements change dramatically depending on the trade-offs between quality and compression ratios. At the lowest audio rate of 2400 bits/s., all ability to recognize the speaker's voice is lost and the audio is barely intelligible. The basic quality telephone standard, known as G.711, uses 64 kbits/s., but the same audio quality has been achieved at 32 kbits/s. using more powerful signal processors. The dependencies between audio quality and bandwidth are summarized in Table 4.2.

Table 4.2 Audio quality and compression trade-offs

Audio quality	*Bandwidth (bits/s)*	*Notes*
Robotic sound	2.4 k	LPC coding
Telephone	32 k	TI DSP
FM radio	132 k	TI DSP
Stereo CD	1.41M	

Video exhibits an even wider range of quality/performance trade-offs. At the most basic level an image can be periodically transmitted, perhaps updated every few minutes or every few seconds, i.e. at the lowest levels video can be regarded as a sequence of still pictures. Fifteen frames per second allows tolerably smooth video, thirty frames per second is perfectly satisfactory. These numbers still allow for enormous scope on the quality of each frame, the variability can be exercised in the number of pels, number of colours and in the correctness of the picture. Many compression techniques depend upon detecting differences between frames and transmitting only the differences. The H.261 recommendation at 64 kbits/s. is just adequate for a small window on a screen showing a talking head, that is a picture with not much movement; 128 kbits/s. makes a noticeable improvement in quality while 384 kbits/s. meets most normal requirements. The bandwidth situation is summarized in Table 4.3.

Table 4.3 Video quality and compression trade-offs

Video quality	*Bandwidth (kbits/s.)*	*Notes*
128 x 120 pels 15 frames/s. 9 bits colour	288	Intel DVI RTV coding (assuming 4 delta frames/ref. frame)
128 x 120 15 frames/s.	64	H.261 recommendation
256 x 240 15 frames/s.	384	H.261 recommendation
256 x 240 30 frames/s.	2,000	H.261 recommendation

The conclusion is that bandwidth requirements range from about 32 kbits/s. for telephone quality, voice-annotated text applications through to 2 Mbits/s. for applications associated with very high quality video.

4.2.2 Latency and jitter

Bandwidth, or the ability to cope with the volume of data per second, is not the only communications requirement to be satisfied. Latency represents the delay imposed by the communication link and is critically important in collaborative working because it affects the natural flow of information between people. The effect of high latency is well illustrated by international telephone calls sent via satellite. The excessive delays confuse the users because they do not correspond to the familiar face-to-face situation. If a speaker stops talking, then an immediate response is normally expected; if the response does not occur the original speaker is liable to speak instead. In the satellite situation, it is not unusual for both parties to end up speaking at the same time—the remote speaker because the message has only just been received, the local speaker because no response was heard in the usual time.

Latency is not a sufficient parameter to characterize networks because their performance may not be constant and bunching of data packets can occur, depending upon the transmission technology and the network loading (see Fig. 4.3).

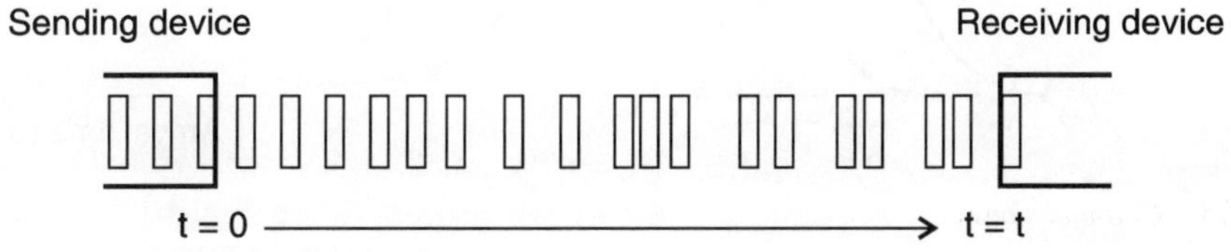

Figure 4.3 Bunching of data during transmission

Latency gives the average delay that can be expected; a parameter known jitter measures the fluctuations in latency that are to be expected (see Fig. 4.4).

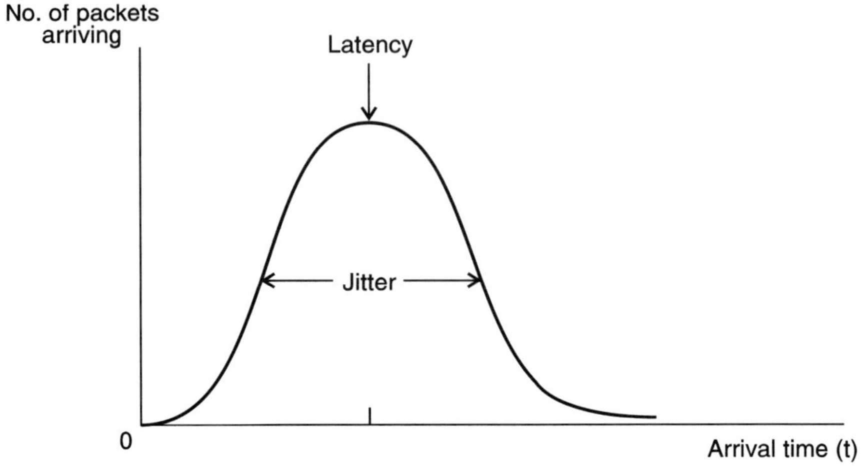

Figure 4.4 Relationship between latency and jitter

The contents of multimedia data streams often have critical time dependencies with each other. An example is synchronization of the audio and video streams associated with a speaker; the video of the moving lips has a critical time relationship with the audio being produced. Another example is given by a speaker identifying features of a picture, where the audio needs to be synchronized with the pointer movement. Skew measures the difference in presentation times of objects which should be synchronized; Fig. 4.5 illustrates the case of pairs of related data packets being transmitted down two channels: A and B. Skew is a measure of the difference in latency between the two channels.

The system requirements for latency and skew are shown in Table 4.4.

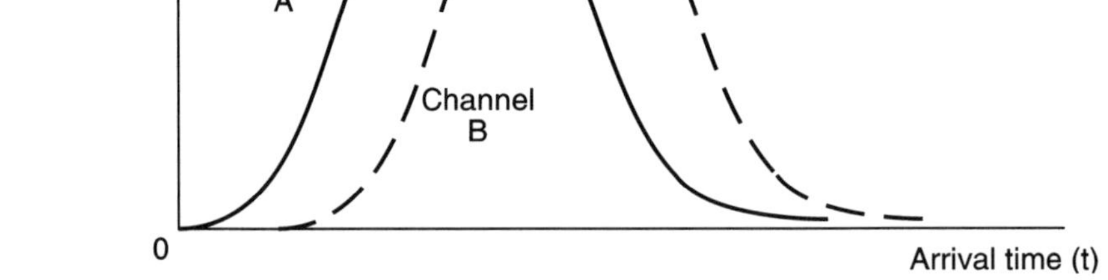

Figure 4.5 Channel skew

The figures supplied in Table 4.4 are subjective and different researchers have come to slightly different conclusions. The audio latency of 150 ms. can be exceeded but other problems increase, for example sound distortions caused by echoes which can, in turn, be minimized by sophisticated signal processing. The video latency appears to be less critical than the audio latency, the eye apparently being more forgiving than the ear. Lip synchronization is

Table 4.4 Latency and skew requirements

Media	*Requirements*
Audio alone	Audio latency < 150 ms.
Audio + discrete information, e.g. slide show	Audio latency <150 ms. Audio/data skew < 1000 ms.
Audio + pointed objects, narration	Audio latency < 150 ms. Audio/data skew < 200 ms.
Audio + lips or other sound effects	Audio latency < 150 ms. Audio advance over video < 20 ms. Audio delay following video < 120 ms.

very important and it is interesting to observe that the brain is less tolerant of audio that arrives early than audio that arrives late. This is undoubtedly a direct consequence of the fact that audio is normally fractionally late because sound travels slower than light.

The requirements for jitter can be deduced from those figures given for latency. One interesting aspect of jitter is that it is also related to data loss in the sense that if a data packet is sufficiently delayed, it is assumed to be lost. Work by the IEEE 802.11 working group has targeted a maximum packet loss rate of one packet per thousand for multimedia traffic over a LAN (IEEE Computer Society, Standards Working Group IEEE P802.11, Document No. 92–20, 28 January, 1992).

The figures in Table 4.4 relate to total system performance. Latency and jitter for audio and video are both much affected by the capture and display process; hence, the latency and jitter that may be introduced by the communication subsystem has to be viewed in terms of the overall system performance. Schematically the total process can be considered as in Fig. 4.6.

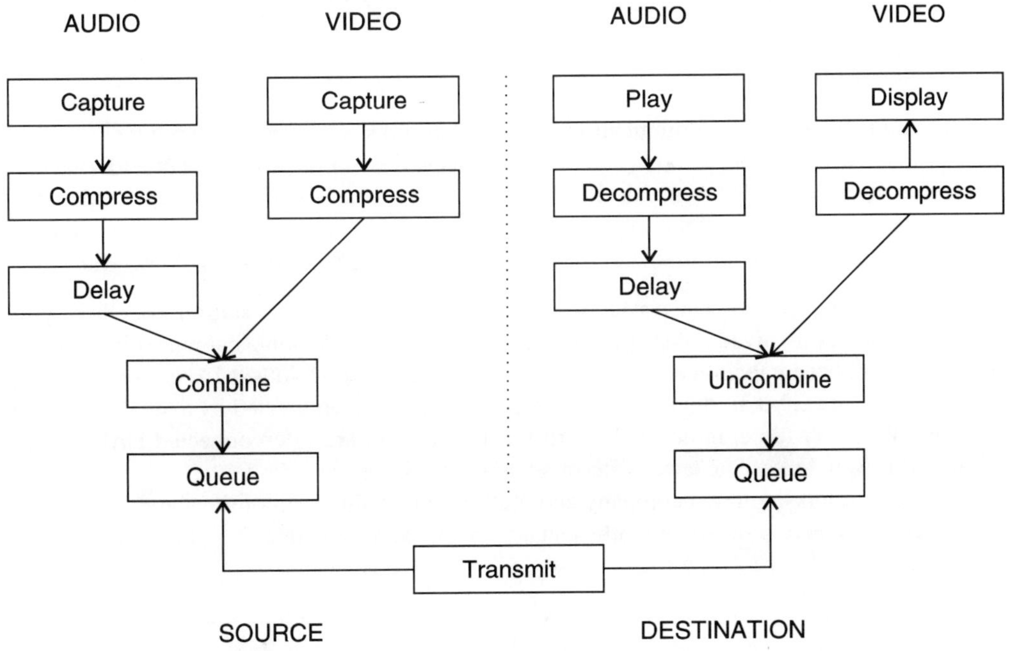

Figure 4.6 Capture and display process for audio/video

The capture process inevitably introduces delay. For video, and possibly for audio, the captured data is compressed to make it more amenable to transmission; compression, especially for video, introduces significant delay. In many cases, video compression involves the comparison of successive frames to detect differences; these video frames must be delayed to allow the comparison to take place. The delay box shown for audio in Fig. 4.6 reflects an audio stream that must be synchronized with video and, therefore, has to be delayed as much as the video, even though there is no processing to perform. The queuing time corresponds to the compressed data waiting for the terminal software, and/or the network, to be ready to transmit the data. Transmission itself takes time, and then the reverse of the capture process is required for display at the destination.

The jitter introduced by all these processes can be handled at the receiving terminal in two ways. The first approach is to buffer the arriving data to smooth out the variable transmissions delays. From this buffer, there will always be data available for the display/play process, thus it can proceed at a consistent rate. The only problem with this delightful scheme is that the buffering introduces additional latency, which is generally unacceptable for person-to-person multimedia. Such an approach is generally acceptable for machine-to-person multimedia, such as the playing of a movie from a file server.

The alternative approach is to reduce the buffering so that the latency falls within the acceptable range or, if this is not possible, to as low a figure as possible. Then jitter will produce situations where data are required for output but none are available. Various schemes have been invented to cope with this situation; for audio nothing very successful exists and the result of delayed data is clicks and other audio artefacts. For video there are more successful schemes and simply reusing the previous data is often sufficient. The other situation caused by jitter is bunches of packets arriving together; in this case all but the latest packet need to be discarded, otherwise the effect is simply to increase buffering and, therefore, overall system latency.

4.3 Networks

A computer network is a communications system that links two or more computers together in order to exchange information. There is enormous variety in the kinds of network that can be created and the challenge for desktop conferencing, to a large extent, is to exploit the installed infrastructure. The technology exists to build new networks with ideal characteristics, but this is seldom an affordable option; much more realistic is a process of evolution.

LANs (local area networks) use private wiring systems to connect workstations together; typically the distances involved are those within a single building. Within a campus it is common to install a backbone capability which interconnects the various LANs. MANs (metropolitan area networks) are city based and are comprised of LANs interconnected by a local telephone company. WANs (wide area networks) cross countries and are interconnected LANs using public and private links. The term 'enterprise network' is used to refer to the entire collection of networks and links within a company and may comprise any or all of the above. It is likely to be a varied collection of subnetworks and *ad hoc* arrangements that do not form a coherent whole.

From a workstation standpoint, the network is apparent as a cable that attaches to a network interface card within the computer (possibly built-in). This card is specific to the network, with the most common of these being Ethernet and token ring, but there are many others, e.g.

FDDI, ARCNET, ATM. Various wiring systems can be used for some or all of these networks, such as twisted pair, coax cable, optical fibre, etc., and similarly there are a number of wiring topologies that may be adopted. All these choices affect network performance. Such aspects relate to level 1 of the OSI model.

Besides these physical considerations there are decisions that can be made about the network access method to be used. The access method determines how the workstation interfaces to the network, for example: carrier sensing or token passing. In a linear topology network such as Ethernet, an attached workstation sends data over the network if no other workstation appears to be using it; if it detects that another workstation is sending data at the same time, then it backs off. In a ring topology network such as token ring, a workstation only transmits if it is in possession of the ring token. Using OSI terminology, these access methods are level 2 and choices here also have performance implications.

Above the access method used by the workstation is the networking support or the networking operating system. In a peer-to-peer network, where all workstations are equal and there is no central server in control, this is usually the networking component of the operating system. In more sophisticated networks, where a network management is in place and central resources are being both shared and managed, a network operating system runs on dedicated servers in conjunction with client networking software. Network operating systems can cover from layer 3 upwards of the OSI model and may reach up to layer 1. Most of such operating systems can be customized in many ways to use a variety of different protocols to transmit information. It is at these levels that it becomes very difficult to make simple statements about network performance and capability. Desktop conferencing does not require a networking operating system; instead desktop conferencing applications require network access and this will typically be expected from OSI level 5 and above.

Figure 4.7 illustrates some common networking environments. The vertical columns reflect network operating systems and, in many situations, the higher layers will either not be present or be replaced by alternatives. Thus, for example, many applications will use NetBIOS session services directly. Furthermore, different selections can often be made at the various OSI layers; thus a NetBIOS interface can be made available over TCP/IP, and the TCP/IP transport/network protocol can be used over a token ring or Ethernet network using an NDIS driver.

Local area networks generally have limits on the distances that can be supported, the number of workstations that can be attached, and the amount of traffic that can be handled. In order to exceed one or more of these limits, LANs can be segmented, that is broken into two or more smaller LANs. These segments can then be joined together with a bridge. A bridge operates at layer 2 of the OSI model and avoids the need for all of the data to traverse all of the network. The IEEE 802 standard provides a media access control specification and the different networks that conform to it may be bridged at this level, for example token ring and Ethernet.

Certain networks can also be interconnected at the OSI layer 3 through the use of routers. These allow separately addressable networks to be linked but not all protocols are supported. Routers can provide route optimization when more than one route is available.

4.3.1 Local area networks

At the physical level, the wiring used in local area networks puts limits on the bandwidth that can achieved. These limits are constantly being pushed higher by improvements in technology but as an approximate guide:

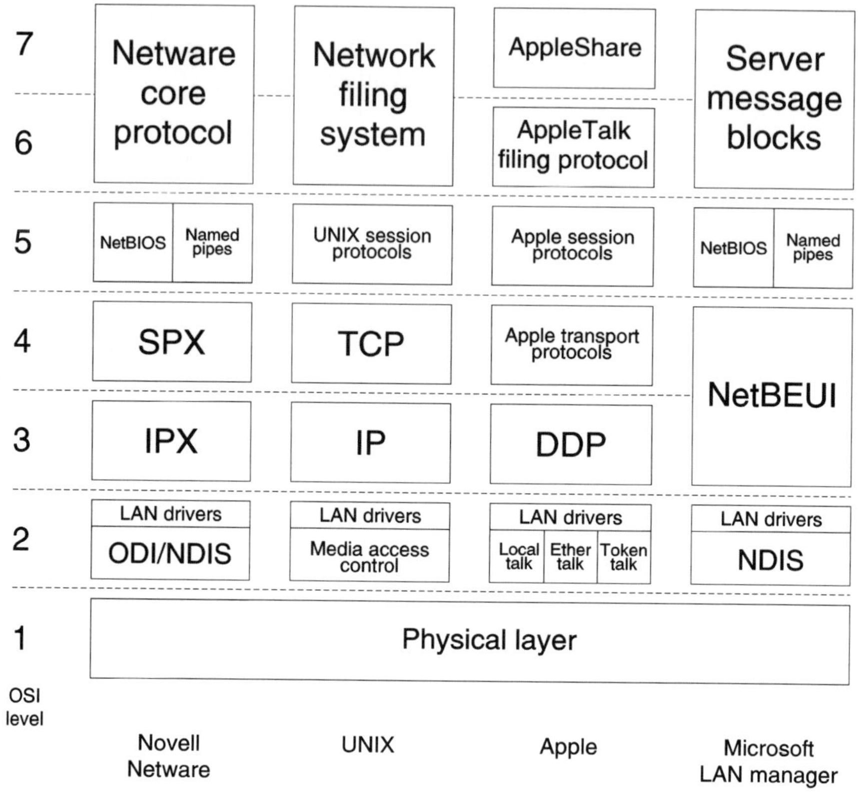

Figure 4.7 Common networking environments

Co-axial cable	20 Mbits/s.
Twisted-pair copper cable	100 Mbits/s.
Fibre optic cable	100 Mbits/s.
Wireless	
narrow-band radio	5 kbits/s.
spread-spectrum radio	250 kbits/s.
infrared	10 Mbits/s.

Three physical local area wiring topologies are possible: linear, star and ring. Linear consists of a single cable daisy-chained from one computer to the next; star requires a single cable from a central point to each workstation; and ring (very rare) connects each workstation to the next and then back to the first. The topology does affect performance; in a linear topology the single linear wire carries all the traffic between all the workstations and therefore its maximum capacity must be shared. In a star system it would be expected that the capacity of the link is available to each workstation; however, in the most common form of star system, token ring, the central point is simply a wiring closet and the connection is logically a ring because the traffic for all workstations runs up and down each arm of the star. As a result, token ring also shares the maximum capacity across all attached workstations.

The most common access methods in use are carrier sensing and token passing; another access method, developed for the 100 Mbits/s. Ethernet standard, is demand priority.

Carrier sensing nodes listen for a carrier tone and transmit when other devices are not themselves transmitting. Carrier sense multiple access/collision detection (CSMA/CD) and carrier sense multiple access/collision avoidance (CSMA/CA) are variations on this technique.

Demand priority access method network access management is performed by a central hub which determines when individual workstations should access the cable.

Token passing a token is passed round the network, which is acquired by a workstation that wishes to transmit.

Carrier sensing methods are normally able to support faster data rates than token passing techniques, but perhaps more important is how network performance degrades as traffic increases. Collision detection becomes very unsatisfactory as network traffic approaches full capacity; token ring has better characteristics in this regard. These considerations affect throughput, latency and jitter and these parameters all degrade on busy LANs. It is this unpredictability, and the lack of any control, which makes shared local area networks such as Ethernet and token ring unsuited to real-time multimedia communications.

The higher level protocol layers affect performance characteristics in many ways. The need to pass the data up and down protocol stacks leads to delays which, at least in the local area, can be significant and usually exceed the transmission time over the physical network. The time-sharing nature of workstation operating systems means that jitter is introduced because the processor may not be continuously available. Different protocol stacks allow different network features to be exploited such as route selection, route optimization, network broadcast capabilities, and so on. Thus the choice of the higher level layers may be critical in determining the actual performance achieved.

Ethernet has been standardized by the IEEE 802.3 committee and the following variations exist:

10Base-5: coaxial, 10 Mbits/s., 500 metres max. per segment, linear topology.
10Base-2: coaxial, 10 Mbits/s., 185 metres max. per segment, linear topology
10Base-T: twisted pair, 10 Mbits/s., 100 metres max. per segment, star topology.
1Base-5: twisted pair, 1 Mbits/s., 500 metres max. per segment, linear topology.
10 Broad-36: coax, 100 Mbits/s., 3600 metres max. per segment, linear topology.
10 Base-F: fibre optic, 10 Mbits/s., 4 kilometres max. per segment, linear topology.
100 Base-X: twisted pair, 100 Mbits/s., hierarchical topology.
100VG-AnyLAN: twisted pair cable, 100 Mbits/s., hierarchical topology.

A recent development of the Ethernet is the so-called is Iso-Ethernet. This replaces the daisy chain topology with a hub configuration. Each workstation gets a dedicated 10 Mbits/s. data connection that uses exactly the same access methods as standard Ethernet and so is totally compatible. In addition, a number of isochronous 64 kbits/s. channels are available, with the hub able to interconnect these among the workstations and thus acting like a telephone switch. These channels are perfectly suited for multimedia communications and standards are being proposed which make these channels compatible with those for ISDN (see later discussion of ISDN channels).

Token ring has been standardized by the IEEE 802.5 committee. The topology is that of a physical star with a multi-point access unit (MAU) providing the hub. There is no logic in the MAU and it exists to allow connections to be made and broken without breaking the logical ring. There are 4 Mbits/s. and 16 Mbits/s. versions in existence and a variety of cable types are defined. The token ring definitions do allow priority to be associated with data packets but this has not been used until recently. Multimedia performance can be improved by distinguishing traffic in this way, but a complete solution also requires bandwidth management across the network to ensure that the capacity is available when required. Various schemes have been proposed under the generic name of iso-token ring.

AppleTalk is the set of specifications that define how Apple Macintosh computers, printers and other devices communicate with each other over a network. It was originally designed for small local networks and used built-in adapters supporting the proprietary LocalTalk cabling system at 230.4 kbits/s. with a limit of 254 nodes per network. Through the EtherTalk and TokenTalk access methods, Ethernet and token ring topologies are supported with a limit of 16 million nodes per network.

FDDI is a fibre-optic cable standard established by the ANSI X3T9.5 committee. It operates at 100 Mbits/s., uses a dual ring technology, and is capable of supporting up to 500 network nodes over a distance of 100 kilometres, with a maximum distance of 2 kilometres between adjacent nodes. A copper version of the standard exists for unshielded twisted pair cable, known as the ANSI TP-PMD standard, with a limit of 100 metres between adjacent nodes. FDDI provides two access services, asynchronous and synchronous. The asynchronous service is token based and the traffic is not prioritized; thus time-sensitive traffic suffers if the network is busy. The synchronous token passing ring mode does allow traffic prioritization and so part of the bandwidth can be reserved for high priority traffic; non-priority traffic competes for the rest. Although this divides the traffic, it does not provide guaranteed bandwidth between any two nodes on the network.

FDDI-II is a development of the FDDI standard designed for networks that need to transport multimedia traffic. It uses multiplexing techniques to divide the bandwidth into dedicated circuits that can guarantee the delivery of traffic. Up to 16 separate circuits can be created that can operate at from 6.144 Mbits/s. each to a maximum of 99.072 Mbits/s. These circuits can be further subdivided to a maximum of 96 separate 64 kbits/s. circuits, capable of carrying either asynchronous or isochronous traffic. Regular timed slots in the ring are used to make guaranteed bandwidth available. The greatest competitor to FDDI-II is ATM technology (see below) which, although originally intended for wide area public networks, is rapidly being adopted for the local area backbone and even for direct workstation connection.

4.3.2 Leased lines

A leased line is a communication circuit, set-up on a permanent basis—that is the opposite of a switched connection. This characteristic alone almost precludes its use for desktop conferencing since it provides fixed remote access; however, leased lines are frequently used to connect local area networks and are thus important in the creation of private networks. Leased lines can be analogue or digital but it is the latter which are of most interest. In the USA, the standard digital line service is known as T1, providing transmission at 1.544 Mbits/s. Using a multiplexor, a T1 line can carry 24 channels of voice and/or data at 64 kbits/s. More capacity is available as a T3 line with 43.232 Mbits/s. (or 28 T1 lines). Less bandwidth can be obtained as fractional-T1 lines, where the capacity available is an integer multiple of the basic 64 kbits/s. channels.

The latency and jitter characteristics of these dedicated lines pose no problems for real-time multimedia communication.

4.3.3 Analogue telephone network

Analogue telephone lines provide dial-up switched circuits. These can be used for analogue audio transmission, as in a normal telephone call, and thereby complement any associated data network transmitting the data component of the conference. However, more interesting is their use for either digital data only, or for analogue audio and digital data together. The digital data component itself can be used as a vehicle for audio and video through an associated codec; for audio this is inferior to the analogue audio/digital data combination but it is used for video, with the video frame rate slowed down to a sequence of still images every few seconds.

Standard modems convert digital signals, i.e. data, to analogue waveforms for transmission over the network and then back to digital again on receipt. They are the most available method for the remote connection of workstations. A family of ITU-T standards defines modem interfaces:

V.21	30 bits/s. full duplex.
V.22	600 and 1.2 kbits/s. full-duplex.
V.22bis	adds 2.4 kbits/s. full-duplex to V.22.
V.23	split speed 1.2 kbits/s. transmit, 75 bits/s. receive; 75 bits/s. transmit, 1.2 kbits/s. receive; 1.2 kbits/s. half duplex.
V.32	asynchronous and synchronous 4.8 and 9.6 kbits/s.
V.32bis	asynchronous and synchronous up to 14.4 kbits/s.
V.32terbo	provides 19.2 kbits/s.
V.34 (V.fast)	provides 28.8 kbits/s.

The bandwidths given above refer to the actual data rates over the link but many modems achieve much higher effective rates through the use of sophisticated compression algorithms, such as the ITU-T V.42bis standard or the Microcom Networking Protocol MNP class 5. Thus a modem that transmits at 28.8 kbits/s. may accept data input at rates around 115 kbits/s. External modems attached to the standard serial port of personal computers have been limited to a maximum error free speed of 9.6 kbit/s. because of the need for frequent servicing of the port by the central processor. However, the need to support high speed modems is leading to its capabilities being upgraded; typically there modems can also be attached to the parallel port where the higher data rates are supported. Integrated ports and modems are also available for direct attachment to the PC bus through PCMCIA or other adapter cards, thus avoiding data rate bottlenecks.

Modems have increased in sophistication considerably in recent years and many techniques are incorporated to handle error recovery over noisy analogue lines, dynamic rate adaptation, and so on. The dedicated nature of the link means that, although the data rates are relatively low, they are guaranteed and end-to-end latency is very low. The widespread availability of the analogue telephone network means that it will continue to play an important role for digital communication for some considerable time.

A recent development has been the data over voice modem. This device allows a conventional voice call to take place while routing data inaudibly over the link at the same time. ITU-T standards are being proposed for such devices but products are already available. In one such modem, the data rate accepted before compression is 57 kbits/s., with a modem transmission rate of 19.2 kbits/s.—which includes the audio stream compressed down to 9 kbits/s. Such products are likely to develop rapidly and are an ideal solution for audio and data conferencing where nothing more sophisticated than an analogue telephone line is available.

4.3.4 Public data networks

Public data networks provide an international network of interconnected access points and switches that can support simultaneous data transmission for many users. Such networks divide into two primary types: circuit-switched and packet-switched.

Circuit-switched networks provide a logically dedicated channel between the parties, for example the ISDN and switched 56 kbits/s. services. Such a service generally involves a bandwidth allocation which is fixed for the duration of the connection. Historically the time taken to establish connection was relatively long, i.e. the order of several seconds, and so connections once established were generally maintained until the end of the call. Modern switching technology has reduced this connection time to milliseconds in some cases and it is, therefore, becoming more common to take down the call if no data is available to be sent and to re-establish it when needed. The dedicated nature of the connection and the guaranteed bandwidth make circuit-switched services suitable for isochronous traffic.

ISDN provides integrated audio, video and data services over the switched public data network. Narrowband ISDN provides from 64 kbits/s. to 2 Mbits/s., while broadband ISDN offers megabit to gigabit rates. This technology is the bedrock of desktop conferencing and is discussed in detail in Chapter 7.

Switched-56 service is popular in the USA, partly because of the relative unavailability of ISDN in the USA in comparison to Europe. It allows data to be transported over switched synchronous lines at 56 kbits/s. or over switched asynchronous lines at 57.6 kbits/s. The channels are dial-up and so used only when needed and are considerably faster than modem rates over analogue lines, but compare poorly with the twin 64 kbits/s. capacity which is the normal basic rate ISDN service over the existing telephony copper wiring. Like ISDN, the service is well suited to audio, video and data.

Packet-switched services provide a connection-less service. Users do not make a connection but instead access a packet transmission service such as X.25. Each packet of data from each supplier carries its destination address as a header on the packet. Exchanges in the network examine the packet address and forward them to the destination. There are many possible routes between the source and destination and the service will use whatever route is available, with the choice being made on an individual packet basis. Some packets may be delayed in the network because of shortage of transmission capabilities. Packet services were designed when networks were liable to high error rates, and it was also assumed that dumb devices would be sending the data and that the network was to be responsible for error checking. As a consequence the packets are continually examined for data corruption. The sender is notified of errors in a packet so that the packet can be retransmitted. Delays occur at the receiving end as packets are reassembled in the correct sequence. Coping with high error rates also leads to a design point based on small packets to avoid excessive retransmission.

A variant on the standard packet-switched service is the establishment of a virtual circuit (or logical circuit). The virtual circuit involves the use of a predefined route through the network and a circuit identifier is added to each packet. This provides some of the same benefits as a circuit-switched service and there is no reassembling delay on receipt.

The X.25 is an ITU-T recommendation that defines connections of terminals and computers to packet-switching networks and offers a virtual circuit. The original standard defined line speeds up to 64 kbits/s., with much of this capacity taken by error checking overhead; a revision in 1992 defined a service up to 2 Mbits/s. The use of shared ports through routers can lead to delays when network traffic from all users becomes heavy. The poor performance of X.25 means that it is ill-suited to most real-time applications.

Frame Relay is a packet-orientated communication method primarily used for local area network interconnection and wide area networking over public and private networks. Most public carriers offer Frame Relay services for the establishment of wide area virtual circuits providing bandwidth in the range 56 kbits/s. to 1.544 Mbits/s. In late 1993, switched virtual circuits were added to the standard. Frame Relay itself is derived from the ISDN definitions. The major difference between X.25 and Frame Relay is that in the latter case the design point is an error-free network and intelligent terminals that can detect and handle errors. Thus there is no error detection within Frame Relay and much data handling in the network is avoided. A characteristic of the technology is that the frames can contain variable length data which makes them very efficient for data transmission. However, the variability in frame size means that one frame can hold up other frames—depending upon its size. This variability means that services based on Frame Relay are not suited to real-time audio and video transmission.

ATM (asynchronous transfer mode) is a service that moved fixed size cells of data between switches in the network and operates at the OSI layer 2 (data link). Like Frame Relay, in many ways it is designed for an error-free network attached to intelligent end-points, but its fixed cell size gives it many advantages. This simplicity means that there is a minimum of complexity at the switching nodes, predictable behaviour, and no possibility that delays can build up in the network. Hence, it is ideal for carrying audio and video traffic. Many services can be offered over ATM technology including transmission at rates up to gigabits/s. Although designed for the wide area, ATM is now available at the desktop through workstation adapter cards.

CHAPTER 5

Audio technology

5.1 The nature of audio

Sound is energy transmitted by pressure waves containing various frequencies and can be converted to an electrical signal by an acoustic transducer, such as a microphone or telephone handset. The electrical output of the transducer is an analogue signal because it continuously varies in value, or amplitude, with time. If the amplitude of the signal is plotted it forms a wave pattern which repeats almost exactly through time. The repeat pattern is not identical because most sounds vary with time, but the pattern is usually obvious for a single continuous note from a source of sound such as a musical instrument. An example is shown in Fig. 5.1.

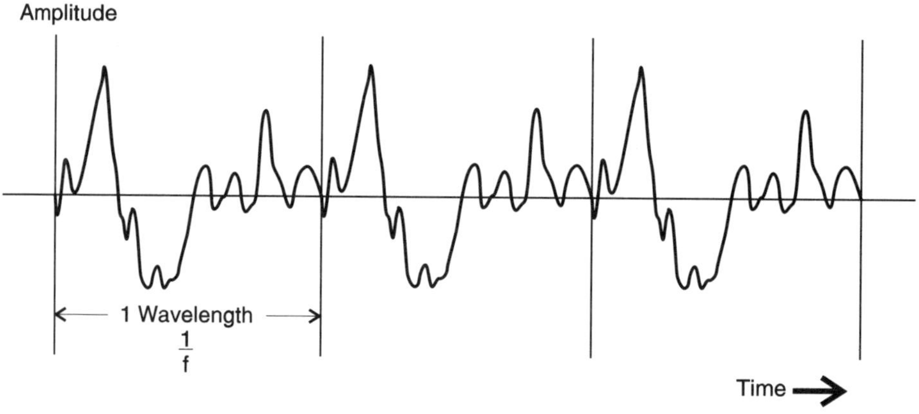

Figure 5.1 An analogue audio waveform

The frequency of a wave is determined by the time that elapses between repetitions, measured in wavelengths/second, usually known as cycles per second. The wavelength of middle A is about 2.273 ms. resulting in a frequency of 440 Hz.

A single frequency results in a waveform that has a true sinusoidal shape. Real sounds are never this simple and depart from the ideal, as does the example in the Fig. 5.1. These differences give sounds their characteristic quality, thus an A from a clarinet has a different waveform than an A from a flute, although both have a basic frequency of 440 Hz. These complex waveforms can be analysed as a basic waveform with overtones of higher frequencies, the overtones being multiples of the base frequency.

Speech is a complex mixture, since the basic frequencies are themselves constantly changing and there is a rich set of harmonics present. Nevertheless, speech is still composed of a range of frequencies. The range of frequencies in speech and the capability of the human ear are shown in Table 5.1, along with the frequency content of some common sources of sound.

Table 5.1 Audio frequency ranges and bandwidths

Audio source/target	*Frequency range*	*Bandwidth*
Human voice	50–15,000 Hz	14.95 kHz
Human ear	20–20,000 Hz	10.98 kHz
Standard telephony	300–3,400 Hz	3.1 kHz
Compact disc quality	50–20,000 Hz	10.98 kHz

The bandwidth column shows the frequency range of the signal, that is the difference between the maximum and the minimum frequencies in the signal. If the multiple audio streams are multiplexed on to a single carrier in analogue format, each stream will need to be allocated its particular bandwidth, though all the frequencies in any one stream will be transposed to avoid overlap with other streams.

ADCs (analogue to digital converters) sample the signal and express instantaneous values of the amplitude in digital form; the process is known as pulse code modulation (PCM). The sampling frequency determines how often the samples are taken, for example 16 kHz; the directly related parameter sampling interval gives the time between measurements. The resolution reflects the accuracy of the digital amplitude representation, for example 8-bit implies 255 sound levels with 0 meaning no sound. ADCs are subject to error and the actual performance may be worse that the quantizing error implied by the resolution.

The maximum frequency that can be reproduced without distortion by digital sampling techniques is exactly half the sampling rate; this frequency is known as the Nyquist frequency. A serious problem, called aliasing, exists when sampling sounds containing frequencies above the Nyquist frequency; the effect is that the higher frequencies are shifted. Thus, if a frequency 15 kHz is sampled at 20 kHz, the signal on decoding will contain frequencies at 20 kHz–15 kHz, i.e. 5 kHz. To prevent aliasing, low-pass filters are used to remove frequencies greater than the Nyquist frequency before the analogue to digital conversion process.

5.1.1 Echoes and signal processing

Transmission of analogue audio is subject to a phenomenon known as echoes, caused by the hardware characteristics of the wiring system. Echoes result in a low volume delayed copy of the audio input being relayed back to the source. Such an echo is disconcerting to the speaker and the longer the delay, the more troublesome the echo. There are two solutions available at the terminal; the first is to allow only half-duplex operation, i.e. when the equipment detects that the local person is speaking, it prevents any audio being heard from the remote destination. This is an inexpensive solution but is an impediment to natural conversation. A second solution is to use sophisticated signal processing techniques which effectively cancel out the echoes by deducting a portion of the outgoing audio from the incoming audio, suitably delayed.

While there is a component of echoes that arises from analogue circuits, there is another component that arises from audio feedback at the terminals. This can be from the earpiece to the mouthpiece, or from the loudspeaker to the microphone via the room. Quality video-conferencing equipment uses loudspeakers for hands-free operation and permits full-duplex exchanges. Signal processors are used to calculate the effects of audio reflections in the room and cancel out them out. The results that can be achieved are quite remarkable, such that all participants are heard with equal clarity irrespective of their distance from the microphone.

5.2 Telephony standards for digitized audio

5.2.1 The G.711 recommendation

G.711 audio encoding is the basic audio digital encoding for telephony. The range of analogue frequencies available on local telephone loops is approximately 300–3400 Hz. This restricted range, without the higher frequencies, is responsible for the poor audio quality of telephone systems but is a direct consequence of the existing design of analogue telephone networks. From a network design perspective, the bandwidth is considered to be 0–4000 Hz, thereby allowing a margin of safety when audio streams are multiplexed together. The sampling rate used is 8000 Hz.

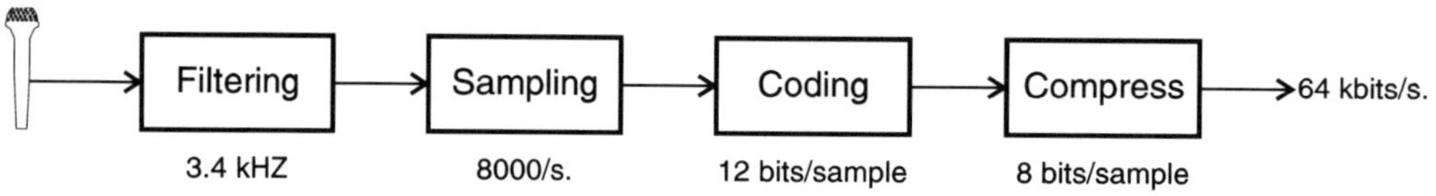

Figure 5.2 The G.711 audio recommendation

Experiments have shown that 12 bits are needed to give an audibly acceptable speech representation; however, it has also been discovered that the human ear is much more tolerant to distortion at higher volumes than at lower volumes. This can be exploited by using a non-linear translation function from amplitude to digital representation, and results in a requirement for only 8 bits per sample (see Fig. 5.2). This transformation is approximately logarithmic; it cannot be exactly logarithmic because the logarithms of numbers less than one are negative, while the transformation must have a zero value for zero amplitude. Unfortunately, two slightly different non-linear translation functions exist. In North America an encoding called μ-law is used; in Europe a slightly different scheme called A-law is standard. Both functions use the first bit in the code to indicate the polarity of the sample; for A-law alternate bits in the code word are inverted to avoid runs of zeros, for μ-law all binary digits are inverted for the same reason. In telephony between Europe and North America, translation between these encodings is performed by the network operators.

The combination of 8000 samples per second at 8 bits/sample results in the 64 kbit/s. standard PCM audio stream.

5.2.2 The G.721 recommendation

G.721 encodes telephone quality speech into a 32 kbits/s. data stream using a technique called adaptive quantization, differential PCM or ADPCM (adaptive differential pulse code modulation); it provides apparent G.711 quality in half the digital bandwidth. The speech is sampled at 8000 Hz and then digitized at 12 bits/sample. Based upon previous values, a prediction is made as to what the value of the signal should be— the difference between this prediction and the actual value is determined and then encoded as follows. Each difference is compared with 16 quantizing levels (4 bits) each a value χ apart. The nearest quantization level is chosen to represent the difference. The expansion or compression of the quantization range is achieved simply by multiplying χ by a number greater or less than unity, depending upon the quantization level selected to code the previous sample. Thus the algorithm adapts to the volume level of the speech (see Fig. 5.3).

The use of predictions and differences in this algorithm is a subtle feature that allows the number of bits used to be reduced. A less efficient scheme would compare each sample directly with the quantizing levels.

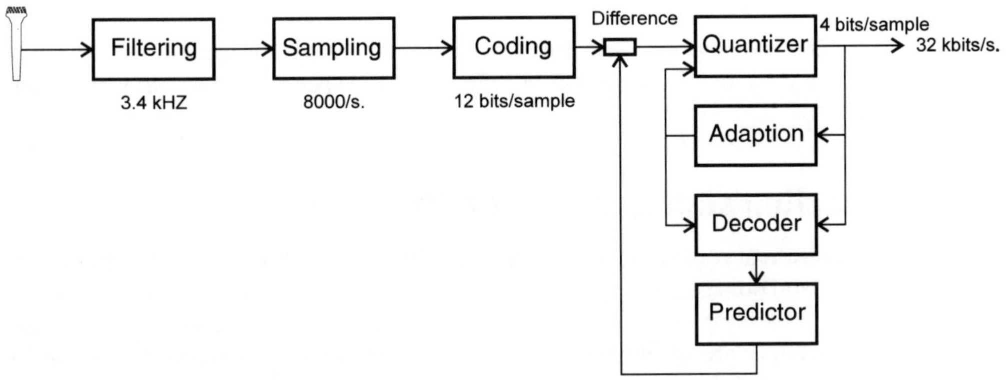

Figure 5.3 The G.721 audio recommendation

5.2.3 The G.722 recommendation

The intention of the G.722 standard was to provide high quality speech in a bandwidth of 64 kbits/s. Most human speech contains very little energy above the 7 kHz frequency limit and, in accordance with the standard, is sampled at 16 kHz and then digitized at 14 bits/sample, making a 'raw' bandwidth of 224 kbits/s. The digital stream is then filtered into two bands, one representing the frequency range 50 Hz–4 kHz, the other 4–7 kHz.

Each band is then sub-sampled from its original 8 kHz bandwidth to a 4 kHz bandwidth data stream—the two bands are then encoded using the ADPCM technique, the low frequency

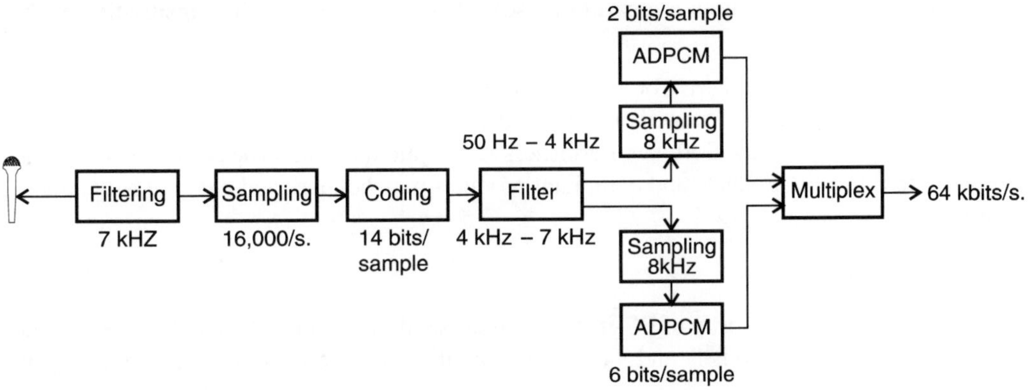

Figure 5.4 The G.722 audio recommendation

band, where most of the energy is, being allocated 6 bits and the high frequency band being allocated 2 bits. The two data streams are then combined in a multiplexor to produce a composite rate of 64 kbits/s. (see Fig. 5.4).

The recommendation also supports the optional provision of a simultaneous data channel of either 8 kbits/s. or 16 kbits/s. within the same 64 kbits/s. overall bandwidth. This is achieved by stealing the least significant 1 or 2 bits from the 6 bits allocated to the low frequency band and using these for data transmission. The effect on the speech quality is scarcely audible.

5.2.4 The G.728 recommendation

The ITU-T G.728 recommendation defines a method of coding speech using a technique known as low-delay excited linear prediction. The result is a speech data stream which occupies only 16 kbits/s.

5.3 Workstation standards for digitized audio

There are many different codings available for audio data on the workstation, and strong links exist between PC and domestic storage formats. While the storage formats are not themselves of direct interest in desktop conferencing, the audio streams resulting from the reading and writing of such devices are of interest. Some of the most common parameters used in PC audio are given in Table 5.2.

Table 5.2 Audio equipment standards

Audio source/target	*Sampling rates (kHz)*	*Resolution (bits)*	*Channels*
PC audio adapters	5.0125 11.025 22.05 44.1	8 or 16	1 or 2
Audio compact disc	44.1	16	2
Digital audio tape	48.0	16	2

The resolution encoding uses a logarithmic scale better to represent the sensitivities of the human ear.

A body to establish standards for multimedia on the personal computer exists called the Multimedia PC Marketing Council or Multimedia PC (MPC), originally created by Microsoft but now a subsidiary of the Software Publishers Association. It establishes standard specifications for multimedia products and compliant products may be marketed with the MPC trademark.

5.3.1 Audio adapters

Prior to 1993 the vast majority of PC-installed sound cards had 8-bit DACs and a monophonic capability, but stereo channels and 44.1 kHz sampling rates are now becoming much more common.

An important standard for the storage of audio waveform data is the Microsoft Resource Interchange File Format (RIFF) wave file, identified through the WAV extension. The file structure includes a header which gives information about the sampling process used to create the file, including the following:

- format of the data (8-bit mono, 16-bit stereo PCM, etc.)
- number of channels
- playback sampling rate for each channel in Hz
- average playback rate
- block alignment of the data

Monophonic samples are stored in a continuous stream, stereophonic samples are interleaved in blocks to avoid delays between the right- and the left-hand channels. The block alignment data is required to keep the right channel aligned. The data rates are much greater than those used in telephony, thus CD quality stereophonic sound equates to 1.411 Mbits/s.

Playback of PCM audio on higher quality audio adapters uses a faster rate of digital to analogue conversion than was used originally to sample the sound—the technique is called oversampling, e.g. 4 x oversampling or even 16 x oversampling. Oversampling involves adding sample values with no amplitude to the original values; thus in 4 x oversampling, three zero values are inserted between each pair of original values. A digital filter circuit then calculates interpolated values for the zero values and these are used in the digital to analogue converter. Four x oversampling on an eight-bit sample produces audio of approximately 12-bits/sample quality.

No final standards exist for compressed audio in the workstation; a number of compressed audio formats exist on CD-ROMs and others for combined audio and video streams. ADPCM technology is likely to form the basis for any emerging standard.

Related to the PC audio standards is the MIDI (Music Industry Digital Interface) format. This is a way of encoding music streams and supports up to 16 signal channels, each of which can be assigned to different instrument voice or device. The commands down each channel indicate when a note is to be played, and also supply the pitch and volume information. Two types of musical synthesizers are supported by the MIDI standard: base level and extended. Base level synthesizers must be able to play three melodic timbres and two percussive timbres simultaneously; additionally, they must be capable of playing six melodic notes and two percussive notes at the same time, i.e. they have eight voice polyphony. Extended synthesizers must be able to play nine simultaneous melodic timbres and eight percussive timbres.

The significance of the MIDI format for conferencing is that, although its use is very specialized, it produces a data stream that is approximately 100 times more compact than the equivalent WAV format. The quality is dependent upon the sound synthesis at the local site.

5.3.2 Compact disc formats

A number of audio formats have been defined for CD-ROM drives and some of these are important in the workstation. In addition to the pure audio formats, others interleave audio with video and/or with data. The important distinction from a conferencing perspective is between the format of the audio data stream that such drives produce and the storage format which dictates how the data is actually stored on a physical medium.

The standard 120 mm audio compact disc, originally intended for use only on domestic CD players, uses the same PCM audio sampling and playback techniques already described for audio adapter cards. The data storage format, known as compact disc digital audio (CD-DA or CDAudio), is quite different from that used in WAV files. CD-DA uses a fixed sampling rate of 44.1 kHz and 16-bit samples as opposed to the options available with WAV files. The drives run at a constant linear velocity so that the spindle speed is automatically varied form around 200 rpm at the outside edge to around 530 rpm near the spindle. The data is organized as 24 byte frames played at a rate of 75 frames per second. Standard CDs have a playing time of 74 minutes 33 seconds. The theoretical maximum number of sectors on a CD-ROM is 330 000 with a maximum capacity of 660 Mbytes, although this is generally reduced to 630 Mbytes by the inclusion of error correcting codes.

Compact disc video (CD-V) combines CD-DA digital audio and laser disc analogue video on to 120 mm CD discs; the same composite format is also available on 8" and 12" discs.

Digital audio tapes (DATs) offer the highest quality commonly available digital sound source, using a sampling rate of 48 kHz and 16-bit samples.

CD-ROMs were originally used for data storage for personal computers and, in this role, adopted byte formats close to those in use on floppy and hard files. However, the applications for pre-recorded data were greatly enhanced if graphics and audio could be added and, accordingly new standards were introduced to support this. The original CD+Graphics format had the dual disadvantages that not only were separate tracks needed for audio and graphics or text, but also the waveform audio format needed intensive CPU processing to create sound.

The CD-ROM XA standard was introduced to solve some of these problems. It interleaves audio, text and graphics within the same file, thus enabling synchronization. Additionally it uses an ADPCM audio compression scheme to reduce storage and therefore also processing requirements.

The standards for CD-ROM media are known by the colour of the Philips publications that describe them:

- The red book describes consumer digital audio CD-DA. It has been adopted as an International Electrotechnical Commission international standard, IEC 908. The MPC specification for devices specifies the combination of features in the standard that must be supported and also lays down other criteria, e.g. block sizes, buffer sizes, mean time to failure and, from a conferencing standpoint:

  an access time of 1000 ms. or less; an ability to sustain a continuous rate of 150 000 bytes/s. while using less than 40 per cent of the CPU processing power (i.e. not quite sufficient to meet the CD-DA audio requirements for 44.1 kHz for 16-bit stereo audio).

- The yellow book describes formats for the storing of data in files such that they can be translated to all the common workstation formats; the standard also includes extensive error detection and correction. Directory structures do not form part of the yellow book but the standards for this component were set by an industry group (known as the High Sierra Group) and have been adopted as ISO standard ISO 9660. ISO 10149 defines the format of the data tracks.
- CD-XA does not have a dedicated book but requires a subset of the green book (see below) plus the yellow book specifications. It enables different kinds of data to be interleaved on the same track—audio data is interleaved with graphics, for example. More importantly, the audio data is compressed using an algorithm based on ADPCM technology. Three qualities of compressed audio are supported:

  Hi-Fi XA: (close to audio CD quality)
  8-bit ADPCM 37.8 kHz sampling rate 20Hz–17kHz bandwidth
  Mid-Fi XA: (narration and background music)
  4-bit ADPCM 37.8 kHz sampling rate 20Hz–17kHz bandwidth
  Speech XA: (narration and other sounds)
  4-bit ADPCM 18.9 kHz sampling rate 20Hz–8.5kHz bandwidth

- The green book describes a format known as CD-Interactive (CD-I) which is an extended version of the CD-XA format.

- The orange book describes a family of re-writable CD-ROMs; orange-book 1 drives are erasable and re-writable; orange-book 2 drives are write-once/read many (WORM). Kodak Photo CD-ROMs are a variant of orange-book 2.

Most generally-available products implement one or more of these standards. High performance CD-ROM drives are capable of transferring data at twice the standard rate, i.e. about 300 kbytes/s. are generally available; products capable of running at four times the standard rate are starting to appear.

5.4 Brief assessment of audio standards

The differences between the telephony and computer industry approaches are very clear. Telephony systems are speech orientated with a basic capability that offers poor fidelity, with just sufficient quality to allow speaker recognition and natural interaction. Within these constraints, however, the emphasis is on compatibility, inter-operability and continued availability. Having achieved a particular service level that has become accepted in the market, technology has first been used to offer that level at lower cost, by using 32 kbits/s. instead of the original 64 kbits/s. The latter standards move the quality level upwards but the focus is primarily on better speech reproduction; music and high fidelity sound are not yet important considerations.

The computer industry started with an interest in sounds for games and a need to add music to enhance the perusal and content of large data bases. As always in the computer industry, many standards exist and the challenge that is being tackled is to develop the workstation into a multimedia machine. High-fidelity sound is the goal and the standard has already been set in the domestic market by the compact disc player; speech is just an interesting subset of that goal. The limited audio formats of telephony have not been used and new standards have been developed which constantly exploit the storage and processing power available. Guaranteed audio performance without break-up is not the primary objective; occasional glitches are undesirable but less of a marketing problem than low quality audio. The multimedia nature of the computer has introduced complex interleaved formats where the various streams to be synchronized are moved together through the various subsystems.

It is impossible to transmit the quality of much of the workstation audio down a telephone line and the formats are completely alien; equally there is little most workstations can do internally with ITU-coded audio data.

CHAPTER 6

Video technology

6.1 The nature of video

A video camera turns an image into an electrical signal, the signal being known as a video signal. This is accomplished by scanning the image in an orderly pattern called a raster. The sensing point is moved over the image fast enough to capture the image before it changes too much. A typical raster is shown in Fig. 6.1

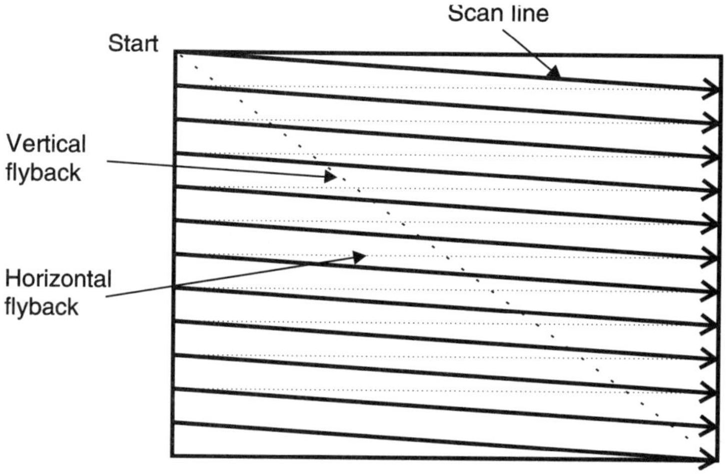

Figure 6.1 Video raster scan

At the end of each scanning line the scanning point flies back to the start of the next line and the sensor is turned off while this occurs; this period is called the horizontal blanking interval. Similarly, when the scanning point returns from the bottom right to the upper left, the vertical blanking interval occurs. Each set of scanning lines is called a frame.

The aspect ratio is the ratio of the length of a scanning line horizontally on the image to the distance covered vertically on the image by all the scanning lines. On existing domestic television standards this ratio is 4:3 and the same ratio is used for PC display adapters.

In order for a video signal to be replayed, additional information is needed to ensure that the monitor scanning will be in synchronization with the camera scanning. This sync information may be included within the blanking period or supplied separately.

The ability of a video signal to reproduce horizontal detail depends upon the performance of the horizontal raster lines and is measured in the television industry by counting the number of black and white vertical lines that can be reproduced in a distance corresponding to the raster height. The representation of abrupt changes from black to white requires corresponding changes in the video signal, and the smaller the scanning spot the more abrupt the change. Representation of such a step function requires very high frequencies—approximately a bandwidth of 1 MHz is needed for each 80 lines of horizontal resolution.

Vertical resolution depends upon the number of scanning lines used in each frame. The NTSC system (established by the National Television Standards Committee), used in Japan and North America, has 525 vertical lines, while the PAL system used in Europe has 625 lines. The vertical resolution response of televisions is not an analogue process in the sense that discrete samples are taken, unlike the horizontal resolution where continuous adjacent samples are used. This difference can give rise to sampling artefacts in the picture. A small number of lines from each frame, typically 40, is devoted to the vertical blanking interval and is also used to transmit other items of data, sometimes unrelated to the television picture.

In order for the eye to perceive a sequence of frames as a continuous and smooth moving image, the frames should ideally be refreshed at greater than 50 frames/s. This requires high bandwidth and television signals achieve the illusion of this through a technique known as interlacing where more than one vertical scan is used to reproduce a complete frame. Broadcast television uses 2:1 interlacing which means that two vertical scans, or fields, are used to make the frame, with one vertical scan displaying all the odd lines and the second vertical scan putting in all the even lines. The NTSC rate is 60 scans/s. or 30 frames/s. PAL is 50 scans/s. or 25 frames/s. Although interlace improves large area flicker it does create other artefacts, such as jagged edges on moving vertical objects and flicker on high contrast horizontal objects. These problems are somewhat obscured by the fuzziness of natural images. Interlacing is not normally used on computer screens because of the need to display graphics detail and small text; require accurate redition of sharp edges, whereas natural images are a small proportion of typical output. Interlacing problems result in video capture cards only using one field of a video image in the still frame.

Colour cameras do not produce a single light intensity signal but instead record three signals, one for each of the three primary colours red, green and blue (RGB). These colours, when added together in the correct proportions, make what we perceive as white. For most purposes, it is inconvenient to handle three separate signals and they are normally combined together in a composite format; the way in which they are combined depends upon the system in use. PAL and NTSC, for example, do this combination differently. All systems make use of the luminance/chrominance principle for their basic structure. This states that any colour signal may be broken down into two parts, luminance and chrominance: luminance is a monochrome video signal that controls only the brightness of the image; chrominance contains only the colouring information for the image. However, in order to reproduce all the colours, the chrominance signal itself contains two signals, each known as colour difference signals.

In a composite system, the luminance and chrominance are combined by frequency interleaving in order to transmit them on a single channel. The luminance signal is transmitted as a normal monochrome signal and the chrominance information is placed in a high frequency subcarrier placed near the top of the channel bandwidth. Careful choosing of the frequencies means that there is very little visual distortion caused by this technique. More importantly, since the eye is less sensitive to colour information than to brightness, the colour resolution is reduced, leading to a bandwidth reduction by a factor of 2 or 4. A composite system using these techniques is able to transmit a colour picture using the same bandwidth as a similar monochrome system.

In the NTSC colour TV system, the luminance signal is called the Y signal and the two chrominance signals the I and Q signals. I stands for in-phase and Q for quadrature, because they are two-phase amplitude-modulated on the colour subcarrier. The Y signal uses the 4.5 MHz bandwidth of a TV channel, the I bandwidth is 1.5 MHz and the Q bandwidth is the 0.5 MHz bandwidth.

The PAL system is also a luminance/chrominance signal. Again chrominance is transmitted on a two-phase amplitude-moderated subcarrier at the top of the system bandwidth, but a more complex process allows both signals to have the 1.5 MHz bandwidth. The difference bandwidths allow a different set of chrominance components to be chosen, these are known as Y and V, instead of I and Q. The NTSC and PAL video formats are presented in Table 6.1.

Table 6.1 NTSC and PAL video formats

System	*NTSC*	*PAL*
Lines/frame	525	625
Frames/s.	30	25
Interlace ratio	2:1	2:1
Aspect ratio	4:3	4:3
Colour matrix equations	Y = 0.30 R + 0.59 G + 0.11B I = 0.60 R–0.28 G–0.32 B Q = 0.21R–0.52 G + 0.31 B	Y = 0.30 R + 0.59 G + 0.11B U = 0.62 R–0.52 G–0.10 B V = -0.15R–0.29 G + 0.44 B

6.2 Video compression considerations

TV video is analogue and, therefore, there is considerable scope in defining a digital representation which contains all of the useful information. A straightforward way is defined in the CCIR recommendation 601 for digital representation, which requires Y to be sampled at 13.5 Mhz and the two chrominance components to be sampled at 6.75 Mhz, each sample to be at 8 bits resolution. This leads to a digital stream of 216 Mbits/s. (or 27 Mbytes/s.) which can be taken as a useful estimate of the bit rate needed for uncompressed video. In order to get video down a 64 kbit ISDN B channel, a compression factor of 3375 is needed.

There are many trade-offs that can be made in video compression and the most appropriate combination is very application dependent. Some of the parameters that can be considered are:

- *Lossless or lossy compression* Lossless compression means that no data has been lost through the compression process and therefore the original signal can be reconstructed without error; lossy compression means the opposite. Better compression ratios can be achieved through lossy compression but some applications are adversely affected. For example, the transfer of digital movies from their originator to a distributor is better accomplished through lossless compression techniques.
- *Latency considerations* Some compression techniques add considerable delay, for example those that look for differences in a series of frames. In a video telephony application, long latencies are unacceptable because they inhibit natural conversation; in a home cinema application, relatively long latencies may pass unoticed.
- *Symmetry* Certain algorithms take much longer to compress than to decompress. A trade-off can be made where very complex and long compression times result in a highly com-

pact video format which can be rapidly decompressed using low powered processors. Such algorithms are excellent for movies but unsuited to video conferencing.

- *Function* Movie applications benefit from an ability to implement the controls of a video recorder, i.e. stop, start, pause, forward, fast forward, backward and fast backward. Such requirements mean that the data stream should be interpretable in either direction, or can be interpreted from a random point. These functions are not necessary for real-time conferencing use and can lead to different algorithms being preferred.
- *Quality* This is the most obvious trade-off. Domestic video quality is far from perfect and will undergo much improvement over the next decade; however, it does set the norm for workstation video. Certain applications, such as many of those in medicine, require much higher quality; others, such as desktop conferencing, can do with less. If the final picture size is very small then quality can be sacrificed without the effects being evident.
- *Movement* Certain algorithms are designed to handle movement well and are suited to applications such as panning cameras, movies and the like, where the scene changes rapidly. Others depend upon there being little change between frames, e.g. the talking head. When these latter algorithms are used on video with rapid movements, the effect is disconcerting: the observed picture quality drops alarmingly and the movements become very jerky until the motion content diminishes.
- *Hardware and software needs* The number and variety of video compression algorithms means that it is increasingly unacceptable to install dedicated hardware for any one algorithm. Given the general purpose nature of the workstation, it is likely that many algorithms will be needed depending upon the current application. Some hardware subsystems are being designed to run a family of algorithms, each optimized for a different class of application. The ultimate goal is to use the workstation processor and implement algorithms totally in software. Not only does this reduce cost, but it gives algorithm independence and allows video performance to improve with better system unit performance.

6.3 Telephony standards for digitized video

6.3.1 The H.261 recommendation

This lossy digital coding scheme is primarily intended for use at bit rates between about 40 kbits/s. and 2 Mbits/s. It forms part of the H.320 series of recommendations and a goal was to enable 46.4 kbits/s. video and 16 kbits/s. audio down a 64 kbits/s. B channel, along with the necessary control and framing information required by the H.221 standard. Amongst the other objectives was that the bit stream produced should:

- be self-contained
- include error detection and correction
- be supportive of multi-point operation
- allow both unidirectional and bidirectional communication
- allow combination with audio

The source video may be either PAL or NTSC and is first converted to a common intermediate format. Two versions of this exist: one known as CIF is for higher quality output and necessarily higher bandwidth; the other, QCIF, is intended for maximum compression and therefore anticipates quality impacts. CIF and QCIF both specify a common luminance/chrominance format—Y, C_B, C_R—with details as shown in Table 6.2:

Table 6.2 CIF and QCIF video formats

System	*CIF*	*QCIF*
Frames/s.	30 (non-interlaced)	30 (non-interlaced)
Luminance sampling	352 pixels/line 288 lines/picture	176 pixels/line 144 lines/picture
Chrominance sampling	176 pixels/line 144 lines/picture	88 pixels/line 72 lines/picture
Resolution per sample	8-bits	8-bits
Colour matrix equations	$Y = 0.30\,R + 0.59\,G + 0.11B$ $C_B = B–Y$ $C_R = R–Y$	$Y = 0.30\,R + 0.59\,G + 0.11B$ $C_B = B–Y$ $C_R = R–Y$

The parameters in Table 6.2 reflect a compromise between the NTSC and the PAL source equivalent numbers. PCM encoding of CIF at 8-bits/pixel would require a 36.5 Mbits/s. data stream; the equivalent figure for QCIF is 9.1 Mbits/s. QCIF support is mandatory in an implementation, CIF is optional.

H.261 uses the following techniques to compress the data:

- *Interpicture prediction* Successive frames are compared and only the differences are transmitted.
- *DCT transform coding* Spatial redundancy is removed through the use of the mathematical technique known as the discrete cosine transform (DCT); the effect of using the DCT is to focus the information transmitted towards the lower spatial frequencies.
- *Motion compensation* Optionally, movement of a region in one frame can be detected and the movement information is sent rather than the changed region.
- *Frame dropping* Where necessary to meet the data rate requirements, one, two or three frames can be dropped between transmitted frames.

The performance of H.261 is such that at 1.5 or 2 Mbits/s. it compares favourably with home video recorders on typical broadcast television pictures. At the lowest rates, around 64 kbits/s., the frame rate on a talking head is 15 frames/s. and the picture appears perfectly recognizable but somewhat fuzzy. In a small window, around one-sixteenth of the screen, the picture quality is towards the minimum of the acceptable range for desktop conferencing. Significant movement in the picture also has a grave impact on the quality. More bandwidth at this low end brings considerable quality improvement.

A follow-on standard to H.261, intended for conferencing over broadband ISDN and ATM networks and generating bit rates up to 50 Mbits/s., is under development and is known as H.26X. It is intended to be a scalable video coding scheme, totally compatible with the international standard established by the Motion Picture Expert Group, MPEG-2, with the existing H.261 as the base level.

6.4 Workstation standards for digitized video

6.4.1 The JPEG standard

JPEG is a standard developed for still images and is the product of the Joint Photographic Expert Group, which is a working party sponsored by the International Organization for Standardization (ISO) and the International Electrotechnical Commission (IEC). The standard is aimed at the compact digital representation of continuous tone images and was intended to have the following characteristics:

- parameterizable with respect to compression v. quality
- applicable to a broad range of images
- allows both hardware and software implementations
- supports four different modes of operation:
  - sequential encoding—where each image component is encoded in scanned order
  - progressive encoding—where an image is encoded in multiple passes with details being added at each pass
  - lossless encoding—where exact reproduction of the source is guaranteed
  - hierarchical encoding—where the image is encoded at multiple resolutions

The lossy methods use a DCT encoding scheme followed by one of two statistical coding methods, while the lossless scheme uses a predictive coding scheme followed by statistical coding. Statistical coding techniques represent values occurring most frequently with small numbers (using fewer bits) and less frequent values with larger numbers.

JPEG compression can be used for compressing digital motion video with appropriate hardware capable of handling 30 frames/s. The compression is not optimal because each frame is treated as though it were a still image, i.e. no attempt is made to discard redundant data between frames. JPEG can compress video streams by a factor of 20–30 with no significant loss of video quality; factors of 200 can be achieved, but with significant picture degradation.

6.4.2 The MPEG standard

MPEG is a standard developed for moving images and is the product of the Motion Picture Coding Expert Group which, like JPEG, is sponsored by the ISO/IEC. The standard represents a toolkit from which a customized alogorithm can be selected. The intention of the standard is to allow:

- symmetric or asymmetric compression/decompression
- random access playback
- fast forward, fast reverse, normal reverse
- maintainance of audio/video synchronization
- control of compression delay
- editability
- format flexibility
- use of low cost chipsets

Many of these objectives conflict and choices must be made when parameterizing the algorithms. MPEG can be considered a logical superset of H.261 and many of the sections in the standard are identical. Its more complex interframe prediction needs larger and higher speed memory. MPEG is not a replacement for H.261 because it adds considerably more latency.

An MPEG data stream contains four different kinds of pictures, depending upon how each picture is to be decoded. An interesting aspect of the algorithm is that the pictures are not necessarily transmitted in their natural order.

- *I pictures* are intracoded, i.e. coded independently of any other picture. Such an I picture must exist at the start of any video stream and at any other access point. I pictures are similar to JPEG images.
- *P pictures* are predicted pictures, which are coded using motion compensation from a previous I or P picture. P pictures require around one-third of the data of an I picture.
- *B pictures* are interpolated pictures, which are coded by interpolation between a previous and a future I or P picture. B pictures take less data than a P picture and the most compression is achieved by having as many B pictures as possible. However, in order to perform B decoding, the future I or P picture must be transmitted before any dependent B pictures can be transmitted—i.e. there is an inherent delay in the decoding proportional to the number of B pictures in the series.
- *D pictures* have a special format relevant to fast search mode.

MPEG provides for a wide range of video resolutions and data rates, but an average figure is around 50:1. During the standard development there was heavy emphasis on 1.2 Mbits/s. performance because this is the CD-ROM data rate. For 30 frames/s. video at 352 x 240 pixels, the video quality is similar to that from a home video recorder. For audio, MPEG specifies ADPCM compression, and the video and audio data is interleaved in the file.

6.4.3 The MPEG-2 standard

The MPEG-2 standard is under development and is targeted at higher quality and bit rates in the range of about 5–50 Mbits/s., sufficient for supporting high definition television. Additionally, MPEG-2 video will be totally compatible with H.262 and will be published as a common text. The audio component is greatly enhanced, with features for five full channels, other commentary channels and further improvements.

The MPEG-2 algorithm is similar to that of MPEG but has additional features to handle interlaced pictures. It is intended that it should be scaleable—that meaningful images should result from decoding only a part of the data stream.

6.4.4 The MPEG-4 standard

This standard is for a very low bit rate coding of audio-visual data and is likely to be developed jointly by ISO and the ITU-T. It has an alternative H series name of H.VLC/L. The goal is to develop algorithms an order of magnitude more compact than H.261 and MPEG. Intended applications include video phones, mobile video, smart cards and hand-held games.

6.4.5 DVI technology

DVI (Digital Video Interactive) technology is different to the other compression standards listed above because it is dependent upon proprietary hardware developed by the Intel Corporation. DVI embraces two distinct compression algorithms, Production Level Video (PLV) and Real Time Video (RTV).

PLV is an asymmetric compression technique that needs very extensive processing to compress the video, approximately 3 s./frame on 250 Mips machine; decompression only needs a proprietary adapter card. The techniques involved are interframe compression, and the combined audio stream uses ADPCM compatible with the CD-ROM XA standards. The compression is parameterized but is typically used to compress in such a way that the result is playable from a CD-ROM, including the audio track.

RTV compression is much lower quality and both the compression and decompression stages can be performed on the DVI adapter card.

6.4.6 AVI audio/video format

Microsoft's Audio Video Interleaved (AVI) format is a special compressed file structure designed to enable video images and synchronized sound stored on CD-ROMs to be playable on PCs with standard display and audio adapters. AVI emulates the interleaved file structure of the CD-ROM XA standard on conventional CD-ROM drives. The slow transfer rate of conventional CD-ROMs limits the picture size to a maximum of 160 x 120 pixels and a frame rate of 15 frames/s. AVI uses symmetrical compression/decompression techniques and PCM audio encoding.

6.4.7 Quicktime

Quicktime is an Apple Computer system software architecture which supports multimedia applications. It provides a set of basic compression/decompression schemes for still images, animations and video. Included are compressors for JPEG, a run-length encoded animation format and a digital video format. The video compressor allows digitized video sequences to be played from a CD-ROM, with no additional hardware. Compression ratios of 5:1 to 25:1 are typical. It has similar performance characteristics to those of AVI.

6.5 Brief assessment of video standards

PC and telephony video standards are currently different but there is a strong move towards standardization based on the same technologies. The convergence of the H.261 and MPEG follow-ons is encouraging for the higher bandwidths and the quality is likely to be good enough for most applications. There remains a mismatch between the bandwidths of the easily-available and affordable communications links on the one hand, and the bandwidths of compressed video streams of high quality on the other. At the low end, the PC industry has a number of incompatible formats, while the telephony world is committed to H.261 over ISDN. Given the intrinsic information content of video signals and the thrusts to improve on domestic television quality, it is likely that both the common video-telephony and the PC industry products will appear deficient for the foreseeable future.

CHAPTER 7

Conferencing standards

7.1 The scope for standards

Standards play an important role in desktop conferencing, possibly a much greater role than is played in comparable application areas such as word processing or spreadsheets. This is because the essence of desktop conferencing is the exploitation of other workstation applications and their data, coupled with inter-communication over a wide variety of communications and networks.

Unfortunately a great many standards in telephony, data processing, personal computing and communications have been developed over the years, and many of them are still important today. Although new standards are constantly appearing to meet new requirements, old standards rarely disappear because of the accumulated infrastructure and the resistance of customers to change. The emphasis in this chapter will be on those standards that have been specifically developed, primarily by public carriers, to promote inter-operability between conferencing systems. These have evolved under the auspices of the ITU, although there has been representation from many of the major players in the computing industry. The primary goal has been inter-operability across the public network, with the focus on ISDN. No obvious attention has been paid to the integration of these systems into the workstation environment; this being left to the individual developers of desktop conferencing products.

7.2 ISDN

ISDN (Integrated Digital Services Network) is a standardized set of services intended to take the digital channels that form the backbone of a modern telephony network, out to the customer premises. ISDN does not specify the network but the various standards defining ISDN determine the interfaces to the network. The basis of ISDN is the 64 kbits/s. circuit switched channel, which historically forms the basis of digital telephony through the G.711 voice encoding standard.

Basic rate user access to ISDN comprises two 64 kbits/s. B channels plus a 16 kbits/s. D channel. This basic rate access is intended, in telephony terms, to be the equivalent of the simple telephone in analogue terms and can normally be offered over the existing twisted pair local loop. The B channels are intended to contain user data, switched by the network for end-to-end transmission; the 64 kbits/s. channels are supported for both directions of transmission (in certain countries the B channels are restricted to 56 kbits/s.). The D channel is for signalling to the network, although in some systems it may also be used to transport user packet data. The ISDN basic rate access terminates in a bus, known as the S bus. This bus can operate in point-to-point mode and support a single attached terminal, or can operate in point-to-multi-point mode where up to eight terminals can be connected in parallel. B channel paths are established by signalling down the D channel. In a multi-terminal situation all terminals have access to the D channel, but each B channel can only be allocated to a single terminal when the call is established. Although the total user data rate on the basic rate interface to ISDN is 144 kbits/s., additional signalling for the physical connection results in the interface operating at a total rate of 192 kbits/s.

Primary rate access to ISDN is intended for PABX or computer bureau connection and offers much higher rates. Interfaces that already existed within the telephony networks have been pressed into service and, in Europe, primary rate is defined as a total rate 2.048 Mbits/s., supplying 1.984 Mbits/s. as 30 B channels and one 64 kbits/s. D channel. In the USA, the corresponding service is a total rate of 1.544 Mbits/s., giving a user rate of 1.536 Mbits/s. as 23 B channels and one 64 kbits/s. D channel.

In some cases, 64 kbits/s. is not sufficient bandwidth to a destination. One solution to this problem is to multiple B channels; however, the effect is not the same as a higher bandwidth channel. There is no guarantee that the B channels will follow the same route and, therefore, no certainty that the delays on those B channels will be identical; although it can be reasonably assumed that, once the channels are established, the relative delays will not change since networks do not normally reconfigure established calls. With this assumption, multiple B channels can be aligned in the terminal by measuring their respective time delays and compensating accordingly. However, this is not a total solution and the need for single channels with a higher capacity remains.

The term 'broadband ISDN' describes ISDN services that offer channels in excess of 64 kbits/s. The ITU-T has identified H_0 channels at 384 kbits/s., H_{11} channels at 1.536 Mbits/s. and H_{12} channels at 1.920 Mbits/s. Even higher rates have been proposed.

Signalling via the D channel can request many different services to be provided on the data channels. The importance of ISDN to desktop conferencing is that one such service is a circuit switched mode, which provides a constant bit rate from terminal to terminal, as opposed to the use of a packet based service which is unsuited to audio (and video). The circuit switched service is implemented via TDM which results in a continuous bit stream, with low jitter and latency.

The interfaces to ISDN at the physical layer are defined in the ITU-T standards I.430 and I.431. Q.921 (also known as LapD) describes the link access protocol and Q.931, the level 3 protocol used to request user services.

7.3 The ITU-T conferencing recommendations

The ITU-T have established, or proposed, a number of recommendations relevant to desktop conferencing. These all build upon the basic standards well established for international telephony. The primary underlying concept is one of end-user equipment attached to a public network, with the network providing inter-working and multi-point services. Since the notion of a public network with private equipment attached is fundamental, the goal is to lay down rules that will ensure that all private equipment meeting the relevant standards will be able to inter-work in a predictable, describable manner. Inter-working is expected, not only between desktop conferencing implementations, but also between other telephony equipment such as telephones, fax machines, video phones, and so on. Various levels of service are considered, from simple point-to-point audio telephony, through to multi-point audio, video and data exchange.

For desktop conferencing, the configurations illustrated in Fig. 7.1 are considered important by the ITU-T.

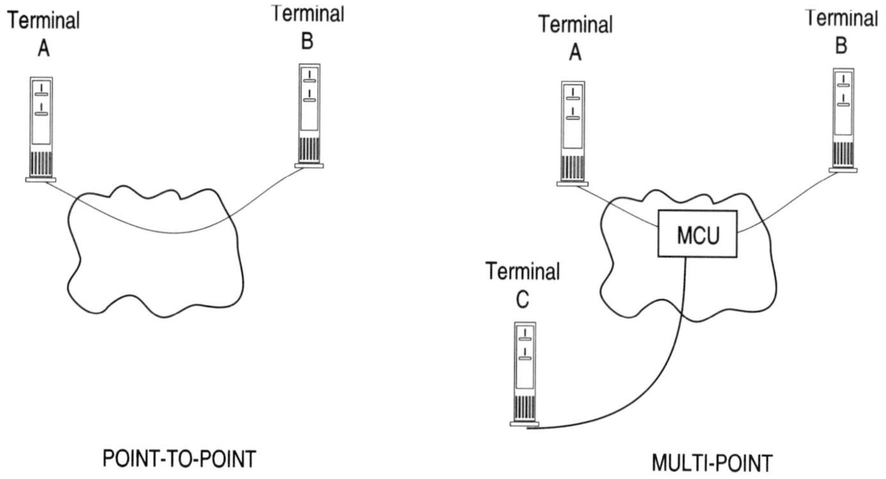

Figure 7.1 Point-to-point and multi-point across a network

Two-party or point-to-point calls, are established by direct connection between end-user equipment across the network. Multi-party calls are established by indirect connection through MCUs (multi-point control units) within the network. MCUs may themselves be hierarchically inter-connected to form larger groups of users (see Fig. 7.2).

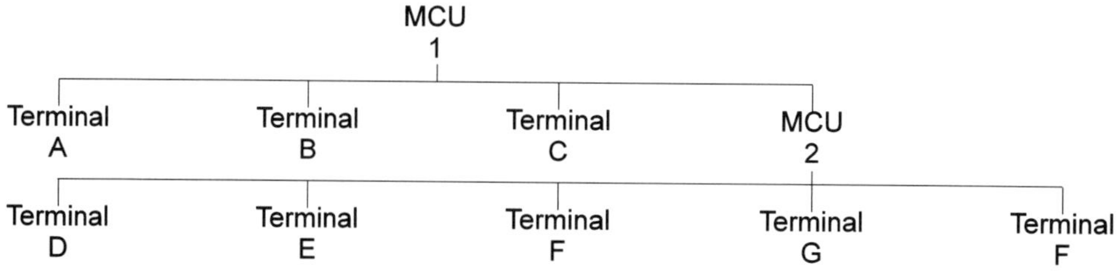

Figure 7.2 Inter-connected MCUs

Only a hierarchical arrangement of physical connections is supported. This hierarchy does not impose a functional hierarchy but it does limit the configurations that are allowed.

7.4 The H.320 recommendation

The H.320 recommendation is intended to cover the requirements for visual telephone services over an ISDN, CSDN (circuit switched digital network) or similar isochronous digital network, covering bandwidths up to 1920 kbits/s. The definition of these visual telephone services is provided in another recommendation known as H.200; in summary, however, these services comprise:

- narrow band videophone (*p* x 64 kbits/s.)

- broadband videophone (a teleservice for broadband ISDN)
- narrow band video conferencing (*p* x 64 kbits/s.)
- broadband video conferencing (a teleservice for broadband ISDN)
- audiographic teleconferencing
- telephony (included for inter-working purposes with telephony equipment)
- tele-surveillance

The H.200 recommendation, besides listing the scope of H.320, also provides a useful bibliography of the relevant ITU standards and recommendations, proposed or approved, for wide area conferencing and visual telephony.

H.320 itself does not define the details of protocols needed to ensure inter-operability but instead, refers to a collection of detailed recommendations that together provide the necessary framework. The full recommendations and their interactions are both numerous and complex, but it is not necessary to understand the detail to gain a good understanding of the approach and an appreciation of what is possible. A high level summary of the H.320 family of recommendations is shown in Fig. 7.3.

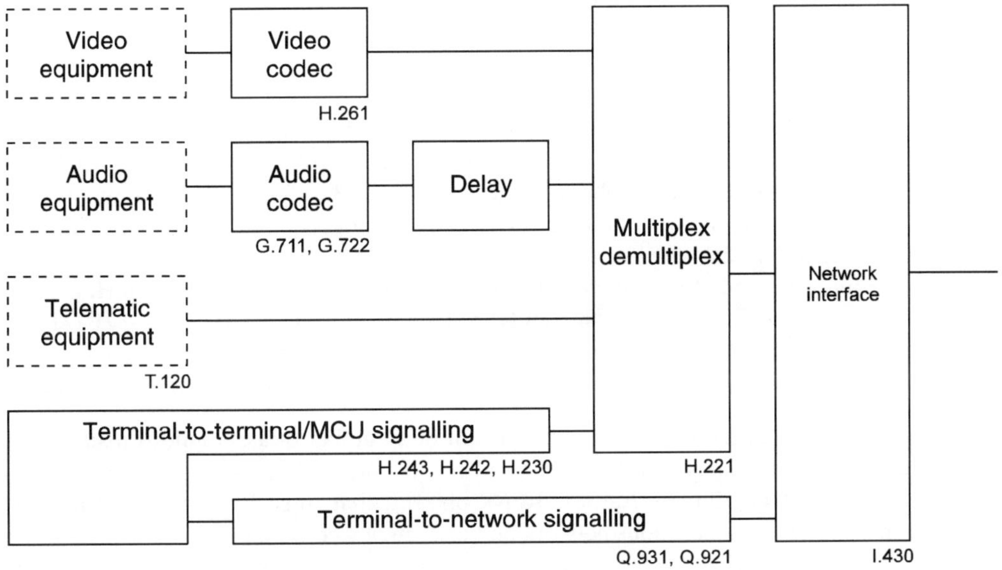

Figure 7.3 The ITU-T H.320 recommendations

From Fig. 7.3 it can be seen that H.320 is based on there being three separate types of information, i.e. video, audio and data, that need to be combined and then transmitted. In the recommendation, video equipment includes cameras and monitors; audio equipment includes microphones and loudspeakers; and telematic equipment includes electronic whiteboards and still picture transmission. For transmission, each of these data types is encoded in a unique way, combined together along with the necessary control information, and then sent over the network. On receipt, the same process happens in reverse. The key elements of the H.320 recommendation can be analysed under the following headings:

- *Video content* The H.261 recommendation defines the method for video encoding and decoding.

- *Audio content* AV.250 is a reference to a series of audio encoding and decoding recommendations including G.711, G.722 and G.728. Audio is delayed on the assumption that the audio stream is related to the video stream and, since video compression/decompression takes longer than audio compression/decompression, a delay must be introduced into the audio process to maintain audio synchronization with video. This delay process is further discussed in the H.261 recommendation.
- *Data content* The H.320 recommendation does not define how data (i.e. that which is neither audio nor video) is to be encoded; thus arbitrary data transmission can be achieved using the standard. This data transmission can occur alongside the movement of the audio and video streams. However, the data formats used are proprietary and understood only by the transmitting and receiving equipment, and so desktop conferencing based on H.320 alone does not provide data inter-operability between different suppliers' equipment. This deficiency is addressed in the T-series set of recommendations, which are a prerequisite to H.320, but are not themselves part of it. In the T-series a format for data transmission is defined and is known as the multi-layer protocol (MLP).
- *Multiplexing of audio/video/data* H.221 defines the way in which the three basic information types and the associated control information are combined for transmission and then separated on receipt. H.221 partitions the available communications bandwidth to support multiple logical streams.
- *System control and signalling* Two kinds of signalling are involved. Control of the network, by the terminal, is transmitted over the D channel for ISDN according to the I.400 series of recommendations. An example of this type of control is the process of establishing the call by providing the telephone number(s). The H.320 family does not modify the way in which calls are set-up and the basic network is not required to provide additional function to support visual telephony.

  Control information between the connected terminal equipment is defined in H.320 and uses controls available in other recommendations, i.e. H.243, H.242, H.230 and H.221. An example of such terminal-to-terminal control is the negotiation of a common capability between the terminals, such as selecting an appropriate audio encoding scheme to be used.

The nature of the H.320 recommendation is a result of a number of assumptions made about the nature of the three types of information to be transmitted over the wide area. Audio is deemed to represent continuous traffic, always present, that must be transmitted in real-time—i.e. it requires an isochronous network and low latency communication is an important consideration. An exception is recognized where voice activation is introduced and in this case audio is only transmitted when it is actually generated—thus the audio stream is no longer continuous. Video is likewise continuous traffic and should generally be allocated the maximum bandwidth available to improve picture quality. The audio and video streams are assumed to be related in the sense that they emanate from a common source and should, therefore, be synchronized. Data, on the other hand, are regarded as only occasionally required but, when present, may temporarily displace all or part of the audiovisual content. Data capability is regarded as an optional enhancement to the basic audiovisual support and is, therefore, only provided if it has been satisfactorily negotiated between the participating items of equipment.

H.320 defines bandwidth usage over the range of 64 kbits/s. to 1920 kbits/s. Within this range, only certain specific bandwidths are allowed and these are restricted to particular multiples of the various ISDN channel types, i.e. as defined numbers of B, H_0, H_{11} and H_{12} channels:

- *64 kbits/s. to 384 kbits/s.* in multiples of 64 kbits/s. (i.e. nB channels where $1 \leq n \geq b$)

- *384 kbits/s. to 1920 kbits/s.* in multiples of 384 kbits/s. (i.e. nH_0 channels where $1 \leq n \geq 5$; 1536 kbits/s. can be $4H_0$ channels or $1H_{11}$ channel; 1920 kbits/s. can be $5H_0$ channels or $1H_{12}$ channel).

The H.320 recommendation then establishes the various combinations of audio and video encodings that are allowed for each of these channel multiples; the combinations are known as modes and each is identified by an alphanumeric code. The modes are shown below, with the code in brackets.

For 1B channel	
Audio without video:	G.711 audio encoding (a_0)
Audio and video:	H.200/AV.254 audio; H.261 video (a_1)
For 2B channels	
Audio and video:	G.711 audio; H.261 video (b_1)
	G.722 audio; H.261 video (b_2)
	H.200/AV.254, AV.253; H.261 video (b_3)
For all other cases:	
Audio and video:	G.722 audio; H.261 video ($c \rightarrow m$)

The 2B channel case is the most important one in the list above since this represents the basic rate ISDN. The 1B channel case is also interesting, partly because it only incurs half the call charges, and partly because it is the mode that a system may be forced into if an ISDN channel fails in a call. The other cases shown above are only available through primary rate ISDN connections.

H.320 compliant equipment is classified according to the combination of these modes that it supports, the classification being known as the terminal type. Thus, equipment supporting multiple B channels is type X equipment; the X being then suffixed with a code that identifies the particular modes supported by that equipment. For example, some of the terminal types are shown below:

- Type Xa: 1B channel; modes a_0, a_1 only supported
- Type Xb_1: 1B or 2B channels; modes a_0, a_1, b_1 only supported
- Type Xb_3: 1B or 2B channels; modes a_0, a_1, b_1, b_2, b_3 only supported
- Type Xb_4: 1B or 2B channels; modes a_0, b_1 only supported

Type Y equipment supports H_0 channels; type Z equipment supports H_{11} and H_{12} channels.

The H.320 recommendation also describes how visual telephone calls are established and terminated by delineating the phases that a call goes through as it is brought up and taken down. There is considerable detail in the recommendation which is generally only important to a designer of visual telephony equipment. From a purchaser and a user perspective, the important elements of the various phases are summarized below.

Call set-up (phase A) The call is established through the normal network procedures, for ISDN by using the D-channel to signal to the network and thereby establish the connection. For type X terminals only, a single B channel connection is used at this point. With this channel opened for bidirectional communication, a structure is overlaid on the bits being transmitted. This structure is defined by the H.221 recommendation and is known as framing. It enables the significance of the bits to be understood by relating each to its position in the frame. At this point the terminal is initialized ready to work in audio-only mode. Thus the call set-up begins with an audio-only call being created, using a single B channel.

Mode initialization (phase B1) After the necessary alignment procedures have been completed following the details described in recommendation H.242, audio is then transmitted between the terminals. An exchange of capabilities between the terminals then follows where each terminal specifies the modes that it is capable of supporting. If additional channels are to be used, the terminal that established the initial call, then sets-up the supplementary channels. This selection of the calling terminal ensures that it is the one that is subsequently billed for all of the channels that are used during the call. Either terminal may decide not to use additional channels in any particular call; thus the maximum common capability does not have to be used in each and every call.

With all the channels to be used now established, the terminals switch to the common operating mode they negotiated earlier; again H.242 describes this process in detail. H.221 framing and the necessary alignment procedures are activated for these supplementary channels. All the channels in use are synchronized; this is a process that compensates for differences in latency between the constituent channels. In ISDN there is no guarantee that different channels will be routed across the ISDN network in the same way and, therefore, a process is needed between the sending and receiving terminals to compensate for any transmission time differences that may exist across the channels.

Establishment of common parameters (phase B2) This phase establishes the common operational parameters to be used in the call. These parameters are specific to visual telephony—for example, whether or not encryption is to be used. Activation of any data capabilities is also part of this phase. The process dictates that the capabilities or the requirements of the receiving side are indicated first and the sending side then decides the operational parameters that will actually be used. Recommendation H.221 defines the process in detail.

Visual telephone communication (phase C) From a user perspective this is the most important phase, since the terminals are now operational and user relevant information can be exchanged. During phase C it is permissible to change modes, for example to introduce a fax capability into the call. The procedures of H.242 are invoked to accomplish mode switching. Likewise, other terminal capabilities may be changed during a call and, again, H.242 defines the process.

Termination (phase D) Termination can be initiated by one of the terminals, either by hanging-up or by a mode change.

Call termination (phase E) The terminal that has initiated the hang-up sends messages over the D channel, with respect to all channels, and idles them so that no more information is sent. Actual disconnection occurs when a disconnect message is received.

The H.320 recommendation also defines the support of inter-communication of type X terminals (i.e. those supporting ISDN B channels) with standard telephony equipment. In the case of a call from such a terminal to an ISDN phone, the call is first placed as an audiovisual call but the ISDN telephone returns an incompatible destination code. The visual telephone is then expected to switch to a normal speech or 7 kHz audio bearer service call. A call from an ISDN telephone to a visual telephone is accepted by the visual telephone because every audiovisual telephone is equipped with this telephone capability as a minimum function.

A call from a visual telephone to a PSTN telephone may be initiated as an audiovisual call, but the network returns a no route to destination error; then the visual telephone may switch to a speech or 3.1 kHz audio bearer service call. The operational mode of encoding is G.711 audio encoding. A call from a PSTN telephone is routed into the ISDN as a 3.1 kHz audio call which is then responded to in the same way an ISDN telephone incoming call. The operational mode of communication in this case is 3.1 kHz audio.

7.4.1 The H.221 recommendation

The H.221 recommendation describes what is known as the frame structure for audiovisual teleservices. In essence, it describes how the overall transmission capacity can be dynamically subdivided into multiple, lower rate partitions for audio, video, data and control information. The overall transmission capacity may be a composite made up from a number of ISDN connections and therefore comprises a number of channels, i.e. 1–6 B channels, 1–5 H_0 channels, or is an H_{11} or an H_{12} channel.

The first connection established in a call is the initial connection and carries the initial channel in each direction; any additional connections carry additional (or supplementary) channels. A single 64 kbits/s. channel is structured into groups of eight bits (or octets in telephony parlance), with the octets being transmitted at 8 kHz. Each bit position in the bytes can be regarded as a subchannel of 8 kbits/s. The eighth such subchannel is called the service channel (see Fig. 7.4). For an H_0, H_{11} or an H_{12} channel a similar scheme applies. These channels may be regarded as a number of 64 kbits/s. time slots; the lowest numbered time slot is structured exactly as described for a single 64 kbits/s. channel, while the other time slots have no such structure. In the case of multiple B or H_0 channels, all channels have a frame structure—that in the initial channel controls most of the functions across the overall transmission, while the frame structure in the additional channels is used for synchronization, channel numbering and related controls.

The term I-channel is used to refer to the initial or only B channel, or the only or the lowest numbered 64 kbits/s. time slot of H_0, H_{11} and H_{12} channels.

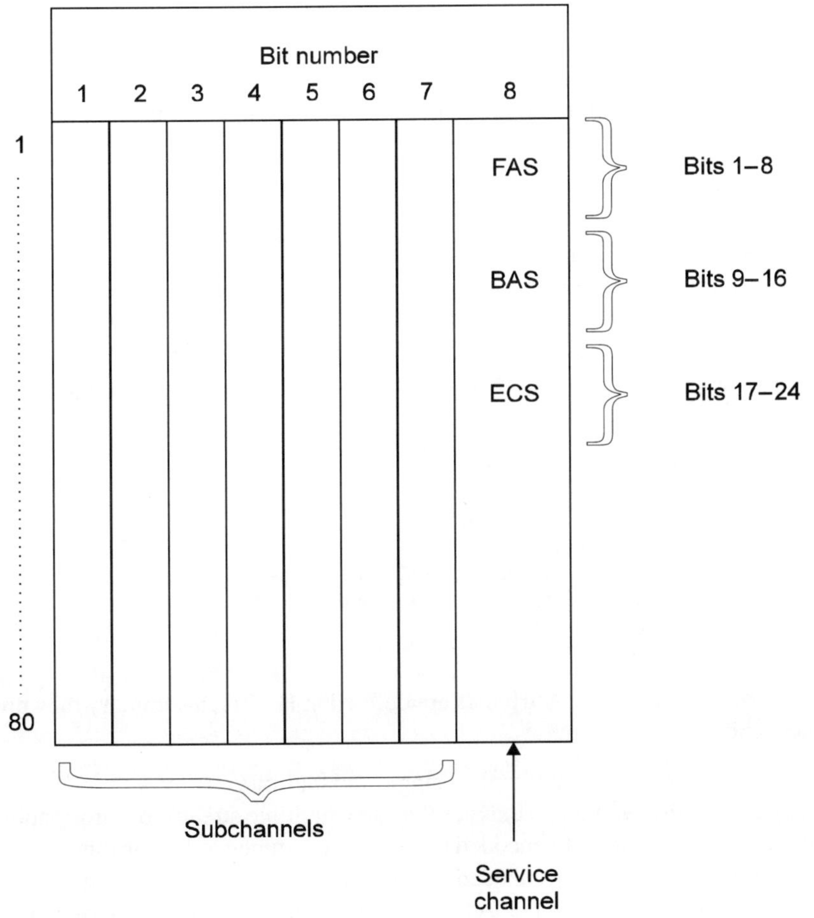

Figure 7.4 H.221 frame structure for an initial B channel

The I-channel and other framed 64 kbits/s. channels are structured by H.221 into frames, sub-multiframes and multiframes.

- *Frames* 80 octets per frame, with the octets being numbered from 1–80
- *Sub-multiframes* groups of two frames
- *Multiframes* groups of eight sub-multiframes

Within a frame, the bits in the service channel are allocated specific functions:

- bits 1–8: frame alignment signal (FAS)
- bits 9–16: bit-rate allocation signal (BAS)
- bits 17–24: encryption control signal (ECS)
- bits 25–80: data

The frame alignment signal is used, as its name implies, to specify the frame structure and to align multiple framed channels. The FAS is not a single value but is a composite value whose constituent parts vary between odd and even frames, and also with the frame's position in the multiframe structure. The scheme is implemented in a way that allows other time slots to be aligned to the first time slot. H.221 defines the process for searching for the frame alignment signal, determining when alignment has been lost and how it should be recovered. Quality monitoring of the connection can be implemented through the use of bits in the FAS.

The bit-rate allocation signal is also sent in a way that allows errors to be detected and corrected. The 8 bit BAS code itself is sent in an even numbered frame and the error correction bits in the succeeding odd frame. The code itself is divided into a hierarchy of attributes:

class (8 classes)
family (8 families)
attribute (8 attributes)
value (32 values)

Class and family are set by one BAS code and apply to successive BAS codes unless changed. Within a class and family, the first three bits of a BAS code (attribute) define the general command or capability, while the other five bits identify the specific command or capability (value). In the class '000' (default class) and the family '000' (default family) the following attributes are defined:

attribute '000' audio coding command
attribute '001' transfer rate command
attribute '010' video, encryption and other commands
attribute '011' data command
attribute '100' terminal capability for audio and transfer rates
attribute '101' terminal capability for video, encryption and other
attribute '110' reserved
attribute '111' escape codes

The values associated with these attributes are defined in H.221. In summary they provide the following capabilities:

- transmission at various total rates and on single and multiple channels.
- ability to partition the available bandwidth to carry multiple streams of information:
  - audio transmission, digitally encoded to various recommended algorithms
  - video transmission, digitally encoded to various recommended algorithms
  - low speed data (LSD) within the I-channel. The format of such data is known only to the source and destination.

  - high speed data (HSD) in the highest numbered 64 kbits/s. channel or time slots (excluding the I-channel). The format of such data is known only to the source and destination.
  - data transmission within a multi-layer protocol, either in the I-channel (MLP), or other channels (H-MLP); this is described later under the H.200 recommendation. The format of this data is defined by the T.120 series of recommendations, described later in this chapter.
- an encryption control signal
- loop back towards the network for maintenance control purposes
- signalling for control and indications
- a message system

The partition of the transmission capacity can be represented as in Fig. 7.5.

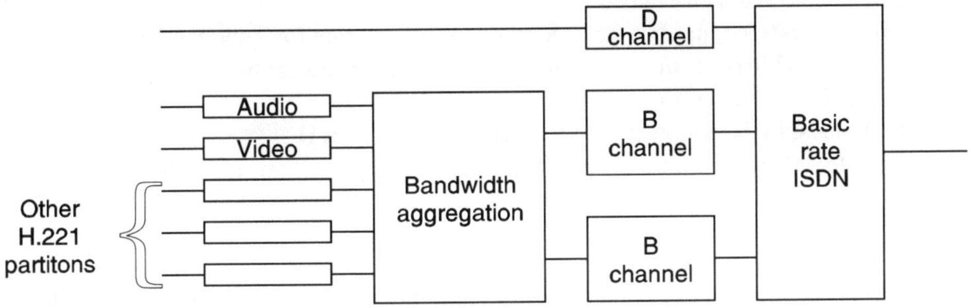

Figure 7.5 H.221 partitions over basic rate ISDN

Along with a definition of these commands, the H.221 recommendation also specifies which bits in a frame are allocated to the various partitions that can be established. The combinations of these partitions that can be created are restricted, but the restrictions are not easily described. The essential requirement is that, in any combination of partitions, a bit cannot be allocated to more than one partition. Thus, the allowed combinations can be summarized as follows:

1 *Audio* zero or one partition only.
   - The partition bandwidth is fixed by the audio encoding scheme selected and may range from 8 kbits/s. to 64 kbits/s. in the I-channel; for H_0 and greater channels, provision is made for audio up to 384 kbits/s. Audio in the I-channel is allocated to the low numbered bit positions.

2 *LSD/MLP* zero, one or more partitions are allowed.
   - LSD partition outside the service channel: 8–56 kbits/s. in multiples of 8 kbits using bit 7 and lower numbered bits as necessary.
   - LSD partition inside the service channel: 300, 1200, 4800 and 6400 bits/s.
   - LSD partition using capacity inside and outside the service channel: 9.6, 14.4 and 62.4 kbits/s.
   - Variable LSD partition occupying all I-channel capacity not allocated under other fixed rate commands (not allowed if a fixed rate LSD partition or a variable rate MLP partition exists): up to 62.4 kbits/s., depending upon other allocations.
   - MLP inside the service channel: 4 or 6.4 kbits/s.
   - Variable MLP partition occupying all I-channel capacity not allocated under other fixed rate commands (not allowed if a fixed rate MLP partition or a variable rate LSD partition exists): up to 62.4 kbits/s., depending upon other allocations.

3 *HSD/H-MLP* zero, one or more partitions are allowed.

- HSD fixed capacity partition:
  - 64 kbits/s. in the highest numbered channel/time-slot. FAS and BAS are removed in the case of multiple B channels.
  - 128-320 kbits/s. in multiples of 64 kbits/s. in the highest numbered time-slots of an H_0 or greater channel.
  - 384 kbits/s. in the highest numbered H_0 channel, or the highest numbered time slots of a greater channel; FAS and BAS are removed in the case of multiple H_0 channels.
- Variable HSD partition occupying all capacity, other than in the I-channel capacity not allocated under commands (not allowed if a fixed rate HSD partition or a variable rate H-MLP partition exists).
- H-MLP fixed capacity partition:
  - 62.4 kbits/s. occupying the second 64 kbits/s. except FAS and BAS positions.
  - 64–320 kbits/s. in multiples of 64 kbits/s. in the lowest numbered time-slots other than TS1, of an H_0 or greater channel.
- 384 kbits/s. in time-slots 2–7 of a greater channel than H_0.
- Variable MLP partition occupying all capacity, other than in the I-channel capacity not allocated under commands (not allowed if a fixed rate MLP partition or a variable rate H-HSD partition exists).

4 *Video* zero or one partitions.

- Video is deemed to occupy all capacity not allocated by other commands. Video cannot be inserted into the I-channel when variable rate LSD or MLP is in progress.

The *command attributes* are acted upon by the frame following their receipt; thus the command is received in one even frame, the error-correcting code in the next (odd) frame, and the receiver prepares to accept the stated mode change beginning from the subsequent (even) frame. A mode change can thus be effected in 20 milliseconds. The *capability attributes* indicate the ability of a terminal to receive and properly treat the various types of signal. The *escape code attributes* are used for a number of purposes. One such use is to set the class and the family; by default, the class and family are both assumed to be '000'. Another use is to send messages, or to point to entries in BAS escape tables. The *individual BAS codes* are listed in the H.221 recommendation; however, their use for the establishment of audio, video and data partitions is specified in H.242 and H.243.

Although H.221 was defined on top of a basic 64 kbits/s. channel structure, ISDN in some countries outside Europe is based on a 56 kbits/s. channel structure. Inter-working between these systems is possible; the technique used is that the service channel for a 64 kbits/s. terminal becomes the seventh subchannel and the eighth subchannel is filled with '1'—later discarded on transmission to the 56 kbits/s. terminal. Certain communication modes are restricted and some command codes are redefined.

7.4.2 Control signals and indications

An audiovisual system requires exchanges of information to take place in addition to the audio, video and data streams that are apparent to the terminal users. Such information may be loosely regarded as signals comprising of controls and indications; controls being concerned with commands to perform certain actions, while indications return data on the state of the system. These control and indication aspects can be further subdivided according to the nature and timeliness of the responses required to the signals:

- Call control—the interaction between a terminal and the network itself. Such control is essentially independent of the use being made of the call once set-up. Call control for ISDN is described in the Q-series of recommendations.
- Transmission signals between terminals that are synchronous with frames, or otherwise require rapid response. These signals are described in the H.230 recommendation.
- Conference, data and other equipment control signals between terminals, not requiring frame synchronization. These can be exchanged privately by terminals using LSD and/or HSD partitions. However, if the T.120 series of recommendations are being used in addition to H.320, this information is exchanged through the multi-layer protocol described in those recommendations and transmitted between terminals using the MLP or H-MLP partitions.
- Certain controls are required to be synchronized with the picture in a conference. These controls are defined in the video encoding recommendation H.261.

7.4.3 The H.230 recommendation

This recommendation covers the control and indication capabilities necessary between digital audiovisual terminals that must be transmitted synchronous with a frame, or otherwise require rapid response. Several of the necessary codes are defined directly in the H.221 recommendation itself as BAS codes and are, therefore, used when appropriate. Other controls require the use of the BAS escape mechanism, i.e. first the BAS escape code is transmitted and then a code defined in H.230 is transmitted in place of a BAS code in the next sub-multiframe.

The codes themselves perform functions which can be summarized under four headings:

1 *Video control/indications* identity of the video source; status of video; information related to video switching.
2 *Audio control/indications* normal audio signal present or not.
3 *Maintenance control/indications* audio, video and data loop back controls.
4 *Multi-point conference control/indications* a set of controls relevant to simple conferences where the MLP protocol is not being used. The commands are for communications between a terminal and an MCU.

7.4.4 The H.242 recommendation

The H.242 recommendation explains how two terminals can communicate audiovisual data using the H.221 frame structure; the recommendation does not consider multi-way communication. An important principle behind the standard is that all audio terminals using G.722 and/or G.711 codings, or any other standardized low bit rate encodings, should be able to be interconnected. Thus, audio is seen as a basic capability and inter-operability with standard telephone audio equipment as essential. This implies that the initial mode of inter-operation is this basic audio capability, followed by a negotiation phase between the communicating terminals to determine what else is possible.

The scheme adopted depends upon each terminal knowing the capabilities of the other terminal to receive and decode signals. This total capability information for a terminal is known as its capability set and is made known to the other terminal through transmission of the H.221 BAS capability marker, followed by all of the current capabilities. Provision is made for specification of:

- *Audio capabilities* G.711 A-law or μ-law; G.725-T1 or G.725-T2; 16 kbits/s. H.200/AV.254; ISO-standard audio at all rates up to 384 kbits/s.

- *Video capabilities* QCIF and/or CIF picture format (see recommendation H.261); minimum picture interval; other video encodings.
- *Transfer rate capabilities* maximum number and type of channels that can be supported.
- *Data capabilities* all the rates that can be supported for the LSD, HSD, MLP and H-MLP partitions.
- *Encryption and extension-BAS capabilities* the options here are defined in H.221.

The H.242 recommendation describes the initial mode to be adopted by terminals and then the details of the initialization and negotiation phases, including the adoption of particular modes and establishment of additional channels if appropriate. A summary of this was given earlier as part of the H.320 recommendation description and will not, therefore, be repeated here.

7.4.5 The H.243 recommendation

H.243 expands the description provided by H.242 to include multi-way communication between three or more terminals. This takes place through a multi-point communication unit or MCU, i.e. each of the terminals to be interconnected is connected not to one of the other terminals, but all terminals are directly connected to an MCU (see Fig. 7.6). The detailed capabilities of these devices are the subject of yet another recommendation, in this case H.231.

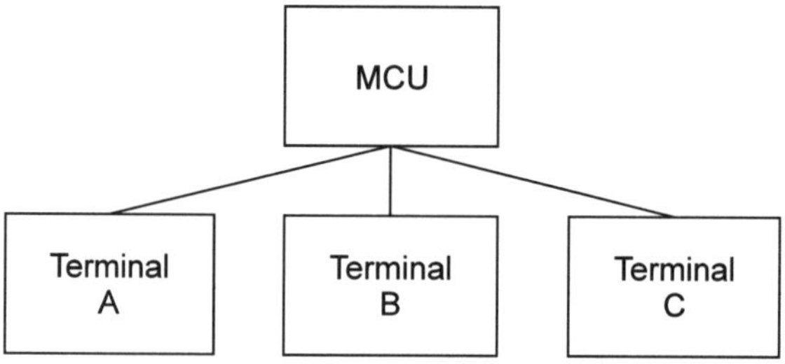

Figure 7.6 Terminals connected to an MCU

H.243 describes not only a simple hierarchy involving one MCU as shown in Fig. 7.6, but more complex hierarchies where MCUs themselves may be interconnected by other MCUs. These aspects will not be considered further in the description that follows.

The signals on each connection to the MCU follow the H.221 recommendation and the BAS commands define fully how the terminals handle the received data. Likewise, the basic procedures for initialization and mode switching are in accordance with those of recommendation H.242 for point-to-point working. However, the multi-point nature of the system requires procedures to be adopted above the level of H.221/H.242 and it is these that are supplied in the H.243 recommendation. The T.120 series of recommendations offers an alternative, and much more sophisticated way, of controlling multi-point operations. MCUs that implement the H.243 recommendation are typically offered by network operators for multi-party video conferencing and are relatively common. Such equipment, however, does not offer a generally useful data exchange capability. MCUs based on the T.120 series are likely to become the standard way of supporting multi-party, wide area, public desktop conferencing and allow the provision of useful audio, video and data services.

It is still instructive, however, to review the scope of H.243 and to appreciate the deficiencies that have led to the subsequent evolution of T.120. Moreover, the T-series is still dependent upon the basic mechanisms of H.320 for its operation.

The capability exchange necessary between terminals, and the subsequent selection of an appropriate operational mode, is more complicated when multiple terminals and an associated MCU are involved. Several approaches are possible: the MCU can have its own, fixed capability; or it can use a capability based upon the capabilities of the terminals attached; or it can adopt some other approach. The procedure for determining this MCU capability is outside the scope of the recommendation. For each conference call, a normal communication mode (NCM) is identified in the MCU, which the MCU strives to maintain between itself and all terminals, and between itself and all other MCUs. The power of an MCU to control the mode transmitted by a terminal is limited to a determination of the rates of audio, video and any data partitions; it cannot—and does not need to—set either the video or audio modes once there is a single agreed bit rate.

At the start of a call, the capabilities transmitted by the MCU are those which correspond to its NCM; any terminal that is found, from its declared capabilities, to be incapable of transmitting the NCM will be connected into the conference with secondary status, which means that it will have an audio-only capability. Later on in the call, it may be necessary for the MCU to change its declared capabilities.

When the first terminal has been connected to an MCU, the terminal sends its capabilities, according to H.221 and H.232. The MCU responds with its NCM capabilities and BAS codes from the H.230 recommendation, indicating that this is a multi-point call, that no other terminals are connected and, therefore, that the user should wait. When the second terminal has been connected, capabilities exchanged, and has been informed by the MCU that this is a multi-point call, the audio and video paths are established. Decoded audio from both terminals is sent to the audio mixer in the MCU and the appropriate mixer outputs transmitted to the terminals. If video signals are being received from either or both terminals, they are forwarded by the video switch using the mode switching procedure defined in H.242.

When a third terminal is connected to the MCU, again the terminal sends its capabilities and the MCU responds as described for the second terminal. The decoded audio is sent to the audio mixer and the appropriate mixer output transmitted back to the terminal. If video signals are being received from either the first or second terminal, one of them (by default the first) is transmitted to the third terminal via the video switch. If video is being received from the third terminal, it may optionally be transmitted to the first and second terminals. Other additional terminals essentially follow this same procedure on connection.

If the intended normal mode of the conference involves multiple channels, then the transmitted MCU transfer rate capability reflects the appropriate rate to all terminals and the additional channels are set-up; terminals that cannot follow suit may be down-rated by the MCU to secondary status.

In a point-to-point call, a terminal is free to change modes at any time, within the constraints of the capabilities it has received from the other end. However, in a multi-point call there are additional constraints which are resolved by the requirement that bit rate changes can only be initiated from the MCU; other mode changes may, however, be initiated from terminals.

The default switching for video is governed by the audio power transmitted from the terminals and is effective from the start of video transmissions, unless overridden by commands. This has the effect that the video from the terminal with the loudest audio is sent to the other participants. It is possible for a terminal to try and force its MCU to broadcast its video to all other connected terminals; this is achieved through issuing the specific BAS code.

Data transmission is controlled by possession of tokens; one token exists for each of the four data partitions, LSD, HSD, MLP and H-MLP. The token commands support:

- claim of a token by a terminal from an MCU
- indication that the token has been given by the MCU
- withdrawal of a token or refusal to give a token by an MCU
- release of a token back to an MCU

Some of the connected terminals may not have a data capability and, therefore, no data partition will be opened to them. If they are transmitting a video signal, this will no longer be at the same rate as those terminals to which the data partition has been opened; this means that their video cannot be forwarded and neither can they be sent video from others during data transmission.

Chair-control is an optional, but relatively simple, feature of an H.243 compliant MCU that allows programmed control of a multi-point conference, without achieving the level of sophistication provided by the T.120 series of recommendations. In order to operate chair-control, at least one of the attached terminals must also be enhanced to support the extended BAS codes necessary to control the procedure. Such an enhanced terminal becomes the chair-controller by claiming a chair-control token in the MCU; the token commands parallel those described above for data partition tokens. Once in control, the terminal can then issue BAS commands which allow it to:

- switch video signals, i.e. determine the source of distributed video. No control is available to determine the video selection to be transmitted to the terminal which has been selected to be the source to others in the conference; the local MCU may forward the previous video signal, or that from the chair-control terminal, or other available signals on a rotating basis.
- stop data transmission by other terminals.
- disconnect a terminal from a conference.

Associated with chair-control is an optional numbering scheme, an H.243 node number, that uniquely identifies the terminals in a conference and can be linked with personal terminal identity numbers or names. These can assist an operator to control the conference.

7.4.6 The G.725 recommendation

G.725 defines how G.722 high quality audio compression encoding should be used in conjunction with H.221. The need for the standard arises because G.722, unlike G.711, is able to operate at a range of bit rates. The following modes of operation are defined:

- *Mode 0* 64 kbits/s. narrow band audio (G.711).
- *Mode 1* 64 kbits/s. 7 kHz audio (G.722).
- *Mode 2* 56 kbits/s. 7 kHz audio (G.722) + up to 6.4 kbits/s. data + 1.6 kbits/s. service channel framing and mode control.
- *Mode 3* 48 kbits/s. 7 kHz audio (G.722) + up to 14.4 kbits/s. data + 1.6 kbits/s. service channel framing and mode control.

Additionally, three types of terminal are defined:

1. *Type 0* (T0) a digital telephone operating in mode 0 (or an analogue telephone connected via a PCM interface).
2. *Type 1* (T1) a 7 kHz audio terminal capable of working in mode 0 or mode 1.

3 *Type 2* (T2) a member of a family of 7 kHz audio/data terminals capable of working in modes 0, 1 and 2. Dynamic mode switching must be provided.

The standard defines that such terminals should initially operate in mode 0 but negotiate to higher modes. BAS codes are used to exchange capabilities and negotiate mode changes.

7.4.7 Brief assessment of the H.320 recommendation

H.320 reflects a natural evolution of basic ISDN services and introduces video telephony as a progression from the standard audio telephony. It organizes the physical connection structure into a hierarchy, with an implicit assumption that multi-point services are offered from within the telephone network. It assumes that speech quality audio is the basis of the service, supplemented by video, with the video stream being assigned all available free bandwidth. A maximum of one audio stream and one video stream per party are allowed. The audio and video are of relatively low quality, well suited to the characteristics of the underlying network. Although the quality is low, the consistency of the service is excellent, built from its roots in a time-division multiplexed, circuit switched network. Data is only provided for as an optional extra—its formats being, to a great extent, outside the standard. Data takes bandwidth away from video on a temporary basis.

The hierarchical nature of the connection structure is appropriate if the multi-point capability is within the network; if outside it, the multi-point capability distinguishes between participants in a way that can lead to unexpected results. Thus, all members of a call are not equal and the departure of one does not have the same effect as the departure of another. Since the hierarchy is also implicitly associated with the billing system, in a public service this may not be a problem; as the basis for a private service its merits are not so apparent.

The true conferencing capabilities offered at the H.320 level are minimal, but may be sufficient if real control is left with the members of the conference. When the usage required is that of a regular voice call over the public network, enhanced by an accompanying video stream with occasional data, then H.320 is a good basis. Its lack of recognition of more complex forms of collaboration, its refusal to accommodate PC standards for audio and video, and its close links to ISDN to the exclusion of personal computer networks and protocols, all make it a telephony phenomenon which fits a little uncomfortably into the workstation world.

7.4.8 Follow-on H.320 series recommendations

The ITU-T has set up expert groups to study audiovisual communications systems for ATM (asynchronous transfer mode) and other network environments, with the objective of producing additional H.320 series recommendations for high bandwidth environments. Alongside, a group is also studying the support of very low bit rates, such as those needed for modem attachment over the PSTN or through a mobile network. The standards under discussion are:

H.32X	Broadband audiovisual communication systems and terminal equipment
H.32Y	Adaptation of H.320 terminals to B-ISDN
H.32Z	Adaptation of H.320 terminals to LANs
H.32P	Portable and low bit rate audiovisual communications systems
H.26X	Video coding for ATM environments
H.22X/H.22W	Multimedia multiplex and synchronization for ATM environments

H.32X is a system overview akin to H.320, but concerned with attachment to broadband ISDN. It delivers new capabilities, beyond those of H.320, and addresses the deficiencies in that standard while exploiting the higher bandwidth. The essential elements are:

- Audio codec based on the recommendations/draft recommendations G.711, G.722, G.728, H.200/AV.255 (MPEG audio)
- Video codec based on the recommendations/draft recommendations H.261, H.262 (a scaleable video coding scheme, totally compatible with MPEG-2, with the existing H.261 as the base level)
- Network adaptation based on the recommendations/draft recommendations H.22W, H.22X, I.363
- End-to-end signalling based on the draft recommendations H.23X (end-to-end control and indication), H.24X (end-to-end communication procedures)
- End-to-network signalling: based on the recommendations of the I-series

H.22X/H.22W are developments of H.221 and are expected to provide two stream functions.

1 Program stream functions, where a program is defined as a collection of media, all with a common time base:
   - multiplexing of data units from media sources (e.g. audio, video, or other), with each unit being of variable length, relatively large and containing data from only one such source
   - timebase recovery (synchronization of sender and receiver)
   - media timing synchronization support (synchronization entities within the media)
   - buffer management
   - security and access control
   - inband signalling
   - error reporting

2 Transport stream functions, a similar list of capabilities but for the transport level, where a transport stream contains multiple programs.

H.32X supports multiple audio and video streams including a concept of programs, for example a paired set of audio and video. Audio streams are supported up to CD standard, along with high quality video and high bandwidth data traffic.

H.32Y describes how existing H.320 terminals may be attached to a broadband ISDN network. Since an H.32X compliant terminal is required to inter-operate with an H.320 terminal, then H.32Y can be also regarded as a subset of H.32X. The differences between H.32Y and H.320 are in the layers defined below H.221, and in the end-to-network signalling. From a user perspective, H.32Y delivers identical H.320 function but the available bandwidth can be exploited through higher quality H.261 video and faster data communication.

H.32Z is an equivalent definition to H.320 but targeted at LAN environments. The audio and data formats are expected to be identical with H.320, with the divergence possibly occurring at the H.221 layer but certainly below, i.e. the LAN protocol and interface. Just as for H.32Y, besides the advantages of LAN connectivity, the benefits to users are in exploiting bandwidth through H.261 and the greater data capacity.

H.32P is a low bit rate protocol being designed for use over the PSTN through a modem. It uses an audio encoding AV.25Y, a very low bit rate video H.26P coding, and a control structure H.24P. Inter-operability is intended with other members of the H.320 and H.32X-Z families.

7.5 The T.120 recommendation

The T.120 recommendation is designed to support what are described as 'audiovisual conferencing services, where a conference refers to a group of geographically dispersed nodes that are joined together and that are capable of exchanging audiographic and audiovisual information across various communication networks'. This equates to the applications areas more commonly known as the combination of video conferencing and desktop conferencing. T.120 itself refers to a collection of subsidiary recommendations, as shown in Fig. 7.7.

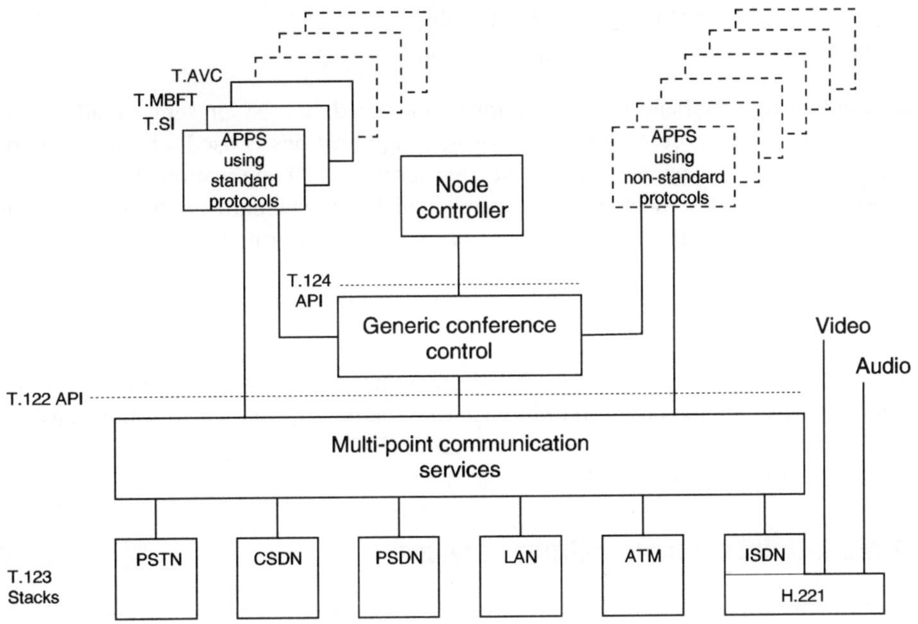

Figure 7.7 The ITU-T T.120 recommendations

Although a wide variety of data transports are supported, it is only in the digital telephony case, using ISDN or switched 56 kbits/s. services with the associated H.320 recommendation, that audio and video are supported. In all other cases, T.120 provides conference control, application definitions and data services but without an available mechanism for the exchange of the associated audio and video streams. Given this characteristic it is likely that, in the near term, T.120 will only be important over ISDN and other circuit switched digital networks for which there is a data, audio and video total solution. Extensions to T.120, to both exploit ATM networks and support the full range of multimedia traffic, are under development.

T.120 requires that the stack from the T.122 API layer and below is used in a compliant conference. Conference control is provided by GCC (generic conference control), and this component can be driven by the user through an application known as the node controller. The functions and protocols generated by GCC are defined and its use is described as conditionally mandatory; this means that if the standardized applications are used then it must be in conjunction with GCC. The node controller is not architected in the T.120 series and thus a variety of user interfaces can be devised.

T.120 also defines the protocols for a number of applications intended for use within the conference:

- T.SI (still image and annotation)
- T.AVC (high level audiovisual control)
- T.MBFT (multipoint binary file transfer)

A number of other applications have been proposed for standardization, including:

- T.Sound (transfer of audio objects)
- T.MPTV (transfer of MPEG encoded video objects)
- T.PRIV (application communication encryption services)

These standardized applications are optional and need not be present in all terminals. However, if the function described in one of these applications is used within a conference, that function must be provided through the appropriate T.120 application stack. The recommendation also provides mechanisms through which non-standard applications, i.e. those which are private to the participating parties, may be invoked during the conference.

All applications use MCS for communication and may also issue commands to the GCC conference control component.

At the time of writing, all aspects of the T.120 recommendation have not been completed and, therefore, the final details may differ slightly from the description which follows. MCS was finalized and adopted in 1993; GCC, T.SI and T.MBFT were approved in March 1995 as T.124, T.126 and T.127, respectively.

7.5.1 Multi-point communications services

The multi-point communication service (MCS) is a generic service designed to support highly interactive multimedia conferencing applications. Through the T.122 API, it supports full-duplex multi-point communication among an arbitrary number of connected application instances over a variety of networks.

MCS domains

The basic concept in MCS is that of a domain; within the domain application clients can send and receive data. MCS establishes a multi-point domain over a collection of point-to-point MCS connections, where an MCS connection is defined as a set of transport connections managed as one unit between two MCS providers. MCS connections are, therefore, logical connections defined across a physical connection, i.e. one physical connection can support more than one logical connection. The creation process is that an MCS implementation at a workstation, known as an MCS provider, establishes a connection to a remote MCS provider and binds this connection to a domain through the use of an MCS primitive, MCS-connect-provider. Other MCS providers can then establish connections to these providers and bind to the same domain; alternatively MCS providers already with connections to a domain can bind further connections to that domain. In this way a domain can be established, which may vary in complexity from a simple point-to-point connection to a multi-branched tree structure of connections. Figure 7.8 illustrates the relationship between MCS providers and domains.

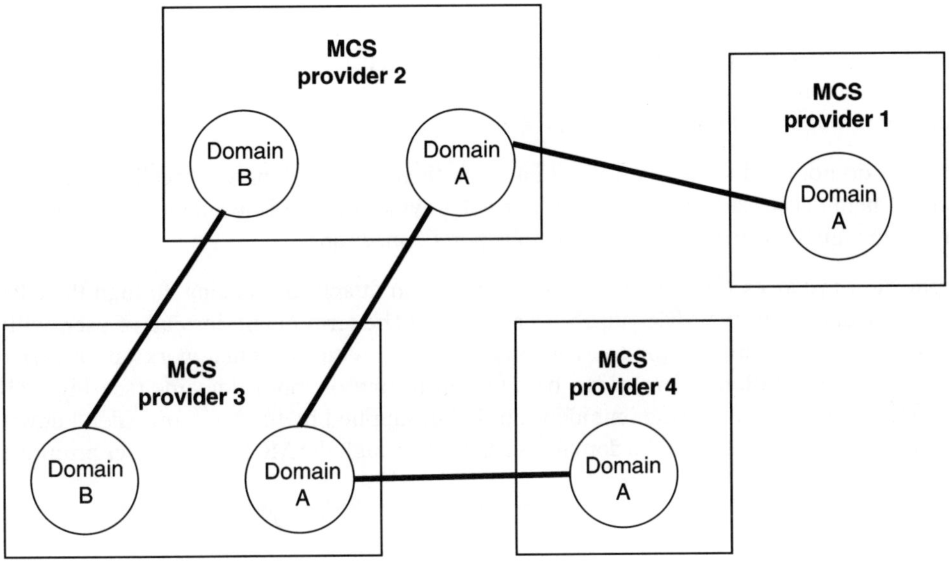

Figure 7.8 MCS providers and domains

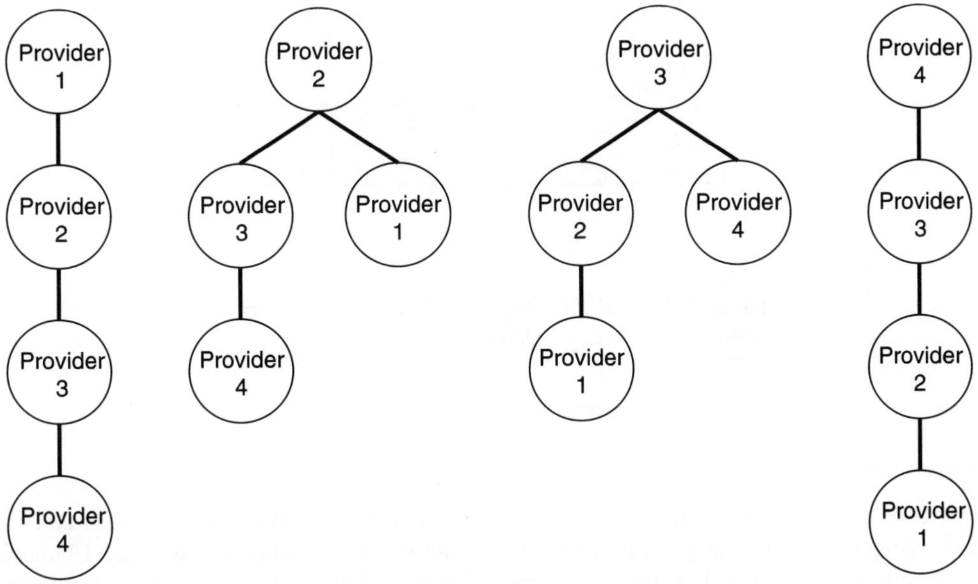

Figure 7.9 Hierarchical structures and domains

Individual domains are each identified by what is called a domain selector. The creation process allows existing domains to be combined into a single domain. A restriction on the establishment of a domain is that it must be created hierarchically; this is enforced by ensuring that, as each binding takes place, the called provider is explicitly positioned as either hierarchically superior or subordinate to the calling provider. This hierarchical structure is key to the implementation of the MCS functions and, indeed, aspects of the architecture. When an

MCS connection is broken, the domain splits into two portions; the portion containing the top provider survives, but the bottom portion eradicates itself. Figure 7.9 shows some of the hierarchical structures that correspond to domain A in Fig. 7.8; one of these alone must have been specified through the domain creation process.

Domains do not need to be multi-point and can, therefore, exist purely locally with no connections being necessary. The MCS-disconnect-provider service is available for a provider to leave a domain; this also disconnects the transport connections.

Application instances (known as clients or users) can attach to domains through their local MCS provider, using the MCS-attach-user service. (The term client, instead of user, will be adopted throughout this section to avoid any confusion with the actual workstation user.) In this way an application instance can be attached to one or more domains (see Fig. 7.10). Client attachment results in a client identifier being supplied by the MCS provider, known as the user id. Detachment from the domain is enabled through the MCS-detach-user primitive.

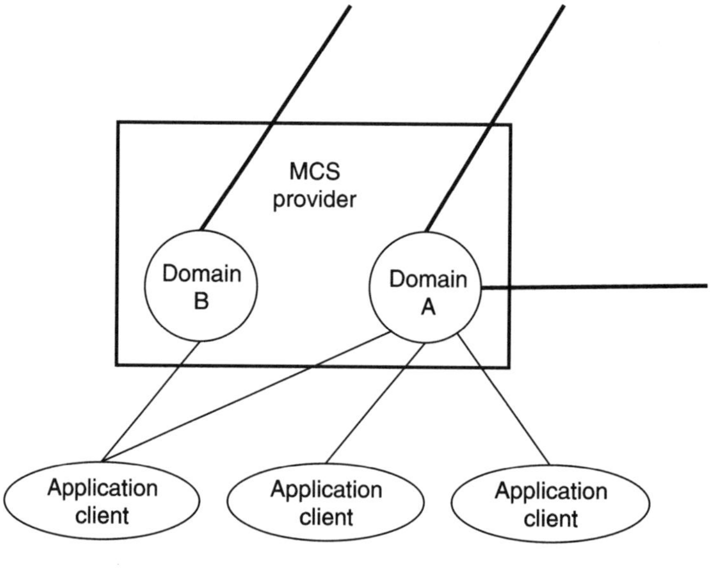

Figure 7.10 Application clients and domains

MCS channels

Once domain set-up and client attachment is complete, the last step necessary before data can be exchanged is for the clients to join the right combination of interaction channels. Channels are effectively domain-wide addresses for the delivery of data to all, or a subset of the clients of a domain and are joined through the MCS-channel-join request. A client does not have to be joined to a channel to send data to it, but must be joined to it in order to receive data from it. Channels are classified as static or dynamic and identified by a numeric id:

Static channels: Channel id (numbered 1–1000)

Dynamic channels (numbered 1001–65535) comprising three types:
- User id
- Private channel id
- Assigned channel id

Static channel id channels are permanently available and any clients can join at will. They provide a mechanism for clients to send data to any subset or all of the clients. For example, the clients in a domain may have a convention to use channel 10 to broadcast to all members; to achieve this they all join channel 10 and send data on this channel when it is to be received by everyone. Particular uses are allocated to individual static channels in other standards, e.g. in the GCC and the T-series applications recommendations.

Dynamic channels require creation before they exist. A user id channel is created by the original MCS-attach-user request and can only be joined by the client with that id; this therefore provides a mechanism for any of the other clients to send data on a point-to-point basis to that client. Private channel id channels are created by any client through the MCS-channel-convene function, with the result that that individual client becomes the owner of that channel and is the only user initially joined to it. This 'owner client' can invite other clients to join the channel using the MCS-channel-admit function, or force clients to leave through the use of MCS-channel-expel. Having been invited, other clients can send data on the private channel or join it to receive data from it. The owner of a private channel may destroy the channel entirely by issuing MCS-channel-disband. Assigned channel id channels provide a mechanism for joining an empty dynamic channel, i.e. one that currently has no clients joined, and is accomplished through a special case usage of the MCS-channel-join primitive.

Clients that join channels may subsequently leave them using the MCS-channel-leave primitive; MCS domain providers can also use this function to force clients to leave channels.

Once the participating MCS providers have connected and bound to the domain, and clients have attached and joined the right combination of channels, the clients are ready to exchange data. Two data services provide the actual transfer of data. MCS-send-data sends data packets on the specified channel to all clients (except the sender) joined to that channel. The data packets from any client are delivered in sequence, but the packets from multiple clients may be interleaved in different orders at each receiving client—a consequence of their being delivered using the most direct route up and down the tree of MCS providers. A variation on send data is MCS-send-data with responses, which requires each receiving client to generate a short response, with the responses from all receivers being gathered at each level and travelling back along the distribution path of the original message. The aggregate response is delivered to the sender.

MCS-uniformly-sequenced-data-send parallels the send data request, but guarantees identical interleaving of data packets. The packets are serialized by being sent to the top MCS provider and from there are despatched, in the same sequence, to all receiving clients and also, in this case, the sender.

Data transmission is associated with a priority specification with four normally available, corresponding to: top, high, medium and low priority. These priorities are used to resolve the contention issues that may arise during transmission. Associated with each priority are throughput (bandwidth) and transit delay (latency) specifications.

MCS tokens

In addition to data transmission facilities, MCS also provides token management services which may be used by clients to control resources. The MCS services available are:

- *MCS-token-grab* Results in the exclusive holding of a token which was previously available
- *MCS-token-release* Return of a held token so that it becomes generally available
- *MCS-token-give* Used to surrender a token to another application client
- *MCS-token-please* Request to hold a token already held
- *MCS-token-test* Determines the status of a token
- *MCS-token-inhibit* Multiple clients can inhibit a token and individually release it. The token is only free when all clients have released. This therefore allows a single token to be used to coordinate a multi-client event.

Other features of MCS

When a multi-point domain is created by the first two providers, a number of domain parameters are negotiated, which are then fixed for all further members. These specify limits such as:

- The maximum number of MCS channels to be in use simultaneously
- The maximum number of users ids to be assigned simultaneously
- The maximum number of token ids to be grabbed/inhibited simultaneously
- The number of data transfer priorities, with their throughput and transit delays
- Minimum data receiving rate enforced
- Maximum data buffer size to be used

MCS provides a mechanism for a number of desktop conferencing workstations and compliant MCUs, to intercommunicate. The associated workstations in a domain are linked hierarchically through (typically) ISDN links, with branches in the tree being created by MCUs in the network. It is possible for a workstation also to behave as an MCU by having multiple logical MCS connections defined over a single physical connection, and/or by multiple physical connections, e.g. more than one ISDN adapter card. The close coupling of the network topology to the associated workstations required by MCS is not normally a problem because the links are usually switched and, therefore, transient.

Applications use the MCS services to exchange data and must be written with prior agreement on the channels to be used, the data formats to be exchanged, and the significance of tokens. There is very little quality of service control available to applications and no means for them easily to negotiate bandwidth. The association between applications in a domain is not controlled; the applications bind to the domain independently, without negotiation with other applications. MCS provides a set of services which may be built upon to implement desktop conferencing—it is not a set of services suitable for independently conceived applications to inter-operate, applications must be in carefully orchestrated communication with each other.

7.5.2 The T.123 recommendation

MCS is defined over a variety of networks, not just ISDN. However, it is the ISDN case that is the most interesting because it is only here that a complete and standardized solution is provided for audio, video and data conferencing—and over a switched network which is generally available. T.123 defines the network specific protocols in any single network connection between terminal and multi-point control unit, or between two terminals directly connected, or between two MCUs directly connected.

Two types of protocol stack are defined, for basic mode service and for extended mode service, depending upon the requirements of the teleconferencing applications to be supported.

The basic mode presents a uniform OSI transport interface and services (X.224) to the MCS layer above and dispenses with the need for presentation and session layers, leaving all the remaining part of the OSI protocol up at the application layer. Connection orientated profiles are provided for circuit switched and packet networks. For computer networks that are not connection orientated the profiles include additional transport layer capability to make them functionally connection orientated. The basic protocol stacks for ISDN, CSDN, PSDN and PSTN networks are illustrated in Fig. 7.11.

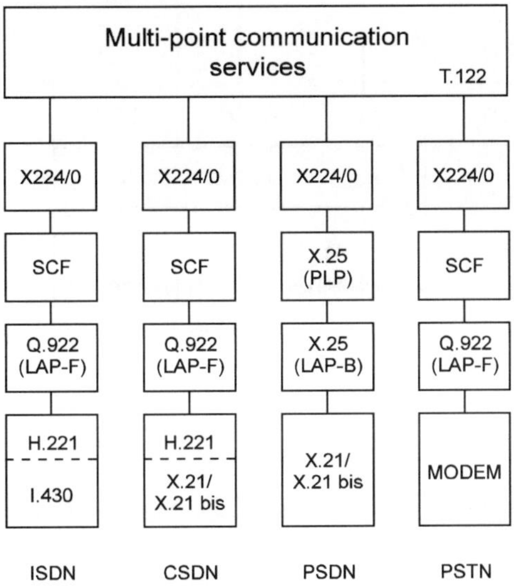

Figure 7.11 T.123 basic protocol stacks

The basic ISDN profile can be expanded to show the relationship to the various ISDN channels more clearly and identify more of the relevant recommendations. Audio, video and the MLP (multi-layer protocol) generated by MCS and MCS applications are multiplexed together at the H.221 layer but arrive through very different routes. Conference control is part of the MLP data stream from an MCS application; ISDN network control, i.e. call set-up for example, is probably generated by that same MCS application but does not reach the ISDN D channel through the MCS/T.123/H.221 stack (see Fig. 7.12).

Q.922 provides a multiple virtual circuit capability at layer 2 of the OSI reference model, and hence multiple transport connections, as are needed to satisfy the MCS channel requirements. However, Q.922 does not support the assignment of a priority classification to each of these virtual circuits, which is another MCS requirement. The synchronization and convergence function (SCF) provides this capability, taking advantage of the control path in Q.922. The algorithm implemented between SCFs at the sending and receiving stacks is described in T.123. SCF provides the layer 3 function of the OSI reference model; it has no effect on the data itself, only on the set-up of the virtual circuits to be used.

X.224, implemented on top of SCF, implements the transport layer protocol specification for open systems interconnection.

It is the basic stacks that are currently in common use. The extended mode stacks are of interest here to show how full OSI conformance can be achieved in the future. The extended proto-

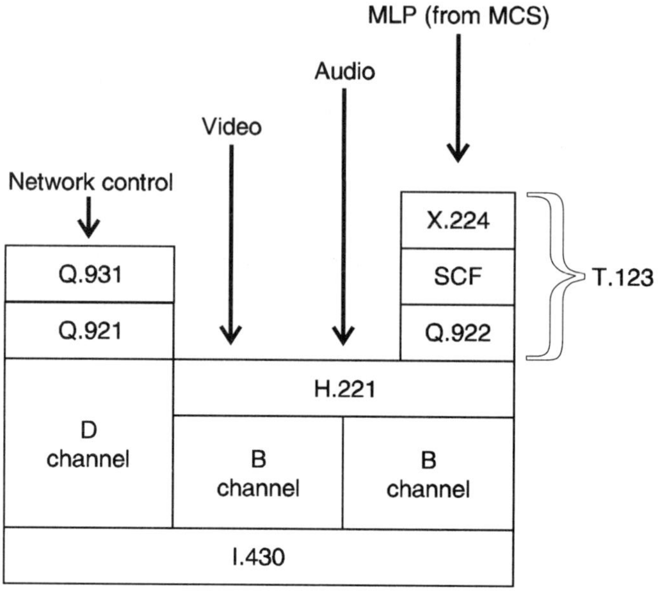

Figure 7.12 The T.120 recommendation over basic rate ISDN

col mode service T.123 stack is an extension of the basic protocol stack, as is illustrated in Fig. 7.13.

X.227 is the association control protocol specification for open systems interconnection, corresponding to level 7 of the OSI reference model; similarly X.226 is the presentation protocol, layer 6; and X.225 is the session protocol, layer 5.

7.5.3 Conference control

T.124 builds upon MCS and provides the specification of generic conference control functions (GCC). The central concept is that of the conference, a real-time collaboration between users. GCC functions include: conference establishment and termination, conference roster management, application roster management, remote application actuation, conference management, bandwidth control, and applications registry services.

GCC conferences

Each node participating in a GCC conference, which is typically a workstation or an MCU, logically consists of the elements illustrated in Fig. 7.14.

The node controller is intended to represent that system component which interacts directly with the user, although it may be embedded in a client application. Its important function is to exploit the GCC agent present on the workstation to produce the required conference personality. Each conference is mapped on to a single MCS domain. A node may participate in more than one conference simultaneously. Conferences are identified by their conference id which is set to the MCS domain selector; they also have a conference name, this name being intended to provide a readable text string to identify the conference to the user. Nodes within a conference are distinguished by their GCC user ids, which are the MCS user ids assigned to the GCC agent at that node.

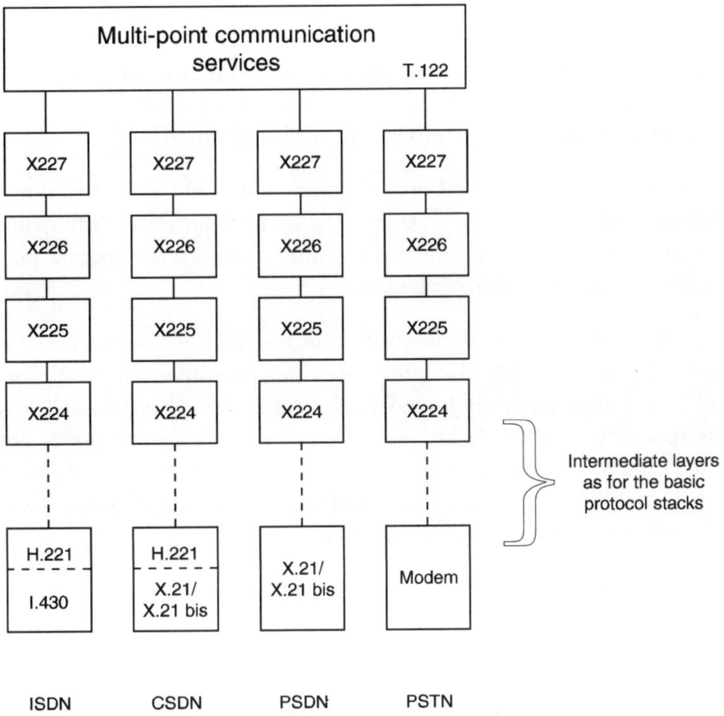

Figure 7.13 The T.123 extended protocol stacks

According to the recommendation, a conference can be viewed as a meeting room in which any number of participants may meet in order to exchange audio, video or other data. Just as for physical meetings, services such as: finding out what conferences are in progress, mechanisms for joining and leaving a conference, ways of restricting access to a conference, etc. are also all required for electronic conferences and are, therefore, provided by GCC.

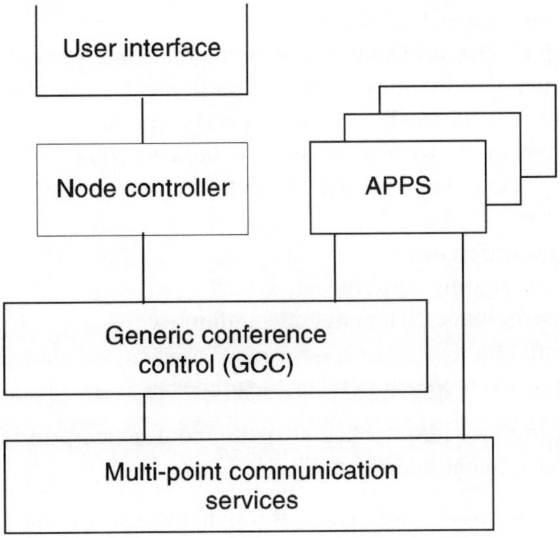

Figure 7.14 The elements of GCC

A node controller can determine what conferences exist at particular MCUs by issuing the GCC-conference-query request. For those conferences which exist and have agreed to be listed, the query returns the conference name and other descriptive data, including sufficient information to allow the node controller to join if this is permitted.

Conferences may operate in conducted or non-conducted mode. Conducted mode structures and orders the course of a conference; it is invoked upon request by participants in a conference. During conducted mode, the applications within a conference require permission from the conductor before interacting with each other.

Conferences can be created by a node controller issuing the GCC-conference-create request to a remote node. Through the MCS-connect-provider primitive, an MCS domain is established, the local node is automatically joined and becomes the top provider. The quality of service required is specified on the GCC request. Both local and remote nodes are members of the newly-created conference. The creator of a conference is known as the convenor. The creation request also establishes the conference profile, a collection of data comprising the key attributes of the conference. These key attributes are:

- *Conference name* A text string that identifies the conference by name, suitable for display to the members of the conference.
- *Conference id* An identifier that uniquely identifies the conference and is set to the MCS domain selector.
- *Convenor id* (optional) A unique identifier that allows the convenor to identify itself in later operations—effectively a private password.
- *Password protected* (optional) Conferences may optionally be password protected; if protected, the password supplied by the convenor must be used by parties joining the conference.
- *Locked/unlocked* Conferences optionally may be locked; unlocked conferences may be joined by parties at their request, locked conferences require the convenor to request parties to join.
- *Listed/unlisted* Conferences may or may not be on the conference list provided when the GCC-conference-query request is issued.
- *Termination method* Choice is available of whether the conference should last until explicitly terminated (manual terminating) or until all participants have disconnected.
- *Privilege lists* (optional) Three lists which specify, in turn, what functions—normally restricted to the convenor—may also be used by the conference conductor, the conducted nodes and the non-conducted nodes. The functions that may be specified, allow or disallow the privileged node to:
  - terminate an entire conference
  - eject a user from an ongoing conference
  - add one or more participants to an ongoing conference
  - lock or unlock conference
  - transfer participants from one conference to another

With the exception of the locked/unlocked attribute, conference profile attributes cannot be changed after the conference has been created.

Other nodes may join the new conference, through the use of the GCC-conference-join request. Alternatively the convenor, or others given the necessary privilege by the convenor, can bring others into the conference by issuing GCC-conference-add, which requests that the MCU dials out to the specified node. As a result of the conference add, the GCC-conference-invite request is then issued to the specified node to invite it into the conference. If the conference is locked, additional members can only be added by invitation.

Conferences can also be created locally at an MCU without the use of GCC primitives. In this case the participants are invited into the conference by the MCU, and it becomes the top provider. Such conferences are likely to be locked and may also be specified as unlisted.

At any time a node may leave a conference using the GCC-conference-disconnect request. Alternatively, the GCC-conference-terminate primitive allows an entire conference to be terminated, disconnecting all nodes. Other GCC commands include: GCC-conference-eject-user which disconnects a specific node from a conference, and GCC-conference-lock and GCC-conference-unlock which lock and unlock conferences. The GCC-conference-transfer request provides for some or all of the members to leave one conference and join another, and the function can therefore be used to split or merge conferences.

The recommendation provides mechanisms which support timed conferences. If the conference has been established as a reserved conference, it will not disappear until explicitly terminated by the convenor or those with the necessary privilege. The GCC-conference-time-remaining request allows the convenor to inform all nodes of the time remaining in a timed conference; similarly the GCC-conference-time-inquire request allows a node to find out from the convenor how much time remains. If a node requires more time than remains, a GCC-conference-extend request can be issued and the response from the convenor states the extra time that has been given, if any.

GCC conference roster

When a node joins a conference it is required to announce its presence to the other nodes in that conference. This requirement is enforced in order to allow each node to build up a collection of information, known as the conference roster, which contains the following for all terminals/workstations, MCUs, etc., identified by GCC user id:

- *Node type* one of:
  - user-terminal (a terminal for a participant with no other terminals connected through it)
  - peripheral-user-terminal (a terminal for a participant connected through a user-terminal/MCU)
  - management-terminal (a terminal intended for conference management, not for normal participation)
  - MCU (a network device intended to allow other terminals or MCUs to connect through it)
  - user-terminal/MCU (both capabilities)
  - peripheral-user-terminal/MCU (both capabilities).
- *Node name* (optional) a text string giving the name of the node.
- *Participants name(s)* (optional) list of names as text strings.
- *Network address* (optional) network address of the node.
- *Alternative node id* (optional) an alternative node number scheme, distinct from the GCC. For nodes supporting H.243 this could be used for the H.243 site id.
- *Node profile id* (optional) capability profile that best fits the node equipment.

The node controller issues the GCC-conference-announce-presence request supplying its own conference roster data. As a result of this request the GCC providers of the nodes in the conference exchange the information needed to update the conference roster to include the newly joined node. The updated conference roster is distributed to all nodes in the conference, generating a GCC-conference-roster-report indication. A node is only a member of the conference when this report has been received. As nodes leave the conference, updated reports are issued in a similar way.

The GCC-conference-roster-inquire request is available to applications and enables them to independently obtain the complete conference roster, for a specified conference, from the GCC provider.

An application instance may attempt to invoke a peer application (or an instance) at one or more remote nodes through the GCC-application-invoke request. The remote node controller receives the indication and can invoke the application (or instance) which may then enrol itself in the conference.

GCC application roster

The collaborative function within a conference is provided by applications. The availability and capabilities of applications are stored in a set of records known as the application roster. This roster consists of two components, the local application roster holding details for each local application instance, and the conference application roster holding details for each instance of every application at every node in the conference.

The local application and the conference roster both contain, for each instance:

- an application record
- an application capabilities list (optional)

Each application record contains:

- *Application key* Used to identify uniquely an application and each instance of that application. Keys may be standard or non-standard indices—standard indices are issued by relevant standards bodies to identify applications; non-standard indices allow proprietary applications to be uniquely identified. When multiple instances of the same application exist, they are distinguished through an instance number being incorporated into the key.
- *Application description* (optional) A text string which describes the application.
- *Application user id* (optional) The MCS user id associated with the application key, if the application has attached to the conference MCS domain through the local MCS provider. The application user id is the only means by which a node can include another node as a participant when convening a private channel for that application to use.
- *Active/inactive flag* Indicates whether the application is ready to receive data.
- *Application profile id* (optional) An optional parameter referencing a standard application profile. The contents of this profile will be defined in a future standard T.PRO.

Each application capabilities list contains:

- *Capabilities* Application specific capability codes.
- *Class specifier* Determines how the capabilities are combined to determine the common capabilities for the conference:
  - Logical—total number of nodes with capability

– Minimum—minimum value from those with capability
– Maximum—maximum value from those with capability

Applications are made aware of the existence of a conference by the receipt of a GCC-permission-to-enrol indication. The application must then issue the GCC-application-enrol request but, before doing so, certain information must be obtained. The indication from GCC supplies the MCS domain selector, which identifies the domain for the conference. The application, therefore, issues MCS-attach-user to attach to that domain and in reply receives its MCS user id, needed for the application record. Similarly, steps may need to be taken to obtain its instance number which is supplied through issuing the GCC-registry-allocate-handle request.

Applications can use the GCC-application-enrol request to decline to enrol, to enrol, to re-enrol to update their application data, or to un-enrol. The local application roster is stored and managed by the local GCC agent. During a conference, any changes in the local application roster are immediately exchanged with other nodes and the new conference application roster is issued—both in its entirety to the node controller, and in the relevant subsets to client applications—through the GCC-application-roster-report primitive.

At any time during a conference, a client application or node controller may issue the GCC-application-roster-inquire request to obtain either their application portion, or the entire conference application roster.

GCC application registry

The application registry is a data base, unique to a conference, which is stored and maintained at the top GCC provider. It offers a service to client applications that can be used to manage channels, tokens and other shared resources in a conference. The notion is that parameters such as channel ids, etc. can be determined dynamically in a general purpose way, rather than being pre-set within applications or exchanged in an *ad hoc* way. The significance of the information in the registry is determined by the applications themselves.

The indices used to store entries in the data base are application-specified registry keys. Both standard or non-standard keys are supported: standard keys consist of the application key combined with a resource id; such resource ids are defined by the applications themselves. Non-standard keys may be proprietary.

The GCC registry requests are briefly described as follows:

- *GCC-registry-register-channel* allows a channel id to be stored and associated with a key
- *GCC-registry-assign-token* given a key, a dynamic token id is assigned by the server and associated with it
- *GCC-registry-set-parameter* allows a string of data to be stored and associated with a key
- *GCC-registry-delete-entry* given a key, deletes the item stored with that key
- *GCC-registry-retrieve-entry* given a key, retrieves the item associated with that key
- *GCC-registry-monitor* provides a mechanism for applications to monitor changes in the registry content for a specified key
- *GCC-registry-allocate-handle* provides a mechanism for applications to request a numerical value, or list of values, to be allocated to that application which will be unique within the conference. Such values may be used by application instances at a node to distinguish themselves from each other.

Entries are owned by the registry agent that created them; owners may modify or delete items that they own at will. Ownership of a key is decided by being the first to create such an entry. Other agents may access data owned by others but may not modify or delete it. When an owning agent detaches, the data in the registry continues; if, however, another agent stored data with that key, the request is allowed and this agent becomes the owner of the entry just created.

To avoid possible conflict with the applications use of MCS token services, the GCC-registry-assign-token request assigns token ids in the range 16384 to 65535; applications can be sure that if they use tokens in the range 1 to 16383, without reference to the GCC services, there will be no conflict. Since this in some way parallels the MCS division of channel ids into static and dynamic, the low numbered tokens are called static tokens and the high numbered tokens, dynamic tokens. At the MCS level there is no significance between static and dynamic tokens.

Conference conductorship

GCC distinguishes between conducted and non-conducted conferences. The recommendation does not define the difference in behaviour between these two modes, but expects that applications will be sensitive to the difference—in particular, that during conducted mode the applications will seek permission from the conductor before interacting with each other. GCC does provide a mechanism for a conference to change mode and for applications to become informed of the current mode.

The node controller at any node may acquire the conductor token in an unconducted conference by using the GCC-conductor-assign request; conversely the GCC-conductor-release request is used to change status from conductor to normal participant. Any change in status of conference conductorship is notified to all other node controllers and all other applications. GCC-conductor-inquire allows either applications or the node controller to determine the current mode and, if applicable, the identity of the conducting node. GCC-conductor-please allows a node to request conductorship from the current conductor; GCC-conductor-give is used to surrender the conductorship to another node.

Miscellaneous other facilities

Assistance from a conference operator may be requested using GCC-conference-assistance. The effect is to broadcast the user supplied data to the node controller at all nodes in the conference. The response is undefined in the standard.

A simple means of sending text messages to the node controller(s), either at one specified node or all the nodes in the conference, is enabled through the GCC-text-message primitive.

7.5.4 Conference applications

A number of applications are intended to be covered by the recommendations of the T.120 series. At the time of writing only sufficient progress had been made on the still image and file transfer applications to allow a full description of their concepts and capabilities; the only other application which has been discussed at an overview level is that handling audiovisual control.

The intention of the T.120 application recommendations is neither to specify an API for application development, nor to specify function. The focus is on inter-operability and the standardization is, therefore, only at the data protocol level, i.e. the information transmitted and received across the network.

Still image application

The T.SI (T.126) recommendation provides the standardization necessary to achieve interoperability for both shared whiteboarding and soft and hard copy still image conferencing, including support for annotations. The definition supports a range of image qualities, ranging from those needed for normal office documents through to high definition photographic image quality. Basic remote pointing and keyboard event exchanges are also included and so participating terminals can implement a basic level of application sharing. Different levels of implementation sophistication are envisaged through the recognition of baseline, standard and non-standard capabilities. The baseline level of function must be provided in all implementations; the standard capabilities are defined within the T.SI specification but must be negotiated before use, i.e. the participant applications exchange capability information and agree the level of support to be used in the conference. Non-standard functions are not defined in the recommendation, but applications are free to negotiate with other applications in the conference to see whether their extra capabilities can be used within the conference.

The recommendation does not define the functionality of the application as seen by the user. It does define the data that will be sent to other T.SI applications and, therefore, the data that must also be accepted; likewise, it defines what use is made of associated MCS and GCC services. Given the primitives provided, there is a great deal of flexibility in the functions and user interface styles that may be presented to users. As an example, although many graphic objects are defined, very advanced graphics functions such as morphing can be offered to users, with the results subsequently being translated into one or more of the supported objects ready for transmission.

For all conferences where a soft copy capability has been negotiated, the available function is based on the concept of a shared workspace. If only a common hard copy capability exists among the members, then a different set of function is available, based on bitmap exchange only. The workspace comprises one or more superimposed data-bearing planes, with the higher-numbered planes appearing in front of the lower-numbered planes. Each plane may contain both images and annotations, depending upon the way in which it was created. Optionally a virtual plane may exist in front of all the data-bearing planes and be used to hold pointers. The workspace model can be represented as in Fig. 7.15.

A created workspace in a conference has the same dimensions at all nodes. All workspace coordinates are specified in pixels and they are assumed to be square in shape. A conference can support one or more workspaces, up to a negotiated maximum value which may change dynamically as new nodes enter or leave the conference. Multiple workspaces are useful for multi-document applications, as well as enabling workstations to pre-loaded data ahead of use. In this way a number of workspaces can be set-up in advance and later revealed, without any associated transmission delays, during the conference. Each workspace is identified by its workspace id (numbered sequentially up to the negotiated maximum).

The colours used within a workspace are negotiated between the participants, with the following combinations defined:

- 2 colour (black, white)
- 16 colour (black, white, two greys, 12 other colours)
- 225 colours (black, white, 32 greys, 191 other colours)
- 24 bit full colour

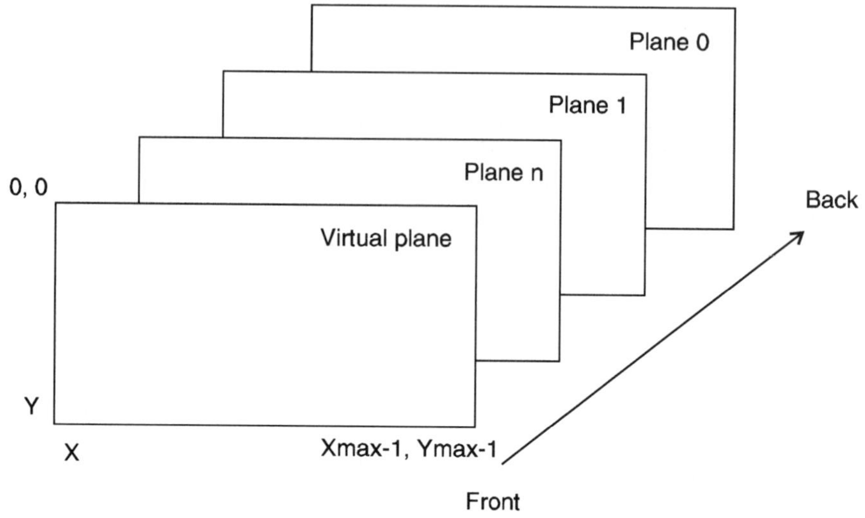

Figure 7.15 Shared workspace model of T.SI

Drawing elements may also be defined as transparent.

Workspaces are associated with a number of attributes when created. These are:

- *Synchronized or unsynchronized* A synchronized workspace is one that is guaranteed to contain the same information at all nodes in the conference (through use of the MCS-uniform-send-data service).
- *Able to accept keyboard and/or mouse information* Remote keystrokes and/or mouse pointings may be directed at the workspace.
- *State* Possible states are hidden (not to be shown to the user), background (display is optional), foreground (display is desirable), and focus (display is mandatory; only one workspace may be in this state at a time).
- *Preserve preference* Any creation of a new workspace should/should not attempt to avoid using this workspace id— use would destroy this workspace.
- *Background colour* This determines the colour of the workspace for a pel, in the cases where that pel in all planes has been set to transparent.

Planes within a workspace have their own set of attributes:

- *Editable or permanent* Editable planes have a data base associated giving the definition of each object, its position and its sequence in the drawing order; permanent planes exist only as the rendered pixels in the plane raster image.
- *Usage* Planes may be marked as being used for annotations and/or images. Annotation usage indicates that annotation objects may be applied to the plane; image usage indicates likewise for image bitmaps.
- *Protection* There are two options here: unprotected (any T.SI application in the conference may write to the plane), and creator-protected (only the workspace creator can write to the plane).

Workspace planes may be copied, in whole or in part, to other planes in the same or different workspaces.

Images and pointers may be exchanged through the creation of bitmaps; however, since bitmaps are also used for annotation, it is convenient to describe them fully later.

Annotations are defined as a collection of objects, the objects being basic shapes, drawing and erasing custom shapes, text and bitmaps. The four basic shapes are:

1 *Open and closed polylines* a sequence of straight lines connecting successive points
2 *Points* a sequence of individual points
3 *Rectangles* defined by the upper left and lower right points
4 *Ellipses* defined by two foci and any point

These have the following attributes:

- outline colour
- line thickness
- pen nib shape
- line style (1 of 5)
- fill colour (not points or open polylines)
- depth order (drawing order sequence)
- highlighting (normal/highlighted)
- selection state (selected/unselected)

Support for drawing and erasing custom shapes must be negotiated between the T.SI application instances; any such shape not thus supported can be realized through bitmap exchange, since one colour allowed to pels is transparency.

Text primitives have not yet been defined within the current level of the standard; meanwhile, text annotation can be accomplished through bitmaps.

T.SI supports the exchange of keyboard and pointing device remote events; since these capabilities are not negotiated, implementation in applications is optional. Their existence is to allow basic application sharing, where one application's window is transmitted to the other members of the conference and the remote sites are able to contribute keystrokes or mouse movements to control the application. The effects are made visible to all. Remote event exchanges use a token mechanism to prevent applications interfering with each other. Requests for workstation printing are also supported by the recommendation.

Both the transactions defined in T.SI, and the ranges allowed for certain parameters, are governed by the conference application roster capabilities profile that is in effect. Application capabilities profiles exist for a terminal operating as a:

- whiteboard
- soft copy image exchange terminal
- soft copy image exchange terminal with annotation
- hard copy image exchange device

The mechanism uses the GCC application roster list support. The following is a summary of the range of detailed capabilities that are negotiated between T.SI applications:

- *Hard copy image capability* workspace dimensions; bitmap formats
- *Soft copy workspace capability* number of workspaces supported, dimensions and maximum number of planes; bitmap formats; palettes and number of colours; workspace editable; scaling rectangle supported; pointer supported with size and format details; annotation capabilities including line thickness, pen shapes, primitives allowed, and highlighting provision

- *Archiving capability* data base read and append support.

Workspace creation requires the associated workspace token to be grabbed. If the token is released, other terminals may subsequently create a workspace to replace it. Normally, however, applications will select an unused workspace id or, failing that, one for which a preservation preference has not been expressed. Deletion of a workspace also requires possession of the associated token. The state, preserve preference, background colour and all the plane attributes of a workspace may be modified after creation, but only by the workspace creator.

T.SI supports the notion of workspace archives using local data bases assumed to be available at all terminals in the conference. Support exists to create such archives, to save existing workspaces, and selectively to load current workspaces with planes retrieved from the archive.

Bitmap creation normally requires possession of a token, but this requirement can be negotiated away during capability exchange. The creation process involves the specification of, among others, the following attributes:

- *Destination address* hard copy device (image bitmaps only), workspace and plane identifiers (soft copy devices only and image, annotation or pointer bitmaps)
- *Width* in pixels
- *Height* in pixels
- *Aspect ratio* hard copy devices and optionally for soft copy workspaces—fax1 (800:385), fax2 (800:770); soft copy workspaces only—square (1:1), cif (12:11), arbitrary (if negotiated)
- *Attributes* region of interest (not hard copy devices), position in workspace, use as an application pointer (pointer bitmaps only), depth order (not hard copy devices), unselected/selected/hidden (display normally/highlighted/no display)
- *Type* pointer (not hard copy), image, annotation (not hard copy)
- *Format* annotation and pointer bitmaps—uncompressed, non-standard (if negotiated); image bitmaps (soft copy workspaces)—uncompressed, JBIG, JPEG, non-standard (if negotiated); image bit maps (hard copy)—T4 (low resolution fax standard), T6 (high resolution fax standard)

Bitmaps may be deleted or have their attributes edited. Pointer bitmaps exist in the virtual plane and can be moved by changing their position attribute; both this function and pointer deletion are reserved to the pointer creator.

Drawing objects may be sent to either the permanent or editable workspace planes. In the case of permanent planes, they overwrite the pixel values over which the drawing objects pass; for editable planes, they are treated as separately editable objects. Drawing objects may be deleted or have their attributes changed.

The standard also defines the impact of conducted and non-conducted modes of behaviour, which can be set using the services of GCC. During conducted mode, a terminal may request from the conductor to be assigned one or more of the following privileges:

- to create or delete a workspace
- to modify an annotation plane
- to modify an image plane
- to create, edit or delete a pointer
- to send remote keyboard or pointing device events

- to request remote printing
- to create or append an archive

Multi-point binary file transfer

T.MBFT (T.127) specifies a mechanism for the simultaneous transfer of one or more binary files in a conference. It enables files to be broadcast to all the participants or to be selectively directed towards a subset of terminals as a private file transfer. No restrictions are placed on the contents of the files being transferred.

Two types of channel are used within T.MBFT: a control channel and a data channel. Control channels are used for managing the file transfer, for example arranging the offering of files, requests for files, and so on; each subgroup of terminals in the conference exchanging file data requires a unique control channel. The data channel is exclusively for the file data itself and, on any one data channel, only one file can be transferred at a time. Thus it is possible for several control channels and data channels to be in use simultaneously.

T.MBFT has one static control channel and one static data channel which allow broadcasting of files to all other T.MBFT terminals in the conference. Further dynamic channels may be added to allow concurrent file transfer and file transfer among a subgroup. Tokens are used to ensure that only one file at a time is transmitted on a channel.

Files are segmented into fixed size data units for transfer, with added sequence numbers to enable applications to recover from disconnections or packet loss.

Broadcast of a single file to all terminals is accomplished by all terminals attaching to the static control channel. The terminal wishing to broadcast acquires the FILETX token and verifies that the CHANLOCK token is free. FILETX ensures that only one terminal is sending a file on the static data channel; CHANLOCK being free guarantees that any previous file transfer has been completed for all participants. The broadcasting terminal then offers the file to all terminals via the control channel; the File_offer primitive provides this function. Nodes wishing to receive the file attach to the static data channel, inhibit CHANLOCK, and indicate their intention to receive through File_accept; nodes not wishing to receive do not attach to the data channel but do send an indication on the control channel, in this case File_reject, that declines to receive. File transfer takes place when all have responded and at least one node requires the file. After the transfer the receiving terminals free CHANLOCK and the sending terminal frees FILETX.

Broadcast of multiple concurrent files to all terminals is similar. The transfer of the first file is identical. The second file is handled by the sending terminal first acquiring a dynamic data channel from MCS and then offering the file, as before, via the static data channel. The file offer includes the identity of the dynamic channel. The rest of the transfer process is self-evident. Further concurrent file transfers are handled in the same way. FILETX*n* tokens are used to control the dynamic multi-cast channel usage; if such a token is available it indicates that such a channel has been created previously and is free. Likewise, for each such channel a CHANLOCK*n* token exists.

The private transfer of files within a subgroup requires the sender to request two dynamic channels from MCS—one for control and one for data. The sender then invites the members of the subgroup to join the dynamic control channel. Once all invitees have joined, the file is offered on the newly-acquired dynamic control channel.

T.MBFT also supports receiver invoked operations, i.e. the receiver requests a file to be sent. This is accomplished by the receiver grabbing the FILERX token and then broadcasting the file request through the File_request primitive. All nodes attached to the static control channel are expected to respond to the request using the File_deny primitive if they are unable to supply the file. A terminal that is able to send the file must first grab the FILETX token and check that CHANLOCK is free, before offering the file for transmission on the static data channel using File_offer—exactly as if it had initiated the transaction.

File transfers can be paused using the File_pause primitive and resumed using File_continue. File_abort aborts the file transfer. The recovery of lost packets is accomplished through the File_retransmit primitive, which allows an application to request transmission of a file from a named packet number.

A conducted mode of operation is defined for T.MBFT. This is not automatically entered when the GCC_CONDUCTOR token is assigned to the node but is explicitly switched on by the use of the **Set_MBFT_conductor_mode** request. In conducted mode, all new file transactions are regulated by the conductor; exclusive rights can be given to a particular terminal to offer data on the static control channel and the need for potential recipients to acknowledge their intent to receive a file can be suspended.

File data is sent with a header in the first packet which is set with the **File_data** request. It includes a great deal of information, for example:

- file name
- permitted actions
- contents type
- date and time of creation
- date and time of last modification
- date and time of last read access
- identity of creator
- identity of last modifier
- identity of last reader
- file size
- access control
- legal qualifications
- compression technique
- path name

Audio-visual control

The T.AVC recommendation sets out the procedures for the management of the real-time audio and video channels in the conference. Unlike the other applications in the T.120 series, the data is not sent via MCS but goes independently, and this exception is made in order to achieve low latency and smooth data flows. T.AVC uses a top priority MCS channel to transmit/receive the control information, not just to the other terminals in the conference, but also to MCS node (or nodes) that are providing the MCU function(s). Thus, T.AVC also receives the audio and video capability exchanges described in H.242 and H.243.

AVC is not mandatory in a conference; if it is not present, audio and video will behave as described in the H.242 and H.243 standards. It is permissible for some terminals in a conference to have AVC and for others in that same conference to rely upon the default audio/video MCU behaviour.

The functions provided in T.AVC allow:

- override of the default video routeing in a variety of ways, e.g.
  - send own video to other terminals
  - specify video stream to be received
  - cycle through available video streams
- override the default mixing of audio
- control for cameras, mixers and microphones, e.g.
  - floor control
  - camera panning

7.5.5 Brief assessment of the T.120 recommendation

T.120 addresses the glaring deficiencies of H.320, namely the lack of standardization for data services. Using the T.120 recommendation it is possible, over an ISDN network, to design audio, video and data conferencing services that will inter-operate between different suppliers' equipment, and over national and international networks. T.120 still suffers from the basic problems inherited from its H.320 base; its limitation to a maximum of one audio stream and one video stream, its relatively low quality audio/video, its hierarchical logical connection structure, its incompatibility with personal computer standards, and its irrelevance to common workstation networks. The definition of MCS over a variety of communication stacks ignores the transmission of audio and video; data-only conferencing is profoundly uninteresting.

The separation of audio, video and data into distinct services, with audio and video being treated in a very different way, is not justifiable from an applications viewpoint. The rigid call management model of GCC may well reflect an important conferencing style, but is likely to be restrictive. Application standardization is important, but many of the useful applications, such as the ability to remotely control existing applications, will necessarily lie outside the scope of the recommendation.

Despite these criticisms, the absence of alternative standards ensures that T.120 will become important, and inter-operability with T.120 compliant products is likely to be a prerequisite for any successful conferencing offering in the workstation market.

7.6 Missing standards

The T.120 and H.320 recommendations, when completed and adopted, will go a long way towards ensuring inter-operability over the public switched digital telephony networks, but they cater only for the directly-attached workstation communicating either with its peers or with existing telephony equipment. Multiple-point services will be provided by MCUs within that switched network.

The majority of workstations, however, are attached to local area networks and use PC industry formats for data, video and audio, and PC communications protocol stacks for networking. Thus, most users do not have a standardized solution to adopt and are dependent upon manufacturers' proprietary systems and, equally important, there is no easy connectivity between the two worlds. The situation cannot be simply resolved by requiring the T.120/H.320 series to be adopted by the PC/LAN community since it fits uncomfortably in that environment in its present form. It fails to take advantage of much of the hardware, software and data that these customers have installed, and, in some areas at least, falls short of existing customer expectations, for example the poor audio and video quality of the 2B channels H.320 products.

A PC standard needs to build upon the strengths of the existing PC product set; thus it should use audio and video that is compatible with what exists and integrate the variety of data services already available. The greatest deficiency in the PC arena is the absence of an easily available, affordable, isochronous local area network, although there are some contenders such as iso-Ethernet and (later) ATM. Video tolerant LANs, using priority schemes and bandwidth management, may perform useful roles in bridging the gap from what exists to what will ultimately become commonplace. Hence a successful PC conferencing standard will establish video, audio and data formats, real-time multimedia communications protocols, distributed object models, compound document formats, and other such items. It will be seen in Chapter 9 that various PC companies, representing a wide range of interests, have seen the need for such developments and established special interest groups to make progress along these lines.

Gateway products are needed to link the two communities; once standards are agreed on both sides, it will become possible to build devices which permit inter-operation. Moreover, the existence of new standards will encourage both communities to evolve towards a uniform system that makes the gateway services ultimately unnecessary.

Unlike the telephone industry where inter-operability has been an essential feature of the business from the early days, and adoption of standards a way of life, the PC industry does not normally operate with that type of mind-set. There is no equivalent body to the ITU-T, the pace of change is historically much faster, and standards in the past have been set by leadership products capturing market share.

CHAPTER 8

The IBM architecture

As will be seen in Chapter 9, that there are many desktop conferencing products available, and almost as many industry alliances and unofficial standardization bodies. Among manufacturers there is full realization of the need for standards in order to grow the market and reassure customers, however, the nature of these standards is open to debate. As has been seen already, the ITU-based standards are incomplete and do not satisfy all the requirements. Moreover, they build on existing telephony designs and do not necessarily provide a smooth migration path for computer users who developed their systems without a bias towards telephony and have a considerable investment to protect. The patchy nature of the standards, and the absence of watertight definitions, means there is no guaranteed specification that can be adopted to produce a universally-accepted solution. Even if there were, manufacturers need to distinguish their products from the competition by adding extra capabilities, since there is an obvious reluctance to compete on price alone. These pressures have resulted in many proprietary systems being developed, which are both genuine attempts to meet market requirements and also ways to establish unique interfaces as *de facto* standards. This has happenned frequently in the past and many of the most successful specifications are exclusively- or largely-based on company initiatives. The availability of the ITU-T T.120 series of recommendations is, therefore, generally regarded as another capability to be accommodated within a manufacturer's specification; not as a limiting definition of product content.

It is not possible in this book exhaustively to analyse all the alternative platform proposals and few have been published in detail. One which has, is the IBM Lakes architecture—a defintion of a real-time multimedia communications platform. It promises full H.320 and T.120 interoperability, as well as overcoming many of the deficiencies evident in the standard.

Since the functions of Lakes and the T.120/H.320 series overlap, it is not surprising that some similar, but not identical, concepts exist. Moreover, each architecture has used many of the same words to describe entities that are related, but different. In the chapters on Lakes, as previously for the ITU recommendations, the names used are not distinguished from identical names in other architecture(s). Later, when comparisons are made, the context of these shared names will be explicitly stated.

8.1 Lakes requirements and overall structure

The detailed requirements for Lakes arose from three sources: the needs of the application programmer; the nature of the networks that form the collaborative infrastructure; and the demands of users and product developers.

From an application programmer perspective, it is preferable if:

- applications can be developed in a platform-independent manner thus encouraging portable code that can be migrated between systems.
- applications can be unaware of the physical communications network and able to operate independently of changes in that network. In other words, applications should operate in terms of the logical rather than the physical properties of a network, typically expressed in quality of services (QoS) parameters such as throughput, latency and jitter.
- the environment supports applications simultaneously interacting with one or more other applications. Such concurrent interactions may be either independent or dependent upon each other. As an illustration, an audio application may wish to handle multiple simultaneous calls, with each call involving multiple other audio applications.
- the cooperation between applications is based upon peer-to-peer responses since, in the general case, there can be no certainty that a central application will be available to mediate behaviour. Peer-to-peer design allows client-server support to be implemented as a special case.
- the applications are able to either handle all aspects of application-to-application collaboration themselves, or delegate functions to others. Likely aspects to be delegated are the association and disassociation phases between applications. Such delegation simplifies the provision of a consistent user interface for call control, yet allows individual applications to specialize in particular collaborative functions, e.g. shared text editing.
- applications are able to collaborate freely, without requiring that they be limited to particular partners. Such a desirable objective is inherently unachievable, but much can be done to help through careful design—for example, by the use of self-describing data streams whose format and content description is available independently of the data itself.
- any applications already written and installed are able to be used collaboratively without modification. This requirement can only be partially satisfied but nevertheless much can be accomplished. For instance, an existing single user application can rarely be made fully multi-user without access to the source code, but can almost always have its inputs and outputs made accessible to remote users.

Other requirements arise from a networking perspective. Thus:

- both digital and analogue networks should be supported. Analogue audio and video capabilities are frequently available at lower cost than their digital counterparts, although this is slowly changing. Ideally, applications should be immune to network migration from an analogue to a digital communications base.
- network traffic in collaborative situations is increasingly multimedia in nature, e.g. it contains not just coded data but one or more audio and video streams. This requires a smooth handling of these continuous data flows, with low latency to ensure the user good usability. A telephony system model, where data flows are directed and connected, is more suited than one in which the applications themselves move data between links and devices.
- historically the networking world has been divided into two camps: the voice network designed by the telephone companies and the data networks designed by computer manufacturers and associated suppliers. Seamless integration of these capabilities is now required, with traditional telephony devices being able to participate in computer collaborations, and vice versa.
- intelligent networks should be exploited, allowing functions such as data serialization to be devolved from applications and implemented within the network itself, i.e. pushed down through the operating system and distributed over the network in some optimal manner.

A third set of requirements emerge from the needs of users and product developers:

- standards compliance is mandatory to ensure guaranteed inter-operability across products. The ITU-T H.320 and T.120 series recommendations are important for the real-time collaborative applications.
- an open architecture is required, with published interfaces and protocols sufficiently detailed to allow independent implementations or extensions.

Lakes meets these requirements by providing an application programming interface which is based only on a view that a network of workstations exists and that application instances are either running at these workstations or may be caused to run. This is intentionally well below any concept of call models and was selected because it reflects the reality of networked applications. Above such an interface, call models can be developed; below such an interface, everything else can be hidden from the application developer. The model, therefore, is a distributed application based model where the applications dominate and determine behaviour. Concepts of calls and other abstractions are built on top of this distributed model and accessed through higher level interfaces.

The overall structure provided by Lakes on a workstation is shown in Fig. 8.1, with the key interfaces identified.

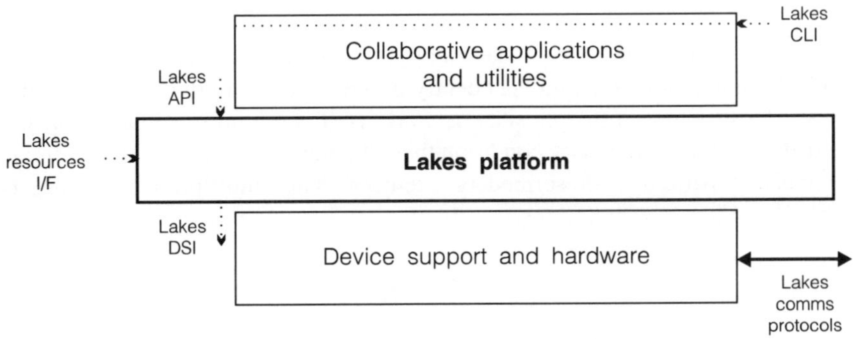

Figure 8.1 Principal Lakes interfaces

Three important open interfaces exist:

- The *application programming interface* (API) which allows applications to request Lakes services.
- The *device support interface* (DSI) which is provided to allow support to be added for different software and hardware subsystems, such as communication systems, video and audio devices, etc.
- The *resources level interface* (RLI) through which Lakes can be integrated into existing network and user data bases containing phone book and related information.

8.2 Principal components of the architecture

8.2.1 Network, nodes and applications

At the highest level, the Lakes programming model presents a representation of a network to an application as a series of interconnected nodes. A node is the addressable entity in Lakes that equals to a user, and comprises an instance of the Lakes API, and typically a set of resources such as application programs, data, etc. Usually a node is a dedicated programmable workstation capable of communicating with its peers; in a multi-user system a node is associated with each user (see Fig. 8.2).

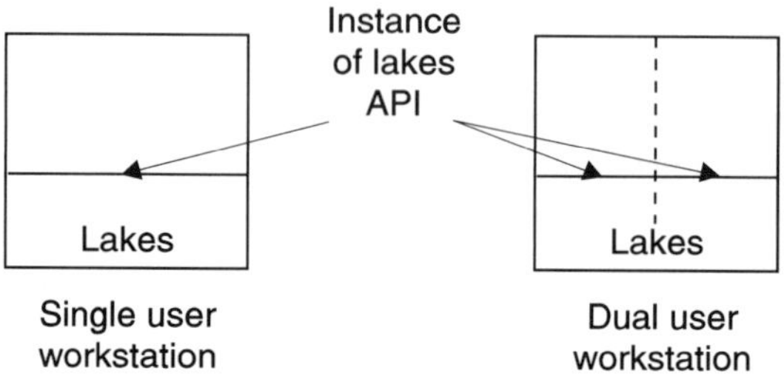

Figure 8.2 Workstations and nodes

Nodes are identified by name; ideally all node names are unique but duplicates can be tolerated as long as their associated nodes are never required to inter-communicate. The node naming scheme is not prescribed by the architecture, but a system, such as that defined by the Internet protocol has many benefits.

A collection of inter-communicating Lakes nodes is called a Lakes network. It is fundamental to the architecture that any node, independently of any others, can dynamically join or leave the network. The structure of the physical network itself is not presented to applications and cannot be deduced. It is a necessary condition that all nodes can be physically interconnected, but no connection pattern is prescribed or excluded. Thus multiple connections between

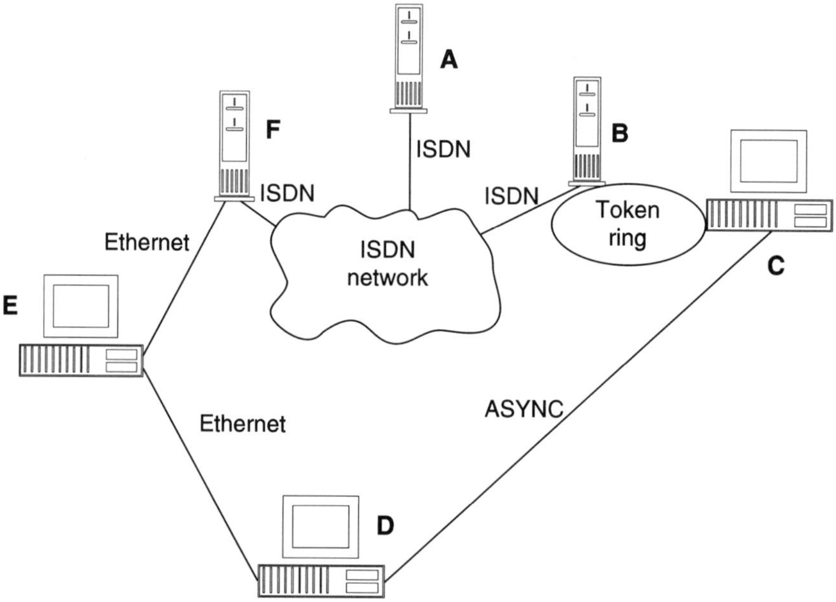

Figure 8.3 A possible Lakes network

nodes can exist, and will be exploited where possible, and the indirect access to one node via other intermediate nodes is possible. The links between nodes can vary in type, capability and protocol. An example of such a Lakes network is given in Fig. 8.3.

Workstations F, A and B all have an ISDN capability and can connect in a pair-wise fashion using the public ISDN network; B and C are also equipped with token ring LAN adapters and can, therefore, communicate with each other over the local area network; C and D have asynchronous adapters and a dedicated link between their ports; F, E and D form an Ethernet local area network. Lakes applications on all nodes will have logically direct access to all other nodes; Lakes itself may realize a connection from, say D to A, either by using E and F or by using C and B; the choice will be governed by the specific quality of service requirements, the state of the network, and by the customization information supplied to Lakes.

Nodes can contain components known as logical devices. These are best understood as software extensions to Lakes that allow an application to manipulate or manage other software entities in a workstation—for example, the system clipboard, or equipment such as a camera or a video player. The intention of logical devices is to provide a general mechanism for adding function to Lakes in a consistent way.

Multiple applications can be executed at a Lakes node, subject to the constraints imposed there by the operating and windowing systems. Applications are classified as being either Lakes-aware or Lakes-unaware; an aware application invokes the services of the Lakes API; an unaware application does not. Both aware and unaware applications will generally be executing simultaneously at a node. Lakes provides facilities for unaware applications to collaborate without requiring them to use the Lakes API directly; the mechanism involves a Lakes aware application effectively surrounding the unaware application, and intercepting and redirecting some of its inputs and outputs. The components typically present at a Lakes node are illustrated in Fig. 8.4.

Although Lakes nodes are generally workstations running applications, it is sometimes convenient if other equipment can be regarded as a Lakes node even if Lakes is not present. A Lakes implementation at one node can allow certain attached devices, such as telephones, video telephones, etc., to behave in this way and it provides this by simulating a virtual node and a virtual application to represent the device. The advantage of this approach is that an appropriate application program, written to communicate with real Lakes nodes, will now also communicate with simulated nodes without device-specific code. Thus Lakes provides two distinct ways of communicating with devices: (a) logical device support that allows full device control, in a device independent way, and (b) virtual node/virtual application support that allows limited device control without the need for any unique application provision.

In order for Lakes to be fully active at a node, one particular aware application must be running at that node. This application plays a unique role and is known as the call manager. The name 'call manager' is misleading and suggests that the job of this application is to provide call management facilities. From a purely Lakes standpoint, this is not true; the job of the call manager is to respond to certain events that are generated by Lakes and to supply installation, application or user-generated information. Although this role will become clearer later, at this stage it is sufficient to state that Lakes frequently requires decisions to be made and needs to know the identity of the application instance that it is to ask for the answers—the instance to be questioned is the one designated as the call manager. Examples of the kinds of question would be: 'An application has requested to be put in contact with a named application at another node—should this be allowed?' and 'Another node wishes to be allocated resources owned by this node - should this be allowed?'

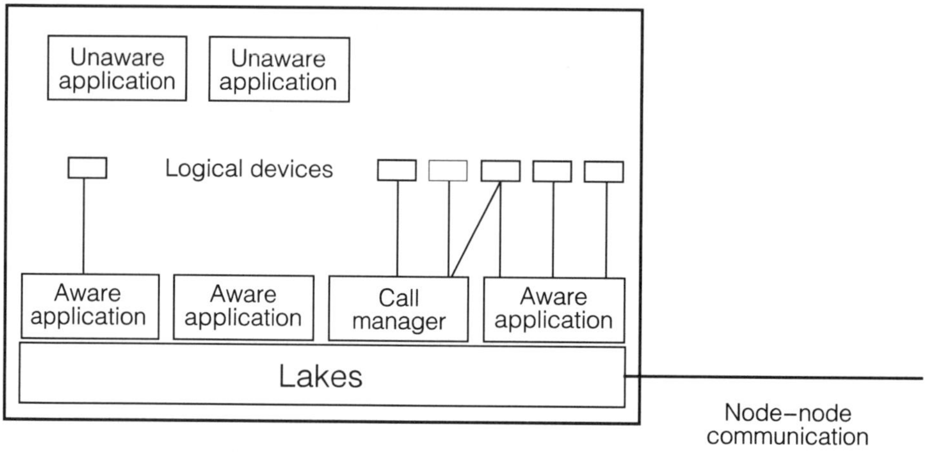

Figure 8.4 Components present at a typical Lakes node

Many call managers may be available for execution at a particular node but, by definition, only one instance of an aware application can perform this role at any time (see Fig. 8.4). This is in no way restrictive; thus it may be designed such that the call manager responsibility can be transferred from one application to another. Alternatively, it is possible for the call manager role to be combined with application functions if that is appropriate. Frequently the Lakes call manager responsibilities are indeed combined with the user function of call set-up and tear-down, but this is optional and is not required by the architecture. The limit of one active call manager at a time does not, even in this case, limit the number of call models that can be simultaneously in use.

A Lakes implementation may request that the resources of one node be made available for Lakes communication between two otherwise unrelated nodes; this is termed passive operation and is an example of the role of a call manager since permission must be granted at the passive node for this to take place. Consider two nodes A and B on a local area network, with a third node C connected to B by an asynchronous communications link. If applications at A and C wish to communicate, the traffic will need to be routed via B. The consent of the call manager at B is required to this use of its node resources.

The most fundamental concept in Lakes is that of the application sharing set. This describes a collection of application instances that have agreed to collaborate. Before joining an application sharing set, applications can reference each other only by name; once a member, each instance has direct addressability to the other application instances in that set. A further consequence of membership is that existing members are informed of any arrivals and departures, through events generated by Lakes. Application sharing sets are each identified by name and any application instance can be a member of none, one or more of such sets. It will be seen that set membership is key to many of the other facilities offered by Lakes for application collaboration.

One way in which applications can join an application sharing set is by initiating a share request using the *LakShareApp* API call and naming: an application sharing set, a target application, and a destination node. This request is first passed by Lakes to the call manager at the sending node, which will typically transfer it to the call manager at the destination node. Usually this second call manager will launch the requested application and transfer the share request to it and, if successful, the source application will be informed. The participation of the call managers in this process allows both local control of the sharing process and other actions to be initiated if necessary—for example, user authentication procedures, security checks, billing, etc. The call managers also play a vital role in resolving the names used by applications to identify other nodes and applications. The symbolic name references are translated into specific node identities and application instances. The sharing mechanism can be cascaded: for example, if two applications are already sharing, one of them can initiate a share with a third application specifying the same sharing set, with the result that all three applications are then sharing with each other.

Applications may also make local share requests on behalf of other applications. It is this ability to perform third party shares which can be exploited to create applications that handle call management on behalf of other applications, i.e. a third party can put the first and second parties in communication with each other. Facilities exist for either the issuer, or the target of the share request to name the application sharing set. These set names are not required to be unique, thus multiple sharing sets with the same name may exist.

Individual applications can cease sharing at any time and thereby withdraw from a sharing set, with the remaining applications in the set being then notified of the application withdrawal.

Figure 8.5 shows a number of applications sharing; the physical network connections are represented by dotted lines and the logical connections, reflecting application sharing set membership, by solid lines.

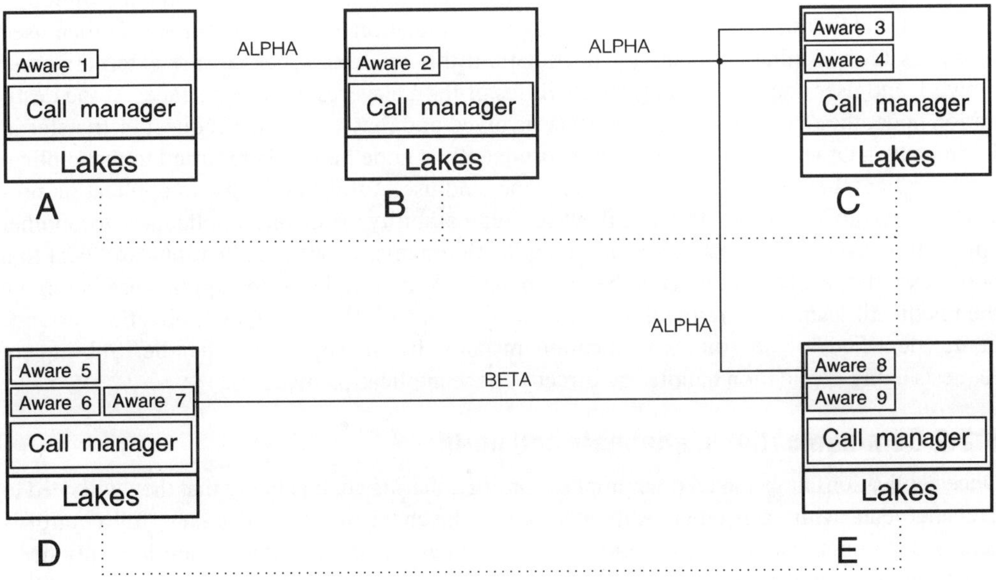

Figure 8.5 Application sharing sets in a network

This figure shows five nodes A–E, seven aware applications 1–7 and two sharing sets, ALPHA and BETA distributed over a network. From an application perspective, the sharing sets are seen as illustrated in Fig. 8.6.

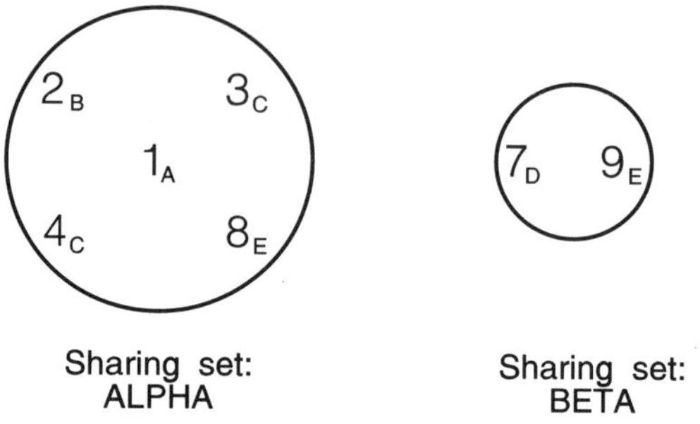

Figure 8.6 Application view of sharing sets

If 8_E was to subsequently share with 7_D naming ALPHA as the sharing set, the effect would be to make 7_D a member of both the ALPHA and BETA sharing sets; 8_F remaining a member of ALPHA only. If both sharing sets had originally both been called by the same name, and 8_F subsequently shared with 7_D using that name, then all the shared applications would become members of one common sharing set.

Information on nodes in the Lakes network is assumed to be held in an address book which Lakes accesses through the resources level interface. The address book may optionally contain a variety of node related information. The API called *LakAddressBookFind* allows an application to search the address book and retrieve parameters, for example node names of interest.

An application initially requests addressability to a remote node by using the node name in a Lakes API call. This name is first passed to the local call manager, which has the option to modify it, unless this has been prohibited by the application. The resultant name is then used by Lakes to determine connectivity information; this requires access to the externally held network and user data base, using the facilities of the Lakes resources interface. At the destination node, the remote call manager gets involved and may accept the request or transfer it. Ultimately, a target node is agreed and subsequently a node handle is returned to the application to reflect this resolution of the node name, and use of this handle by an application provides direct node addressability. Likewise, addressability from one application to another application requires the resolution of an application name. If both applications are local to a node, then the resolution involves the call manager at that node; if one application is remote then both call managers are involved. The resolution results in the target application instance being identified to the source application instance by an application handle. Subsequent requests using application handles go directly to the application instance.

8.2.2 Communications, channels and ports

Once applications have joined other applications in a sharing set it is likely that they will need to exchange data with each other. Although various mechanisms exist in Lakes, full control is achieved through data communication links known as channels. Channels are logically dedicated, unidirectional pipes, with application specified transmission characteristics. Unidirectional channels are used as the basic communications building blocks to efficiently support both broadcast and two-way communications, where the requirements might vary with direction. Lakes channels are always defined by the sending application and go from that sending application to a receiving application. This approach is used because only the sending application can be aware of the properties of the data that dictate how it should be transmitted. The ends of channels are known as ports; thus each channel has one sending port and one receiving port. A sending port sends data blocks down the channel; a receiving port receives data blocks, in the order in which they were sent down the channel. Both sending and receiving ports can be shared between different channels. There may not be a direct mapping between the logical channel structure seen by the Lakes-aware applications and the physical communication network in existence between the nodes; the mapping that does exist is not identifiable by the applications. A complex example of channels, ports and applications is illustrated in Fig. 8.7.

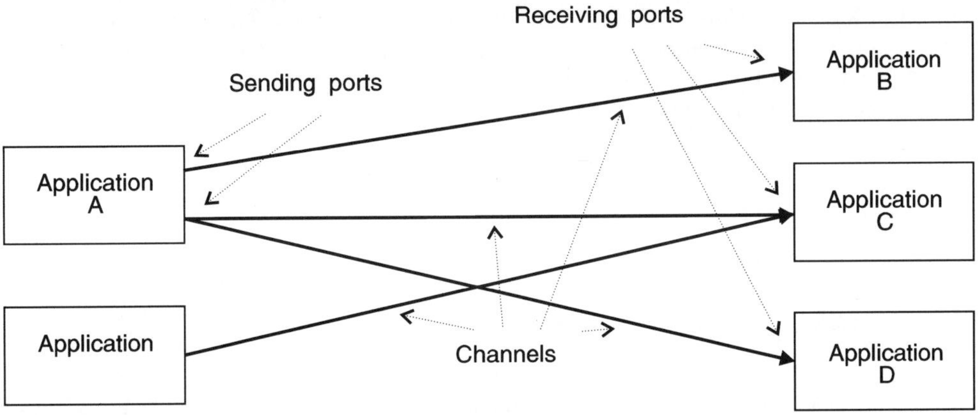

Figure 8.7 Channels and ports

An application is expected to establish multiple channels to another application as a convenient way to separate data traffic of different types. Thus, if an application wishes to send audio, video and image application data it would be normal for the application to create three such channels. The characteristics of each of these channels would be specified differently, to suit the intended traffic. If the destination application wished to send data back, it would have to establish another set of channels suited to move data in the opposite direction. Lakes may map some or all of the logical channels on to a single physical link, but this will be invisible to the application.

The capabilities of a channel are governed by its quality of service characteristics, initially negotiated with Lakes during the creation process, which allow data transmission capabilities to be tailored to the requirements of the expected traffic. Such parameters are defined according to the signal type, which distinguishes analogue from digital data. Typically for digital data, quality of service is defined in terms of parameters such as throughput, latency and jitter. Rather than have applications express these parameters directly, it is preferable if they use symbolic references to collections of values, thus allowing individual parameters to be changed independently of the application. Such a symbolic reference might be, for example: 'Audio, G.711', for an ITU-T G.711 compliant audio stream, with the translation into detailed communications characteristics defined elsewhere. These symbolic collections of values are known as the data classes that are to be transmitted down the channel. Channel QoS parameters may also be left unspecified; this allows a channel to be created, the operational characteristics of which depend upon the resources available when data is being sent down the channel. This reflects the reality of many existing data networks, where behaviour cannot be guaranteed but is wholly dependent upon the activities of the other simultaneous users; token ring and Ethernet local area networks fall into this category.

A feature of Lakes is that channels may be collected into named sets; such named sets are known as channel sets and each must also be associated with a channel set type. Four such types exist: standard, merged, serialized and synchronous . The names assigned to channel sets names are local to an application sharing set; thus duplicates may exist in other sharing sets.

Standard channel sets provide a convenient way of referring to a collection of channels, e.g. for channel managements, but the individual behaviour of the constituent channels is not changed in any way. Thus, in the example in Fig. 8.8, application A is sending squares to application C, while application B is sending circles. At C, two ports exist: one terminates the channels established by A and from it C receives squares; similarly, the second terminates the channel established by B and from it C receives circles.

Figure 8.8 A standard channel set

The merged channel set groups a collection of channels together in such a way that, for any single application, the sending ports and receiving ports for all channels in that set are each combined by default into one such port. A typical use of the facility is an application that wishes to send data to multiple destinations; it can achieve this by making all the channels to those destinations members of a merged channel set—then the data presented at the single sending port will go to all destinations. More importantly, an application can often arrange that channel creation in a merged channel set is handled automatically by Lakes, and so as receiving applications come and go, the data is sent to all the correct receiving ports without further programming. Figure 8.9 illustrates two examples of the merged channel set; the first is identical to the example used earlier for a standard channel set, where applications A and B are sending squares and circles respectively to application C. The specification of a merged channel set means that the receiving port at C for the first channel is used when the second channel is created, and thus both circles and squares are available there. The identity of the sender is not lost through the use of a merged channel set and thus each data block is presented along with its originator's identity.

The second case shown in Fig. 8.9 is more complicated in that A is first sending data to C, and when later B sends data to D through the same merged channel set, this is interpreted to mean that all the senders of the data are sending to all the receivers. Thus, both C and D receive all the blocks sent by A and B. There is no attempt to interleave the data in an identical way and, therefore, although C and D receive all the data, and they both receive A and B in the order in which it was sent, it may be that the interleaving of the blocks is seen differently by C and D.

The serialised channel set is closely related to the merged channel set and performs the same functions. It has the additional property that the interleaving of data from the various sources is per-

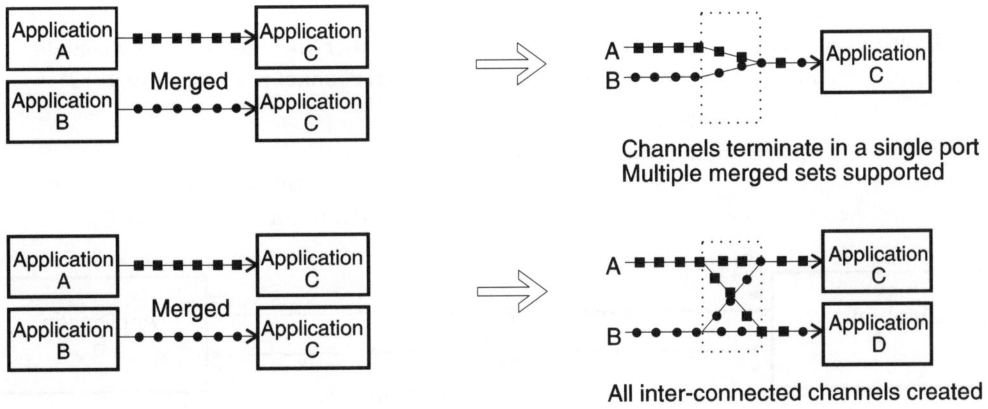

Figure 8.9 A merged channel set

formed identically for all receivers. If serialization could be implemented without affecting quality of service, then the serialized channel set could always be used in place of the merged channel set. However, since this is not the case, it is necessary to offer both capabilities to applications.

The serialization process can be understood by considering all the senders to send one copy only of their data into a common queue, with each data block entering the queue being stamped with a list of all its destination addresses. Data can then be thought of as emerging from this queue, block by block, with each block in turn being cloned as many times as necessary and the individual blocks then being delivered to the required destinations. This notional queuing implies a time delay, and it may well be that the order in which the data items appear in the queue is not exactly the same as the order in which they were sent to the queue. Clearly, if two items are sent at precisely the same time, it is necessary to impose an order, albeit an arbitrary one. A measure of the quality of the implementation of data serialization is the size of the added delay and the fidelity of the data ordering. In practice, it is not always necessary to implement the function in this centralized manner and algorithms have been developed to distribute the serialization process over a network. See Fig. 8.10 for an illustration of a serialized channel set.

Figure 8.10 A serialized channel set

An example of the use of data serialisation is provided by a shared drawing board application (see Fig. 8.11). Two identical applications, A and B, allow their users to draw on a single shared surface. In order that the users at A and B see identical results, all the drawing orders must not be processed immediately at A, but instead must be sent to some serializing process that similarly also receives all the drawing orders from B. This process transmits the drawing orders to both A and B, ensuring that both receive the same sequence of data. The applications each then update their shared drawing board display using this data. In Lakes, this is accomplished by A and B each transmitting their own data both to each other and to themselves, over four channels, which are each members of a common serialized channel set.

The fourth channel set type, the synchronized channel set, exists to allow data blocks to be synchronized so that the blocks transmitted on multiple, otherwise independent channels, are tied together in time, yet delivered through their individual channel ports (see Fig. 8.12).

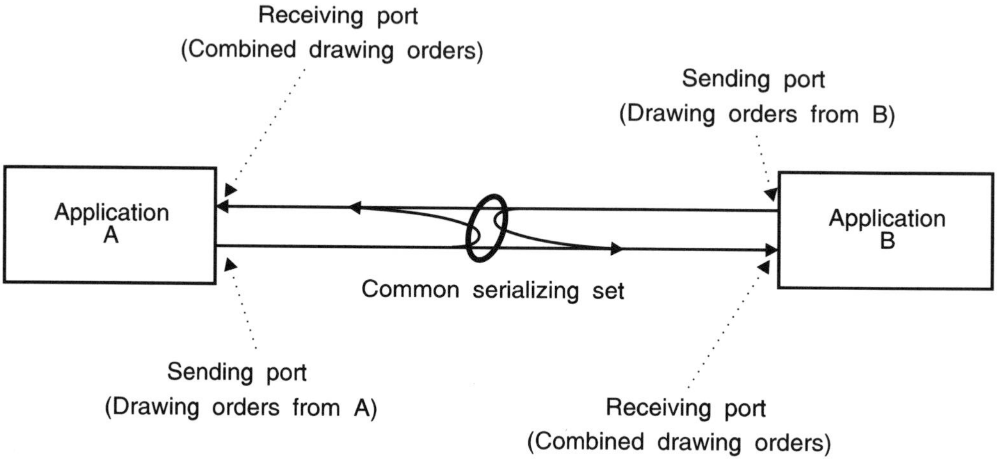

Figure 8.11 Lakes serialization example

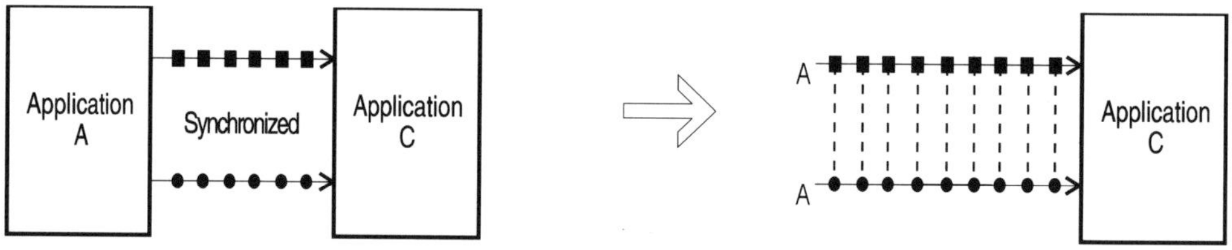

Figure 8.12 A synchronized channel set

Data synchronization is illustrated in Fig. 8.13 by an application A that needs to send synchronized video, audio and data to application B. The video and audio reflect a person speaking; the data corresponds to a pointer being used by the speaker to identify parts of a chart on the display. All three streams are, therefore, related to each other in time. Three channels are used for the transmission, each being a member of the same synchronized channel set.

Channels, and their associated ports, can be created explicitly or implicitly. Explicit creation

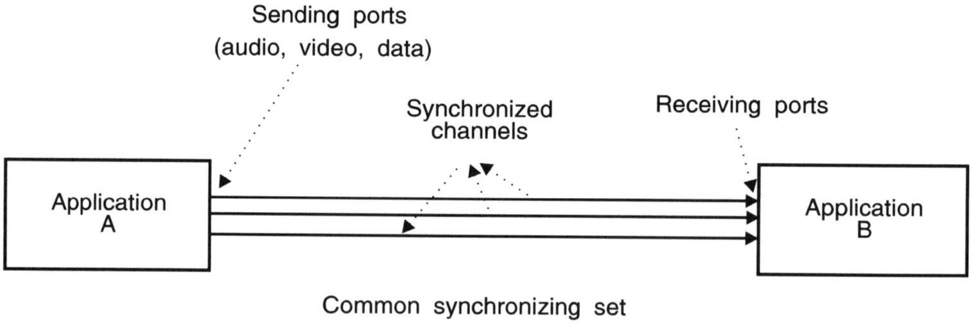

Figure 8.13 Lakes synchronization example

uses the *LakCreateChannel* request, specifying the required channel characteristics; likewise new channels can be added to an existing port through the *LakAddChannel* request. This mechanism also allows a port to be shared across channels belonging to different channel sets: for example, data can be sent from a single port to one set of destinations belonging to a merged channel set, and to a second set of destinations belonging to a serialized channel set.

Channels can be implicitly created as a consequence of an application being, or becoming, a member of an application sharing set. For example, if unshared applications already have a merged or serialized channel, and the channel set name used is identical across these applications, then when the applications share with each other, the additional channels required will be created automatically. Implicit channel creation is illustrated in Fig. 8.14.

Applications A, B and C in Fig. 8.14 all have explicitly created a single serialized channel to themselves, using the same channel set name. On being shared into a common application

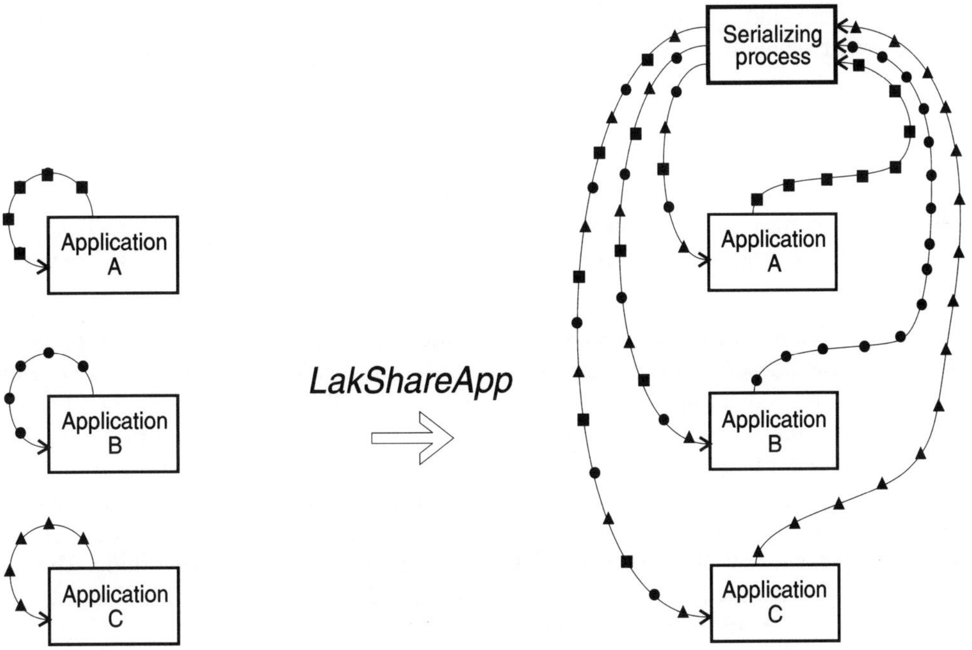

Figure 8.14 An example of implicit channel creation

sharing set, additional channels are created by Lakes such that they all receive all the data that the three applications are sending, and they each receive it in an identical sequence. If a fourth application was to join later, all the necessary additional channels would be also created automatically. Similarly, when applications leave, the channels are appropriately reconfigured.

The result obtained is independent of whether the share precedes or follows the explicit channel creation. Applications are notified of channels implicitly created in this way and have the same ability to accept or reject as they have for explicitly created channels.

A channel, however created, can be deleted through the *LakRemoveChannel* request; the channel to be deleted being uniquely identified by specifying both its sending and receiving ports. Certain quality of service characteristics of channels, such as throughput, can be changed after channel creation through use of the *LakChangeChannel* request.

The sending and receiving ports which terminate channels have an assigned connect type: event, command or null, and are associated with a port event handler. Event ports generate an event when data are either available or are required; command ports allow the application to drive the receipt or supply of data to the port. Null ports are ports that are unable to supply data to an application, e.g. ports associated with analogue channels, such as the sending port of a video camera. A port can be controlled through commands specified in a *LakSignalPort* request. Signal commands are issued to the local port and can be passed to the next port or the end port in the channel or channel set. Normally, the signal commands for channel ports will be sent to the port event handler of the application either supplying or receiving data, and may be used, for example, to stop, start, decrease or increase the data flow. The order of signals between a source and a target is maintained. Signal commands sent to receiving ports in a serialized channel set are serialized with the data, so that all destinations receive the same sequence of commands and data. A receiving port can cause the sending port to stop sending data down the channel by issuing a *LakSuspendPort* request, with the option to either discard or deliver the remaining data in the channel. Suspended data transmission can be restarted by a *LakResumePort* request.

User exits can be optionally associated with ports. These allow monitoring or manipulation of the data, after they have been supplied to a sending port, or before being presented by a receiving port. In the case of synchronized channels, synchronization is carried out from after the data leaves the sending port user exit, and up to the data being presented to the receiving port user exit.

Ports are associated with a data class which specifies the data type and data sub-type that is sent by a sending port down the channel, or received by a receiving port; this approach means that the data class is determined by the application owning the port. The data type identifies the nature of the data, for example, audio, video, file, etc. The data types are further divided into sub-types according to the precise format of the data; examples of audio sub-types are G.711, G.721, G.722, etc. The list of recognized data types and sub-types is specified at each Lakes node in its customization information. The data class may be queried by an application independently of the data stream itself; this facility assists application inter-working. The data sub-type may be specified differently at the sending and receiving ports of a channel, with Lakes performing the conversions below the API.

Certain characteristics of ports, such as data class, event handler address, user exit and user information, can be changed after port creation through the *LakChangePort* request.

Channel merging and serialization operations are independent of the data class; thus there is no merging or combination of the contents of data blocks. All data blocks travelling down a channel carry the identity of the sending port, and therefore the receiving application can, if necessary, distinguish data from different sources.

Ports can be connected together, via the *LakConnectPorts* request, to establish channel-to-channel communication, so that an application may redirect its inputs to another application for processing. When ports are connected, and providing user exits have not been established, no further application involvement in the data flow is required but is allowed, e.g. *LakSignalPort*. This allows the streaming of data between applications and devices. Connected ports can be subsequently disconnected, using the *LakDisconnectPorts* request.

Connected channel ports may also be welded using *LakWeldConnection*, so that the connection is permanent and persists even when the local application has terminated; no reversal of a welding request is allowed. Welding removes any user exits which may be present on the connected ports. The resulting channel behaves as though it had been originally created to run from its source directly to its destination. Figure 8.15 illustrates port connection and welding.

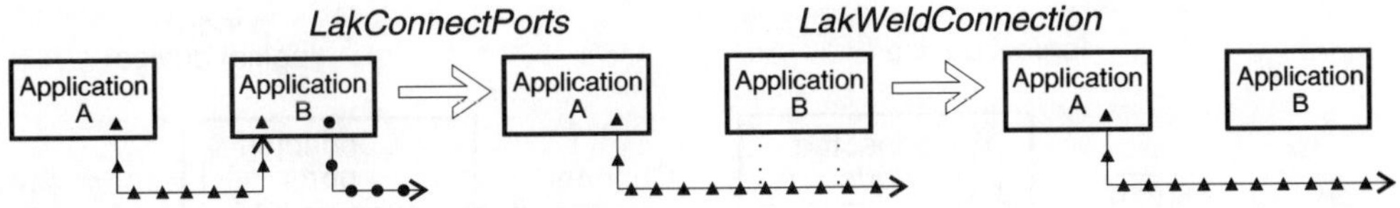

Figure 8.15 Port connection and welding

Connection and welding of channels allows the transport of data to drop below the API. Lakes has the option, in some cases, of effecting the connection either at a very low level at that node or re-routeing the flow away from that node.

8.2.3 Logical devices

Logical device support in Lakes enables:

- easier access to system resources and devices, such as the clipboard, DDE, printer, and video devices by providing a generalized abstraction of device function and control.
- unaware applications to be used for collaborative working, for example by giving access to the window contents and file activity of an unaware application.
- end-to-end data streaming without application involvement, apart from set-up and tear-down.

A logical device can be represented as in Fig. 8.16.

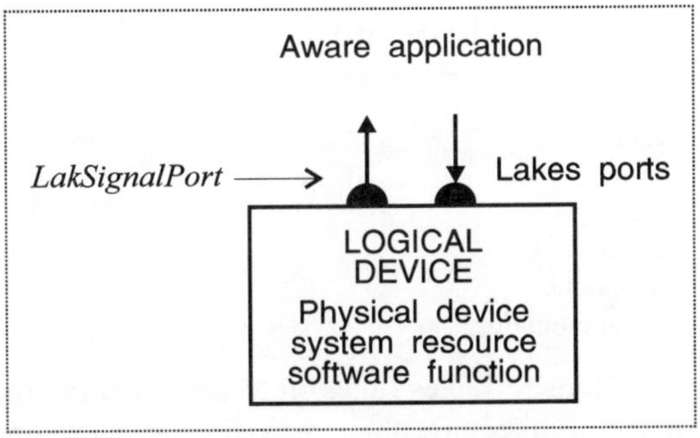

Figure 8.16 A Lakes logical device

Logical devices are identified by name. When opened with the *LakOpenDevicePort* request, they present a port to the application; a single logical device can have multiple ports and, moreover, a device can simultaneously present ports to different applications at the same node. The *LakOpenDevicePort* request allows characteristics to be established, peculiar to that device, for example the data formats to be used. Opened logical devices can be controlled through commands sent via the *LakSignalPort* function request, the commands being specific to the particular logical device. Typical commands to a device port are “rewind” or “pause” to a tape drive, or "change paper size" to a printer device. Device status, indicating, for example, whether data is available, can be determined via the *LakQueryDeviceStatus* call.

Applications can connect ports on logical devices to a channel port; this enables data to flow to or from the device and across the channel. This data flow does not require further application involvement once the connection has been made. This is illustrated in Fig. 8.17.

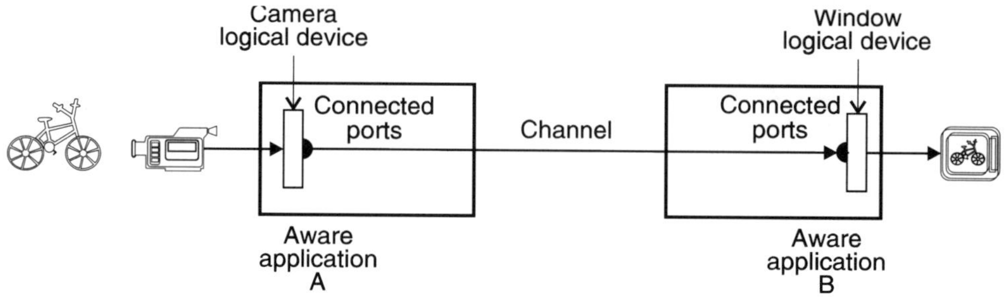

Figure 8.17 Connecting a Lakes logical device to a channel

Data from the camera is streamed through the camera logical device, across the channel, and then displayed by the window logical device. The application can control the two logical devices via the *LakSignalPort* call; when the transmission is no longer required the application can disconnect the ports, close the devices and remove the channel.

Device ports cannot be welded to channel ports because this would allow a device to exist which is outside the control of a local application.

Logical devices are permitted to issue Lakes API calls and, in this regard, act on behalf of the owning application, i.e. that application which issued the *LakOpenDevicePort*. Devices, for example, can cause their owning application to share with other applications, create channels, and send or receive data.

Potential logical devices which could be defined include:

system clipboard	window
printer	LPTx
connector	serial
file	DDE
audio	codec
video	telephone
printer emulator	serial emulator

Logical devices allow extensions to Lakes function to be added but their detailed operations are outside the scope of the architecture; their provision is, therefore, dependent upon the implementation. The Lakes API provides prototype logical device calls and events for consistent access to such platform extensions. The relationship of logical devices to Lakes can be represented as in Fig. 8.18.

The Lakes logical device interface (LDI) is distinct from the Lakes API. It describes a set of calls used inside the logical device implementation to allow integration into the platform; thus, for example, it provides initialization and termination services.

An example illustrates some of the possibilities. The window logical device provided with Lakes provides a way of: (a) capturing an existing visible window on the workstation desktop

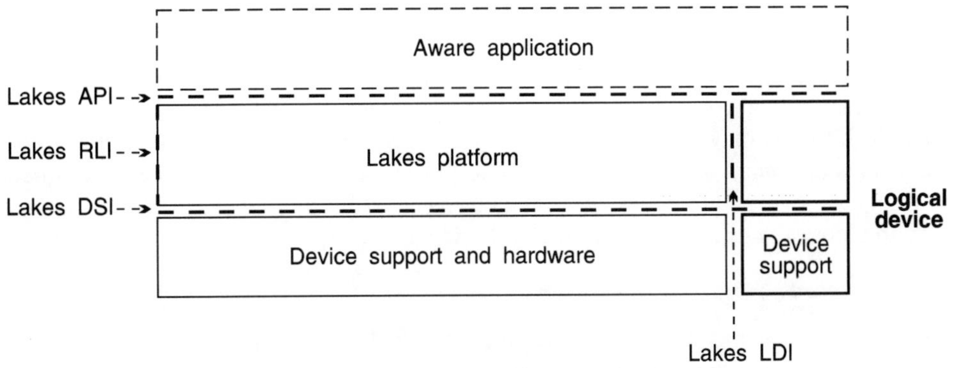

Figure 8.18 Lakes logical devices as extensions of the architecture

and sending it out through a Lakes port on the device, and (b) displaying captured data in an existing visible window. Facilities include capturing the system pointer or allowing the system pointer to be used as a shared pointer. A device of this type could be used to share the window contents of unaware applications, as shown in Fig. 8.19.

In the example in Fig. 8.19, application programming is limited to the user interface considerations, creating the channel and opening and connecting the devices.

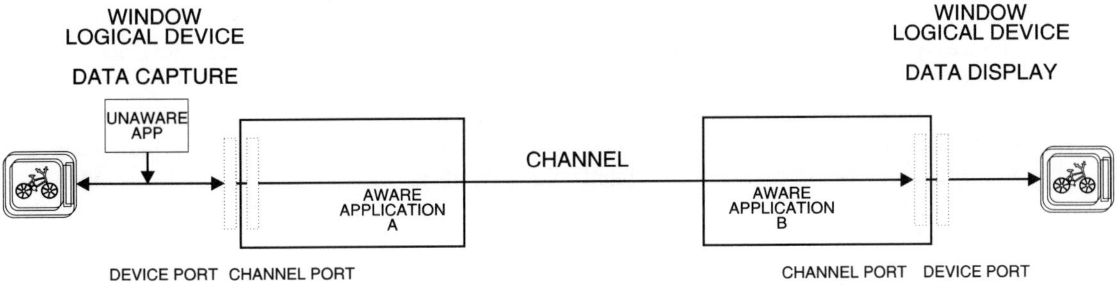

Figure 8.19 Sharing of an unaware application window using logical devices

8.2.4 Tokens

Collaborative working frequently requires that resources owned by a node, for example a printer device, can be shared with other nodes. Such resources are considered to be global and application access to them is controlled through the holding of global tokens. Other resources are local to application sharing sets, for example a shared pointer, and access to these resources is managed through the holding of application tokens.

A token owner determines the significance of a token and allocates it on request. At the discretion of the owner, queued requests may be permitted, and more than one concurrent holder of a particular token may be allowed. Token owners can optionally force holders to hand back tokens.

Global tokens

Global tokens share a common name space throughout the Lakes network, but since applications are expected to know the identity of the node holding the required globally available resource, duplicate global token names are permitted. Facilities for the broadcasting of global token availability information are not provided; instead, the call manager at the node with the global resource is responsible for resource management and, therefore, holds any global tokens. Such tokens may be held by an application instance on an exclusive or shared basis; token ownership cannot be transferred via Lakes. Requests for a global token may be queued, with the queue being held above the API and managed by the owning node call manager. Access to global tokens is not restricted to a sharing application set.

Application tokens

Application token name space is restricted to the application sharing set. Tokens may be owned by one member application and ownership can be transferred. Application tokens may be held on an exclusive or shared basis, and requests for tokens queued, with the queue being held above the API, and managed by the current application token owner.

8.3 Lakes operations and use

8.3.1 Profile data

Customization information, and other node specific data for Lakes, are held in a configuration profile unique to each node. Access to these data is via a profile interface module which forms a part of the resources level interface. The profile interface module is replaceable and its identity is supplied as a run time parameter to the Lakes executable module—thus allowing information to be stored in a data base of arbitrary structure. Similarly, channel quality of service and related information is held in a quality of services profile; again accessed through the profile interface module. In both profiles the data are structured into sections headed by identifiers, with each section containing keywords with associated values. Applications may also choose to use additional private profiles or may use their own sections and keywords in the configuration and quality of service profiles.

The configuration profile contains information on configuration and start-up options, including the local node name, the call manager executable, communications options, logical devices, aware application executables, and associated parameters. The quality of service profile contains information relating to the data classes and sub-classes associated with channels.

Calls to access and update the profiles are provided in the Lakes API. *LakReadProfileString* returns the string value for an identified keyword in a specified section of the named profile; *LakWriteProfileString* writes the string value.

8.3.2 Initialization, application execution and termination

Lakes is started by the execution of a Lakes module. This module accepts run time parameters: the first of these identifies the dynamic load library that initializes Lakes; the second specifies the profile interface module to be used to access profile data. Any further run time parameters are passed to this profile interface module and can be used, for example, to specify a particular file or a data base access string. Lakes gains access to the customization profile and retrieves the identity of the call manager; this program is then started by Lakes. The call manager uses the *LakRegisterApp* request to identify itself as an aware application; in the return data it receives its application and node handles. Following that, it issues the *LakSetCallManager* request which establishes this particular application as the call manager for that node. After this call, Lakes is fully active at that node and can process incoming events and Lakes requests.

Normal operation of Lakes depends upon the presence of a call manager. A replacement call manager can issue the *LakSetCallManager* request, in which case a CALL_MANAGER_REQUEST event will be raised at the existing call manager. This existing call manager has the option of allowing the transfer of the call manager function to the new application, or rejecting the request.

Any aware application can be initiated by the user through the usual operating system procedures, for example a double click on a program icon. Such an application will identify itself to Lakes via the *LakRegisterApp* request and, on the return data, receive its application and node handles. The call manager is notified of this registration itself via an appropriate event, and is supplied a handle to the application.

Applications may also be initiated by aware applications at the same node through the *LakLaunchApp* request. The launching application is returned a handle to the application; this handle is only valid in very restricted circumstances until the launched application has identified itself to Lakes as an aware application by issuing a *LakRegisterApp* request.

Applications may revert to unaware application status by issuing the *LakDeregisterApp* request; the deregistering process includes dismantling all the channels, tokens and application sharing sets, and raising appropriate events to inform the local call manager and other affected applications.

The *LakShutdownNode* request can be issued by an application to close down a Lakes node in an orderly manner. A NODE_SHUTDOWN_REQUEST event is raised in the local call manager and, if the call manager accepts the request, then all other applications receive a NODE_SHUTDOWN event. The applications then prepare to close down, finally issuing a *LakDeregisterApp* request. The call manager receives APP_DEREGISTERED events corresponding to each such request. When all such events have been received, or on some other appropriate criterion, the call manager itself issues a *LakDeregisterApp* to complete the shut down.

8.3.3 Application sharing

Applications may join other applications in a sharing set by issuing the *LakShareApp* request and naming an application sharing set; the normal case being where the target application and node are both specified by name. If an application at one node wants to share, by name with an already existing instance of an application at another node, Fig. 8.20 shows the overall flow of control, assuming sympathetic call managers.

The dotted line in Fig. 8.20 reflects the application view; the solid line reflects the actual process of the share request. Application 1 at node 1 issues a *LakShareApp* naming application 2 and node 2 as the target. This first raises an event, the SHARE_REQUEST, at the local call manager and, assuming that call manager agrees, the event is next raised at the node 2 call manager. Once again, if that call manager agrees, then the target application receives the event. The sharing process is complete when this target application accepts the share request. This is a somewhat simplified description, since many more events are also raised to keep the various parties informed, but the important aspect is that, for an application to share with another, the local call managers and the target application are all involved. At the conclusion of the sharing process, the two applications have each other's application and node handles and, from this point on, can therefore address each other directly.

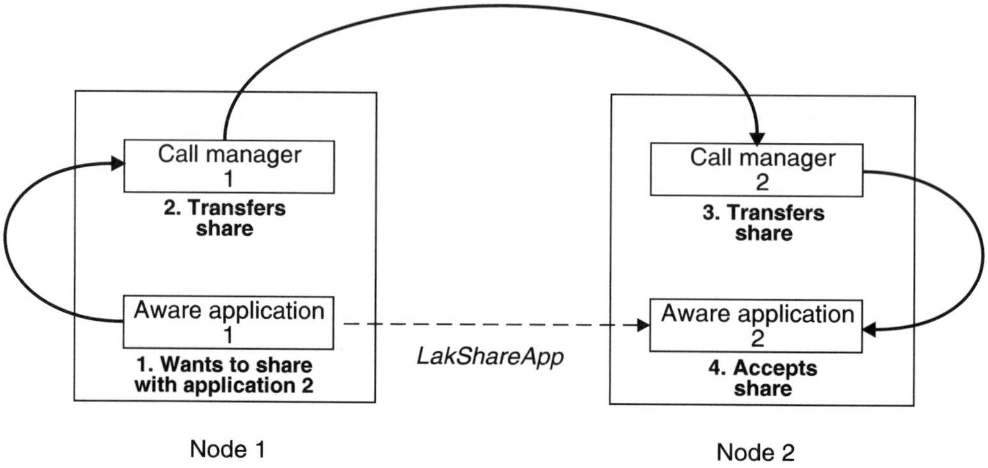

Figure 8.20 Sharing of two applications by name

This scheme provides for considerable flexibility in application sharing. Each call manager is aware of the share activity at its node, whether applications are the source or target of *LakShareApp* requests. Moreover, the call manager, and those applications that are the target of *LakShareApp* requests, can respond in a number of different ways. The options are illustrated in Fig. 8.21.

The transfers can be cascaded from application to application; this process can be controlled by the issuing application through an ability to protect the target application address from

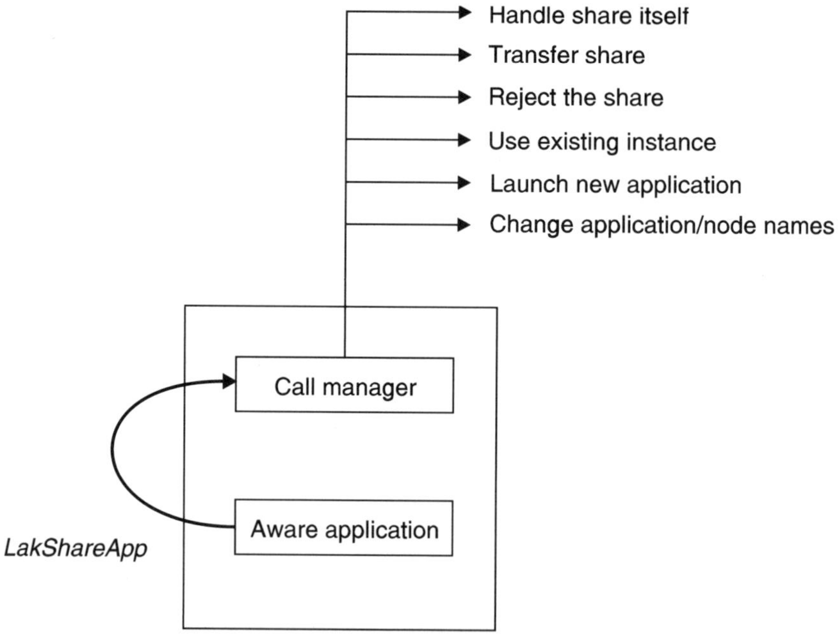

Figure 8.21 Call manager options for share request processing

subsequent changes. The *LakShareApp* request also allows a local application to share on behalf of others. If the call manager is written to share on behalf of a local application instance, it specifies the source application and node handles, with the target application and node names. Third party shares require the concurrence of the source and target applications. An example of this technique is illustrated in Fig. 8.22.

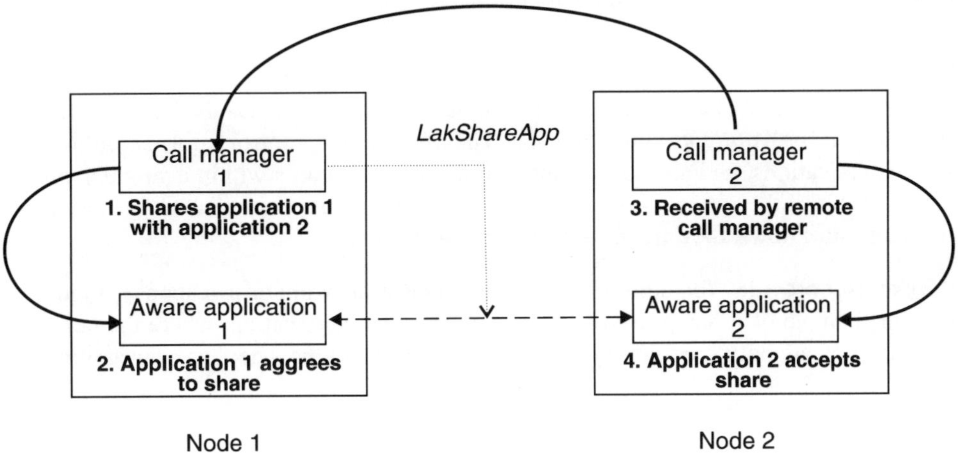

Figure 8.22 Call manager sharing on behalf of an application

The *LakShareApp* request issued by the call manager raises a SHARE_REQUEST event in the source application. If this application agrees to be shared with the target, the SHARE_REQUEST event is raised at the target call manager, which responds in the usual way. This greatly simplifies application programming since the source application, apart from agreeing to be shared, now just receives an appropriate event corresponding to each new share and no longer has to initiate any actions. Third party shares may also be issued by local applications which are not the call manager; the process is similar, with the local call manager being first involved.

An application is not a member of an application sharing set when launched. When the source application issues a *LakShareApp* request, it has the option of naming the resulting sharing set; if it does not name the sharing set, the target must supply the name. After the share, both the target and the source join a new sharing set with this name. If either the source and/or the target were already members of a sharing set with this same name, then those sharing sets are merged with the newly-created sharing set.

Applications can leave a sharing set using the *LakUnshareApp* request. All remaining members of the sharing set are informed. A local application can also unshare on behalf of another application, with the concurrence of that application.

8.3.4 Data transmission and receipt

Lakes provides four mechanisms for applications to exchange data:

- user information strings
- signal function and signal port calls
- channel transmission
- logical devices

User information strings

User information may be supplied on a number of Lakes function calls; this information is then passed to the target application in the appropriate event. It provides a convenient but application specific way of indicating additional information associated with the function call.

Signal function calls

An alternative method of application inter-communication, is provided through *LakSignalApp* and *LakSignalAppWithReply* function calls. They both allow control information to be sent between applications, and are not restricted to those applications within a single application sharing set. Since these two calls use the communication paths established by Lakes for its own data control flows, they are limited to light data traffic.

LakSignalApp provides for unidirectional communication without a response. Figure 8.23 shows an example of it being used to communicate to an application, where the target node and application are both specified by name—a compliant call manager has been assumed.

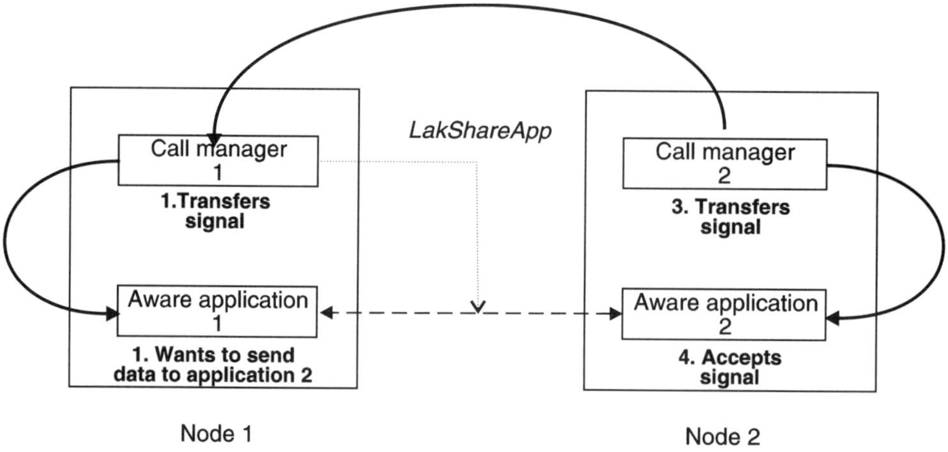

Figure 8.23 Use of signal for named application communication

Figure 8.23 is almost identical to Fig. 8.20 which illustrates an application wishing to share with a remote application by name, and exactly the same considerations apply. The two local call managers are involved and have the same abilities to approve or re-direct the signal. *LakSignalApp* can be used for direct application-to-application communication using instance handles. In this case, the call managers are not involved. If a response is required, the *LakSignalAppWithReply* is used instead; it acts as a simple string-oriented remote procedure call.

The ability of an application to signal to ports provides a specialized mechanism for applications to exchange certain kinds of control information.

Channel transmission

Channels are intended to support the transfer of volume data between applications. They provide the only means of controlling the transport characteristics. The use of channels is restricted to applications within the same application sharing set.

A simple example of channel creation is illustrated in Fig. 8.24, with application 1 creating a channel to application 2.

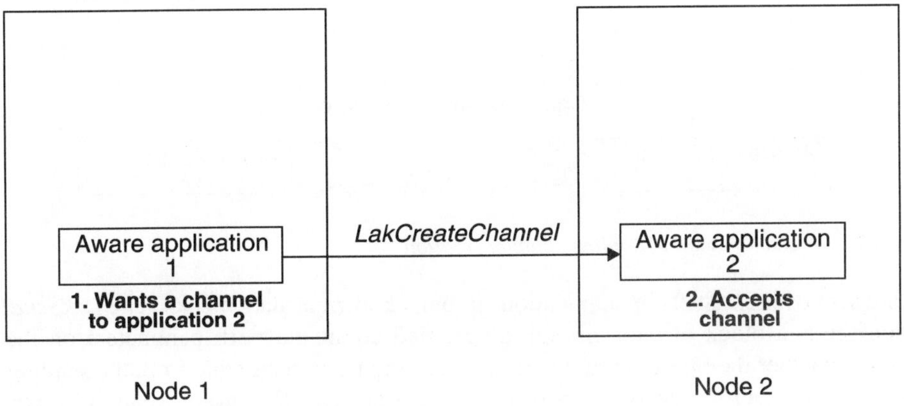

Figure 8.24 Channel creation between two applications

Application 1 issues a *LakCreateChannel* function call specifying:

target application handle	node handle
channel set type, identifier	quality of service
data class	connect type
maximum buffer size	port event handler
user exit	user information

This results in a PORT_REQUEST event at application 2. In accepting this event, application 2 must specify:

data class	maximum buffer size
connect type	port event handler
user exit	user information

Creation of the channel is indicated by CHANNEL_CONFIRMED events being sent to both applications. Application 1 can add further channels to the same sending port using the *LakAddChannel* request; the call and event sequence is almost identical to that described above. Digital data channels may be established with the port connect type being independently specified by the sending and receiving applications.

An alternative approach to channel creation, is to take advantage of the channels that Lakes attempts to create when applications, with existing merged or serialized channel sets, are involved in application sharing. An example of implicit channel creation for two applications sharing is shown in Fig. 8.25. Each application, before the share takes places, has a serialized channel to itself; these two channels are assumed to be already defined as belonging to the same channel set.

The sequence of requests and events is identical to that described earlier for application sharing, with the addition of two CHANNEL_CONFIRMED events for each application. These inform each application of the two new channels that have been created: the channel from application 1 to application 2, and the channel from application 2 to application 1. No additional data are required from the applications since the ports already exist and the new channels take their characteristics from the existing channels.

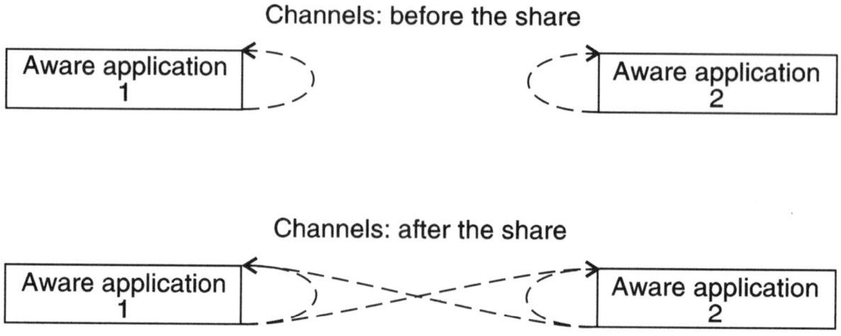

Figure 8.25 A channel view of implicit channel creation

Data are sent over channels by applications in units known as data blocks. The *LakSendData* function sends a block of data through a specified command port; parameters on the call determine whether the block is sent to all the receiving ports accessible from the sending port or whether a specific receiving port is to be selected. For event sending ports, the DATA_REQUESTED event is raised to the port event handler of the application instance that is to supply a block of data to a channel. The following acknowledgement options are specified either on the *LakSendData* request or on the DATA_REQUESTED event; the responses are returned via DATA_CONFIRMED events:

Transmit:	when the data block is transmitted
First:	when the first receiving node responds
All:	when each receiving node responds
Last:	when the last receiving node responds
Progress:	requests progress information
None:	no acknowledgements

For a command type port, *LakReceiveData* calls are used to receive the data blocks; for an event type port, a DATA_AVAILABLE event is raised to the port event handler when a data block is available. The identity of the source is provided with each data block.

Certain data are spoilable, i.e. under certain conditions, if they cannot be delivered in time to meet the quality of service requirements, then they may be discarded. Spoilability involves a parameter on the *LakSendData* call or on the return to the DATA_REQUESTED event; it allows some blocks to be marked as spoilable blocks, and other blocks to be marked as spoilers. A spoiler block, if present, will cause the removal of those spoilable blocks with which it has been associated. This technique supports, for example, the implementation of buffer management schemes for video, where certain blocks are delta frame blocks and others are full frame blocks. Selected sequences of delta frame blocks can, and must, be deleted if a full frame block is available. Another possibility is to mark blocks simultaneously both as spoilers and spoilable; this has the effect that any such block will replace any previous such block.

When a channel is created, one of its quality of service parameters is related to encryption. By this means an application can, on a per channel basis, ensure that data encryption is used for all data being transmitted down that channel. The parameter identifies an encryption/decryption routine and when data is to be sent down such a channel, e.g. by *LakSendData*, a CIPHER_KEY_REQUEST event is raised to the port event handler for that channel, requesting the completion of a cipher block. This provides the encryption routine with the encryption key and also allows the option of requiring the CIPHER_KEY_REQUEST event to be raised for each subsequent data block down that channel. This facility, therefore, allows dynamic encryption keys, changed on a data block basis.

Data receipt at the destination port behaves in an analogous way with the quality of service parameter identifying an encryption/decryption routine and the CIPHER_KEY_REQUEST event being raised to obtain the key for decryption. Establishment and passing of encryption keys between applications is an application responsibility.

Compression specification is handled in a related way to encryption; the quality of service parameter in this case identifying a compression/decompression routine, invoked as appropriate.

Incorporating encryption and compression routines into a Lakes implementation is accomplished through the services provided in the resources level interface.

Logical devices

In certain specialized situations, it is appropriate to use logical devices to exchange data. A single logical device can present ports to multiple applications; the logical device can then move data between the ports. This transport mechanism is not restricted to applications within the same sharing set and, therefore, overcomes a limitation placed on channels; however, logical devices cannot span across nodes. Moreover, any necessary quality of service support must be explicitly provided for by the particular logical device.

8.3.5 Negotiation of channel quality of service

Applications communicating through channels have many requirements for both quality of service, including throughput negotiation, and control. Accordingly, Lakes provides mechanisms to allow:

- applications to request unspecified quality of service and be given whatever is dynamically available
- applications to request a particular quality of service
- applications to manage their own communications resources
- the call manager to manage communications resources across applications

Lakes meets these requirements by providing abilities:

- to allow applications to request undetermined quality of service and be given whatever is dynamically available
- to allow applications to query what is currently available and request a particular quality of service
- to allow applications to manage their own communications resources
- to allow the call manager to manage communications resources across applications

For those applications that are satisfied with unspecified quality of service characteristics, channels may be established using the *LakCreateChannel* request leaving the quality of service parameters empty. Throughput and other characteristics will not be guaranteed by Lakes and may change dynamically, depending upon availability. Such channels will take from whatever bandwidth is currently available; this includes taking from a bandwidth that may have been reserved but is not actually in use.

Certain applications have fixed quality of service requirements for the channels that they need to communicate with other applications. In these cases, each channel may be established directly, using the *LakCreateChannel* request. The resources are allocated by Lakes if they are available, without any other considerations being taken into account. Likewise, if the channel characteristics are changed or the channel is deleted, any freed up resources are returned to Lakes.

Some applications are more flexible in their quality of service requirements and need to establish whether an acceptable range is available to a particular node before creating the channel. Although this can be accomplished through the *LakQueryResource* request, specifying the target node, unfortunately, if used in this way, the call only returns what is dynamically available and there is no guarantee that this will still be the case when a subsequent *LakCreateChannel* is issued. One way of avoiding this situation is only to issue the *LakCreateChannel* to attempt to establish an appropriate channel, and to back-off to a lower quality of service specification if the attempt fails.

Other applications have flexible quality of service requirements, but need the ability to manipulate the allocation of communications resources. For example, a desktop conferencing application may wish to use all the bandwidth available, all the time, and allocate it to a combination of video and audio channels. However, when data services are required, it may wish to temporarily reallocate some video bandwidth to data, restoring it to video use later. If the channels are requested directly from Lakes, there is no guarantee that bandwidth, once freed up, will be available to that application later. This problem is overcome by the concept of named resource sets. Applications can request that communications resources to a remote node are allocated to an application-owned resource set, where such resources are identified by the appropriate quality of service parameters. Channels are then allocated from this set and any resources freed up are returned to the source set. Only the call manager can request resources directly from Lakes; other applications must request resources from those acquired by the call manager—either directly or indirectly from other applications This scheme gives the call manager the ability to manage competing requests for resources between applications. An example of the need is the situation that arises when multiple independent applications are involved in a desktop conferencing session, for example chat, chalkboard, video and audio applications. Each of these is unaware of the others, but all desire bandwidth to the target node. The call manager can police their resource requests and allocate accordingly.

In some cases, the call manager needs to negotiate with applications to determine what resources are available and to defer any reallocation until the negotiations are complete. For example, a movie application starting part way through a call may require a certain minimum bandwidth that is not available. Other applications may be already running that, between them, are using more than that bandwidth and each also has the ability to be flexible in its usage. Lakes provides a set of requests that enable the call manager to ask applications to free up bandwidth, and then to commit those changes if sufficient total bandwidth is available.

8.4 The resources level interface

The resources level interface (RLI) provides access to installation-specific external data and services, that is:

- profile data access
- address book data access (including custom link selection)
- channel data compression and encryption routines

The RLI structure can be illustrated as in Fig. 8.26.

8.4.1 Profiles

Node specific, local data needed for Lakes operation, are held in profiles which are logically local to each node. Lakes requires that two such profiles be present, these being the configura-

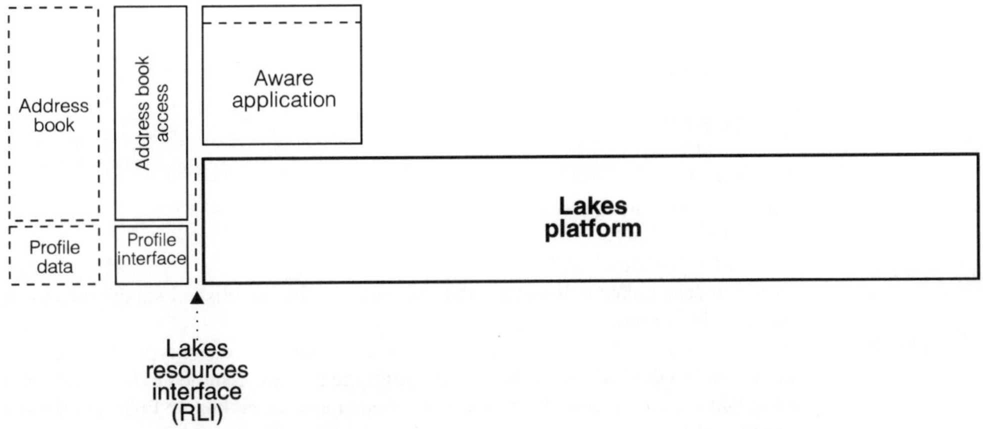

Figure 8.26 *Resource level interface*

tion profile and the quality of service profile. Other profiles, owned and managed by applications, may also be present. Lakes access to the profiles is via a profile interface module which is required to implement the following four RLI calls to:

- initialization
- read values associated with keywords
- write values associated with keywords
- termination

8.4.2 Address book

The address book data contains information on nodes in the Lakes network. The data base is logically assumed to be organized as a set records of many different types; such record types may each have their own format. All records in the data base are logically required to have a type field and a bookname field. The type field identifies the logical record type; the bookname field is significant only to the address book access module used to access records of that type, but typically it may be used to identify a subset of the records. Any other fields can also exist, subject to the considerations below.

Lakes itself accesses node records, i.e. records with a type field of value NODE. The default call manager and address book manager also access list records, i.e. records with a type of value LIST.

Node records contain information on Lakes nodes; any single node can be described by multiple node records. The following field names within node records are used by Lakes and, therefore, must be present:

type	*NODE*
bookname	a name field whose value is significant only to the address book access module used to store and access the record
nodename	name of the destination node (this field must be present)
linktype	how to connect to the given node name. A given node must have at least one record containing a linktype field. This is mapped by Lakes to an LSM, through a section with that name in the configuration profile; this LSM is responsible for providing that particular type of connection. Examples of field values are:

ISDN
ASYNC
TOKEN_RING
TCP/IP
LAN0
MEM

The linktype field value can also take the form:

NODENAME
NICKNAME

in which case Lakes will assume that the link is to be established via the intermediate node identified.

linkvalue	this field provides the connection string for the associated linktype. The contents are passed to the LSM identified by the linktype and are assumed to be sufficient to establish the connection. In the case of a node name or nickname linktype, the link value contains the relevant node name or nickname.
QoS	quality of service parameters required for the connection. This field is optional but, if present, it overrides the defaults supplied in the quality of service profile for that linktype.
order	the order in which this record should be considered for use by Lakes when more than one suitable link exists. This field is optional but, if present, overrides the defaults supplied in the LSM-owned section of the configuration profile for that linktype.
timeout	the timeout value; after the timeout has expired, Lakes will assume no response over that link. This field is optional but, if present, overrides the defaults used by the LSM.
switched	indicates whether the link is a switched link or not and, if switched, the time that the link should be held beyond the last communication. This field is optional but, if present, overrides the defaults supplied in the LSM-owned section of the configuration profile for that linktype.

The following field names within node records, while not used by Lakes, can be used by the default address book manager:

nickname	short name used to identify the entry (this field is optional)
lastname	the last name (surname) of the person located at the node
forenames	the forenames of the person located at the node
phone	the (audio) phone number of the person located at the node
user	a user-defined string associated with the entry

Only the first node record for a given node can contain these additional fields. Subsequent records for that node merely define additional links and the associated QoS and order information.

The following field names within list records are used by the default call manager and address book manger:

type	*LIST*
bookname	a name field whose value is significant only to the address book access module used to store and access the record
listname	the short name of the list
list	a list of nicknames or node names, separated by commas and enclosed in parentheses

An example of the address book data scheme is given in Table 8.1.

Table 8.1 Address book data base example

type	*nodename*	*nickname*	*linktype*	*linkvalue*	*order*	*QoS*
NODE	FFlintstone	Fred	ISDN	0962841122	1	64kb/s VIDEO
NODE	FFlintstone		NODENAME	BaRubble	9	32kb/s
NODE	WFlintstone	Wilma	NICKNAME	Fred		
NODE	BaRubble	Barney	ASYNC	0962842200		64kb/s
NODE	BeRubble	Betty	NICKNAME	Barney		32kb/s

type	*listname*	*list*
LIST	Flintstones	(Fred, Wilma, Barney, Betty)

Given these entries, a request to connect to Betty, node BeRubble, would result in Lakes retrieving the record for BeRubble, examining the link field and using it to retrieve the record with the nickname Barney, that for node BaRubble. This means that node BaRubble can be used as an intermediate step in connecting to node BeRubble. It is assumed that when such a request reaches Barney's node, his address book contains more information about how to connect to Betty.

Address book access is via the installation-supplied address book access module. All such modules are required to support the logical address book structure and to provide seven RLI routines to access and update the data.

- Module initialization
- Open address books
- Close address books
- Find records
- Insert records
- Update records
- Delete records

Address book access modules can support additional RLI calls for use by applications.

Calls to the address book access module routines can be issued by Lakes applications but, if used, it is the application's responsibility to ensure that the values returned are consistent with those obtained by Lakes itself accessing the address book data. The default call manager and address book manager behave in this way. The Lakes API provides a call *LakAddressBookFind* which is functionally equivalent to *LakfindRecord* and is guaranteed to return values consistent with those obtained by Lakes.

Address book access modules can support additional RLI calls for use by applications.

8.4.3 Compression and encryption

Channel data compression and encryption is invoked by an application through the channel quality of service definition, which specifies a keyword identifying an appropriate routine. Such routines must provide the following functions:

- Module initialization
- Compression or encryption
- Expansion or decryption
- Termination

8.5 Overview of the device support interface

8.5.1 Link support

An application can specify quality of service characteristics when creating a channel, or when reserving resources for later allocation to channels. Channels are mapped by Lakes on to physical links. Two kinds of physical links are relevant: (a) those that allow data packets to be transmitted independently of each other, for example, a token ring local area network; and (b) those that allow bit streams to be transmitted, for example the use of H.320 protocol over an ISDN link.

Links are characterized by link type, order, and by their quality of service. Link type identifies the link support module (LSM) that is to be invoked to communicate over that link. Order determines the order in which Lakes will attempt to use links for data transmission, assuming that there is a choice of links available with suitable data transmission characteristics. Quality of service information characterizes the communications capabilities of the link. For each link type, the link selection order, and defaults for the quality of service characteristics, are stored in the configuration profile. Link descriptions, which associate remote nodes with link types and optionally include quality of service characteristics, are stored in an address book external to Lakes. The data base is accessed by the address book access module.

The quality of service parameters relevant to digital links are:

signal tpe (value = digital)

throughput	latency
jitter	frame size
frame error rate	max. packet size

Throughput describes capacity in bits/s.; latency describes the average transit delay, in milliseconds, of a data frame; jitter characterizes the variation in transit times for individual frames. Frame size specifies the unit of transmission recovery in bits. For (a) a packet based network, this represents the unit size sent over the network; for (b) a bit stream network, such as H.320, it represents the transmission frame size. Frame error rate denotes the average proportion of such frames that are received with errors. Max. packet size reflects the maximum number of bytes that can be accepted at a time for transmission over the link.

Lakes logical channels are also normally associated with quality of service information. This can be set explicitly when the channel is created or can be set implicitly by the use of defaults related to data types and data sub-types. This default information is held in the quality of service profile. The key parameters used to characterize the quality of service required by applications over logical channels are:

signal type (value = digital)

throughput	latency
jitter	max. block size
block error rate	encryption
compression	priority

Most of these parameters mirror their link counterparts with the following exceptions: encryption and compression are used to invoke software routines for the data being transmitted over that channel and are not used for link selection purposes; channel priority specifies the order in which Lakes will attempt to service data transmissions over all the channels at that node, assuming that there is resource contention between the channels. Max. block size gives the maximum size of a block of data that Lakes will use when it supplies data to an application through an event sending port; it also controls the maximum size supplied to encryption/compression routines. Block error rate specifies an acceptable random proportion of such blocks that need not be delivered due to loss or error in transmission—note that this is an expected maximum error rate that will be tolerated by the application, but conformance to this limit is not guaranteed by Lakes. Setting this limit to zero guarantees that Lakes will attempt to deliver all blocks, notifying the application in case of failure. The channel latency parameter reflects transmission times only and, therefore, excludes time spent in user-specified data compression and encryption routines.

Lakes uses a subset of the quality of service parameters to select a link that is suitable for carrying a particular channel; the values in brackets indicate various permitted values:

- *Channel QoS parameters used:*
  - throughput (bits/s.; unspecified)
  - latency (bits/s.; unspecified)
  - jitter (bits/s.; unspecified)
  - block error rate (0; ratio of blocks)
- *Link QoS parameters used:*
  - available throughput (bits/s.; unspecified)
  - latency (bits/s.; unspecified)
  - jitter (bits/s.; unspecified)
  - frame size (number of bits)
  - frame error rate (0; ratio of frames)
  - max. packet size (number of bits)

The selection process is illustrated in Fig. 8.27.

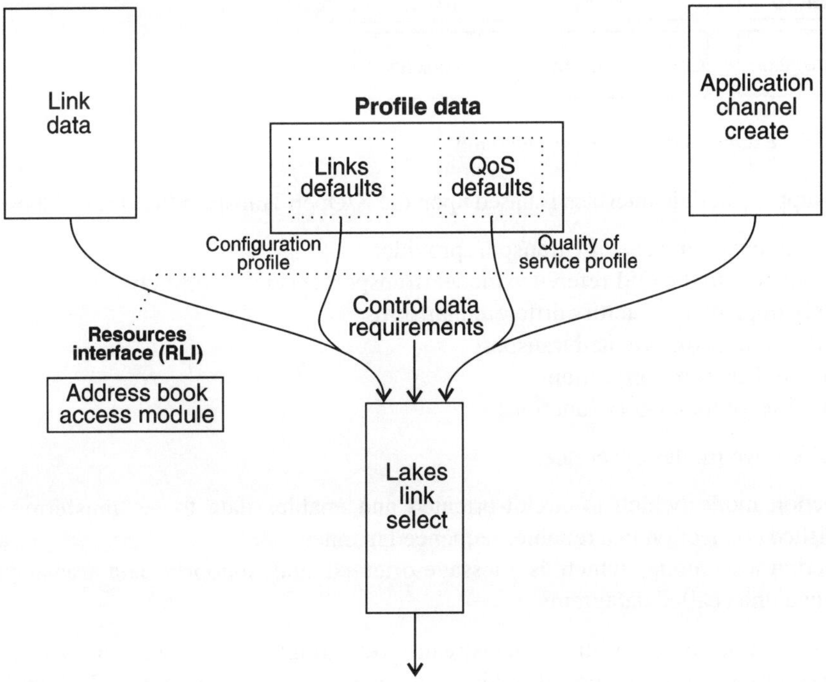

Figure 8.27 Link selection process

Defaults in the profile data are used, if necessary, to expand both the link data from the address book and the channel data supplied by the application. Lakes then selects an appropriate link to use based upon matching the fully-resolved channel requirements with the fully-resolved available links information, taking account of: (a) the need to exchange Lakes control information; and (b) the order values associated with the links. In order that the complex process of route selection can also be performed outside Lakes if desired, the RLI call *LakFindRecord*, used to retrieve link information, also supplies all the required channel quality of service characteristics. Through this means, the address book access module can itself determine the appropriate route and return that route to Lakes. This could be useful, for example, if transmissions costs vary with the time of day and such costs should be taken into account in link selection.

The IBM-supplied link support modules can interface through a broad range of industry standard communication protocols. An example of the relationship between link support modules and communications device drivers is shown in Fig. 8.28.

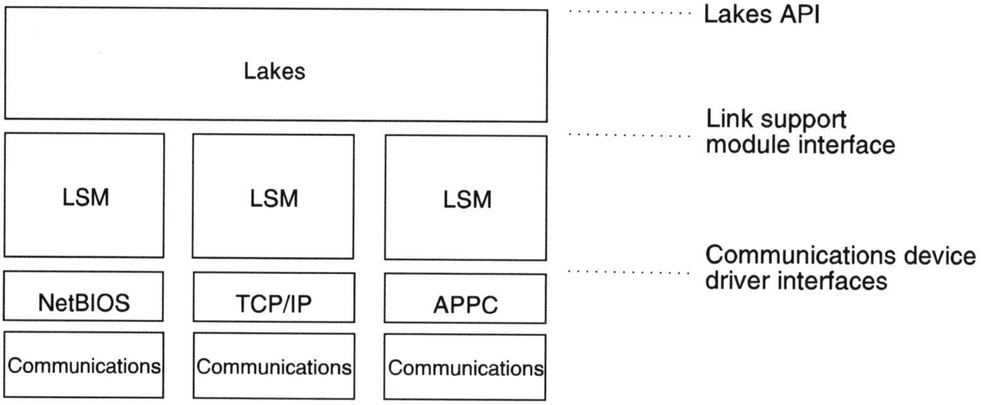

Figure 8.28 Examples of link support modules

The link support module interface is based upon the X/Open Transport Interface XTI because it:

- is independent of any specific transport provider
- is compliant with the OSI reference model (transport service definition)
- is widely implemented across different platforms
- supports connection-oriented transport
- supports full-duplex connections
- is a small set of mandatory functions

XTI provides two modes of service:

- connection mode, which is circuit-oriented and enables data to be transferred over an established connection in a reliable, sequenced manner
- connection-less mode, which is message-oriented and supports data transfer in self-contained units called datagrams.

Lakes requires relatively long-lived, datastream-oriented interactions, e.g. once a call is established from one node to another, it is likely to persist. Accordingly, the LSM interface only supports the connection mode of operation.

XTI supports synchronous and asynchronous modes of operation:

- Synchronous mode—primitives wait for specific events before returning control to the user.
- Asynchronous mode—primitives return immediately to the user.

The LSM interface supports asynchronous mode only and uses a call-back to report events to Lakes.

The functions to be provided by an LSM are as follows:

- support for a given network protocol (one LSM may interface to several adapters)
- send/receive point-to-point connection to another node
- flow control for a specific connection
- determining optimum frame size for a physical connection
- incoming call notification

Some LSMs are able to set up multiple point-to-point connections over a single adapter (e.g. NetBIOS), whereas others (e.g. ASYNC) are only able to set up a single point-to-point connection over a single adapter. The LSM masks completely any and all network specific flows, protocols, events or errors from Lakes, to realize a network independent interface.

Typical network protocols supported by LSMs are:

- TCP/IP
- NetBIOS
- ASYNC
- ISDN
- APPC

As part of the optimization of network usage, the LSMs within the same node need to be able to communicate with each other. When an application connects or welds channels together, or when a node is providing a passive link, the data flow is then passed efficiently through the node rather than being delivered to an application.

8.5.2 Video and audio support

Video and audio support is mainly provided through the logical device mechanism. The video logical device is structured in a way that allows a range of video support to be added without replacing the entire logical device. This is illustrated in Fig. 8.29.

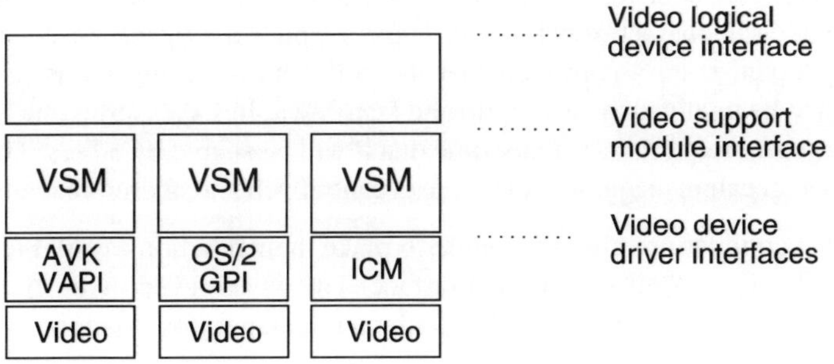

Figure 8.29 VSMs and the video logical device

For example, the Installable Compression Manager (ICM) for MCI, interfacing to the default video support module (VSM), gives access to a broad range of the video hardware and software support. Additional VSMs may be added to extend the range of video formats, and hardware and software equipment that can be accessed.

In a similar manner, audio is supported through an audio logical device, and audio support modules (ASMs) provide subsystem independence.

8.6 Introduction to the Lakes utilities

The structure of the Lakes platform, including applications, is illustrated in Fig. 8.30.

All of the modules surrounding the Lakes platform are independently replaceable or extendable, this includes: device and network support, interfaces to the network data base, interfaces to repositories of customization information, and all applications. Two of these applications are different from the rest in the sense that they are not themselves collaborative, but are there to assist users with conference control.

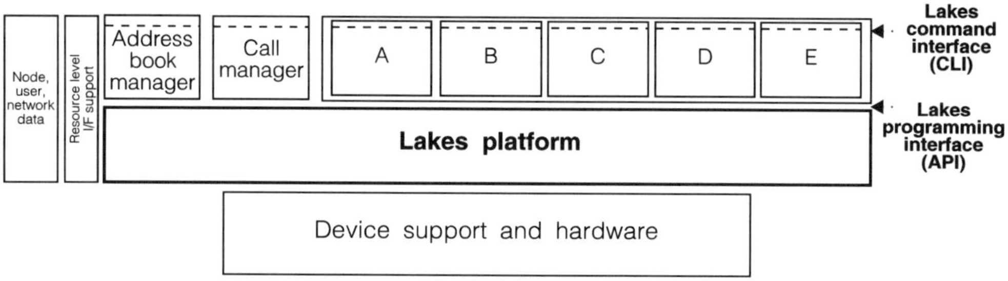

Figure 8.30 Lakes utilities overview

The address book manager is a means of accessing and updating address book data, i.e. the names and details of parties to be called, with associated connectivity information. The default address book manager provides user functions to access, search and update entries. Since it interfaces to the address book data base via the RLI, it can operate with any installation-determined data bases.

The call manager establishes calls and manages applications. The terminology is confusing because the default call manager application is more than a Lakes call manager. The general functions of a Lakes call manager have already been described; the default call manager application implements a particular set of call policies and supplies a user interface. One of the (arbitrary) policies adopted is an assumption that the collaborative applications in a call will not themselves wish to be involved in call set-up and tear-down. In Lakes terms, such an application will not issue the share request but will assume that it will be shared by others. This has usability advantages in that all call management dialogue is centralized and, therefore, consistent.

It is desirable that applications should be able to make their functions available to other applications, independently of their own user interface. This is achieved by each implementing a command interface (CLI). The CLI to the default call manager, for example, is a key interface in the Lakes architecture.

The command interface can be realized by structuring an application in two portions, one an engine portion providing the function, the other a user interface portion. This approach has been adopted in the default call manager as is shown in Fig. 8.31.

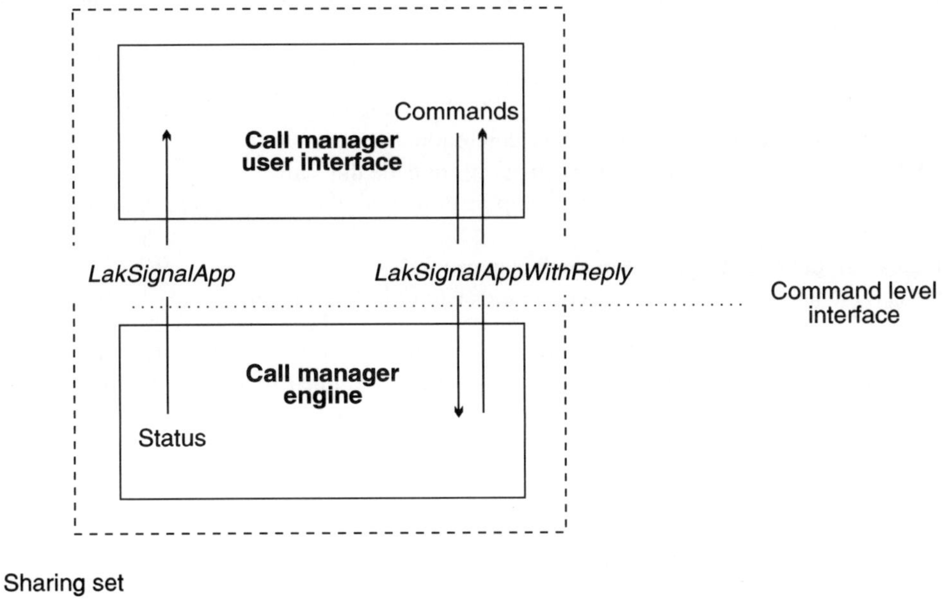

Figure 8.31 Call manager command level interface

It is desirable, but not necessary, that both constituent applications belong to a common application sharing set. The user interface controls the engine through commands and responses exchanged via the *LakSignalAppWithReply* call, using application handles. The call manager can asynchronously send status to the user interface via *LakSignalApp*. Other applications can control command the engine in an identical way.

8.6.1 The default call manager

The IBM call manager application allows the user to select other users that he or she wishes to work with, and allows the control of collaborative applications. It does this through presenting a call model comprising users, calls and applications. The current call manager only offers a single call model, or one set of policies, although this can be customized to a limited extent. As described earlier in this book, one call model cannot satisfy the varying demands for different forms of collaborative working and other call models need to be added. The requirement for inter-operability with ITU-T T.120 compliant equipment also gives rise to the need for a specific call model to reflect the nuances of that particular environment. Such extensions can be made by modifying the existing IBM call manager or by replacing it with a more sophisticated implementation. Although the Lakes architecture permits only one call manager to be active at any one time, this does not preclude the use of a sophisticated call manager which provides multiple concurrent styles of interaction. Local initiation of a particular style may be selected by the user from an appropriate menu item or application; local responses to a particular style of incoming call can be triggered from information that can be associated with the Lakes SHARE_REQUEST event.

A call, as defined by the IBM call manager, refers to a group of users collaborating by using shared applications. Such calls are superficially similar to telephone calls, for example, in that parties can be selected, connected to, added or dropped. The parallel is not close because of the richness of the interactions possible with a computer versus a telephone. The specific policies enforced are:

- a call must comprise at least two parties
- any party to a call can invite others to join, without reference to any existing parties
- an external user can request a party in a call to join that call
- applications in a call cannot share with parties outside that call
- when a call is terminated, any shared applications in that call are unshared but continue to execute
- Lakes cannot be shutdown when a call is in progress
- the call manager will only accept commands from local applications

Using the IBM call manager, more than one call can exist at any time, users can be in more than one simultaneous call, and copies of an application can be executed in multiple calls. For example, the users A, B and C can be in a call, *x*, to review a document; all may be using audio communication with each other, A and B may also have a video link, and A and C may have, in addition, a shared chalkboard. Meanwhile, A, B and D may be in a second call, *y*, to review a different document—with A and D using another chalkboard, and B and D using audio links.

The IBM call manager lets the user initiate the following actions:

- start a new call
- extend a call by adding a new person to it
- leave a call
- cancel an outgoing request to join a call if the callee is not responding
- launch a Lakes application
- add an existing unshared application to a call
- remove an existing application from a call
- shutdown the Lakes system at that node

In addition the call manager handles certain events, usually from other nodes:

- a request to join a call
- a request to share a new application into an existing call
- a request to use this node in order to make a connection between two other nodes
- a request from an application at the local node to be shared with other nodes

The user can also set various options, for example, to indicate if incoming calls are to be automatically accepted or rejected, and how requests for passive working are to be handled. Activity during the call is made available in a log. Additionally, the call manager provides a simple messaging facility between members of a call; the messages are logged in the activity log and, optionally, can also be logged on an individual call basis.

The default call manager does not provide access to address book data; it does provide a user interface that allows the default address book manager to be invoked and communicates with it through its own command level interface.

Implementation of the call model is achieved through the use of application sharing sets. Within a single call there are one or more sharing sets, each with the same name, known as the callid. Within each sharing set is one application from each node in the call, assuming all nodes have all the necessary applications available.

Figure 8.32 illustrates the scheme used.

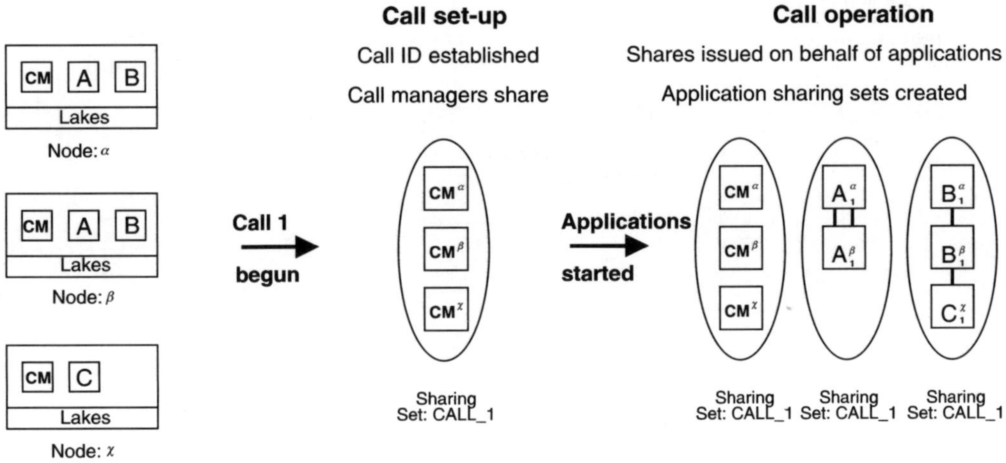

Figure 8.32 Call model implementation in the default call manager

A user at node α wishes to establish a call with nodes β and χ. The call manager at α creates a callid, CALL_1, and then shares with the call managers at β and χ. This application sharing set, CALL_1, containing the call managers, represents the call. When an application A, at α, is started by the user, the call manager at α attempts to share it with an equivalent application at the other nodes, resulting in the establishment of a second sharing set called CALL_1. In the example in Fig. 8.32, no matching application exists at node χ. Similarly, when application B is started at a node β, the call manager there attempts to share it with equivalent applications at the other nodes; in this case resulting in application B at α and application C at χ joining a third sharing set CALL_1. When the user at α wishes to terminate the call, the call manager there issues an unshare on behalf of the shared applications A and B, and then finally unshares itself.

Applications that behave in this sympathetic way with the default call manager must have been written with that objective; use of the Lakes API, *per se*, does not guarantee this result.

The call manager application as seen by the user is actually two applications: the call manager engine and the call manager user interface, each with a command level interface. This is illustrated in Fig. 8.33.

Figure 8.33 shows not only the call manager user interface and associated engine; it also shows how other Lakes applications can drive these two components and how additional user interfaces can also be concurrently active if required.

Instances of applications simultaneously driving the call manager engine are known as master applications and must be members of a common command set, so called because it is a common application sharing set whose name must begin with the word 'command'. The default address book manager is an example of a master application. Within a command set, one such application instance is known as the call manager user interface application, generally because it assumes responsibility for communicating with the user. Multiple user interface

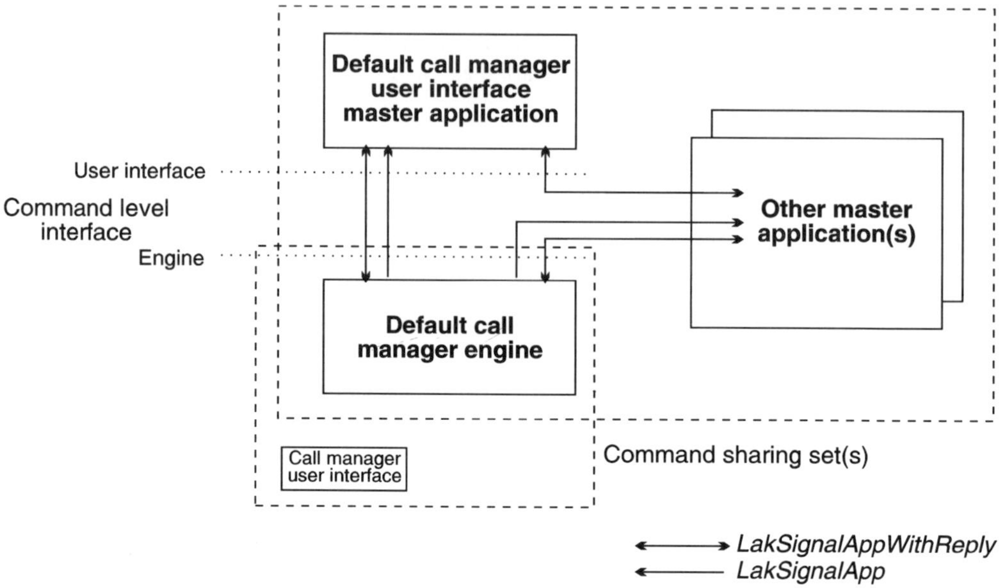

Figure 8.33 Call manager application structure

instances can simultaneously exist, but each must be in a distinct command sharing set with the call manager engine. Other aware applications, affected by the call management operations but not involved in call control, are known as slave applications.

Each aware application instance within a command set is associated with a unique identifier, the applid, allocated by the call manager. Similarly each call, within a command set, is uniquely identified by a callid. For those applications within calls, the call manager maintains the association between applids and callids.

In a command set, the user interface application is privileged in that it receives more status- and call-related information than any other master application. The identity of the user interface application can be set with a CLI call; by default, the engine assumes that the first other application in the command set is the user interface application.

Members of a command set can establish a new call specifying the nickname of the called party or parties. The nickname is subsequently resolved by the engine, to one or more node names, through calls using the RLI. An option prohibits any changes being made to the destination node address, by any intermediate nodes that may be involved in establishing the call. Additional parties can also be added to an existing call.

Application instances can be created at the local node through CLI specifying the application name and the appropriate information in the configuration profile is used to specify the launch parameters. The issuing application receives an applid for the new application instance which does not become a member of a call.

Slave applications joined into a call specifying the applid and callid. An entry for that application in the configuration profile is inspected to determine if the incoming share request can be satisfied without asking the user. Similarly, information there also determines whether an already-existing instance of the application can be used or whether a new instance must be created. Conversely, application instances can be removed from a call; these instances are unshared but continue to exist.

A node's participation in a call can be terminated and all of the local applications are unshared. An appropriate signal is sent to the remaining members.

Other facilities exist in the call manager engine CLI to support, among other things:

- message text to be returned to the caller when an incoming call is automatically answered or rejected
- message text to be returned to the caller when an incoming share is automatically answered
- signalling to parties in the call
- options to determine how incoming calls are answered
- time-outs for responses
- passive working
- Lakes shutdown

The call manager user interface also accepts commands from master applications. These can be used to control the logging options, window positioning, sound effects, user options and names of recently-called parties. Furthermore, the association between the call manager user interface and the application to handle address book access can be changed through the call manager user interface CLI.

8.6.2 The default address book manager

The IBM-supplied default address book manager is designed for a small organization which has no existing address book or phone book application. It can be used to access and update existing data bases through an appropriate installation-supplied address book access module. Alternatively, the default access module will use flat ASCII files. The function provided is limited to browsing and editing address book entries, and adding and deleting entries. Simple searching is provided, with limited support for user-defined information.

Access and updates to the address book data base use the six mandatory calls provided in the RLI, plus the additional calls *LakRefreshAddressBook* and *LakSaveAddressBook*.

The default address book manager CLI allows other applications to update the address book data base and access its contents. Find, delete, insert, update and query functions are available. Nicknames, node details and link data can be accessed. Named lists of node names and nicknames are also supported.

8.7 System considerations

8.7.1 Monitoring, audit and control

Lakes allows applications to monitor requests and events at a Lakes node. A *LakBeginMonitor* request starts monitoring; specific classes can be set and, within these sets, individual requests and events selected. Control of one application by another is accomplished through audit managers and is provided to allow access policies to be implemented or for the provision of costing and billing. At any node, a Lakes application may request to be an audit manager through issuing the appropriate API call. Two kinds of audit managers are supported: local and remote. Both receive information on application activity and may be required to approve certain actions; additionally, local audit managers give permission for their node to be remotely audited.

The process of becoming an audit manager requires the specification of:

- the target to be audited, i.e. the node and optionally, an application at that node. If no application is specified, all applications are assumed.
- the scope of the audit:
  - applications
  - channels
  - quality of service
  - tokens

Depending upon the scope, almost all activity by an audited application raises either an information event or an authorization event, first at the local audit manager(s), then at the remote audit manager(s). Information events do not require the audit managers' approval, e.g. removing a channel; authorization events do require all the audit managers to approve.

The facility may be used to implement a security application that has control of, for example:

- what applications may be run
- when applications may be run
- how many applications may be run
- how many channels can be created
- what type of channels can be created
- what quality of service an application can use

Logging and audit trail information can be collected to identify 'who' did 'what' and 'when'. The statistics data for billing and costing purposes include:

- bytes sent down a channel
- bytes received from a channel
- quality of service requested
- application start and finish times

8.7.2 Intelligent networks

Lakes permits intelligent value-added networks to be exploited. Thus, the following functions can be supported in the network and implemented at locations which can, at least in principle, be dynamically changed as circumstances require. For example, in order to respond to network congestion or node workload and availability:

cloning of data	data routing
merging of data	data serialization
data conversions	data synchronization
data compression/decompression	

This is illustrated in Fig. 8.34.

One way of considering this is that the use of the Lakes architecture by an application removes the need for it to handle many of the complexities of application association and real-time multimedia communications. Lakes takes those off-loaded functions and, depending upon the implementation, pushes them out from the workstation into the network. It is only in the network itself that sufficient information exists to optimize the execution of the application communication and data requirements.

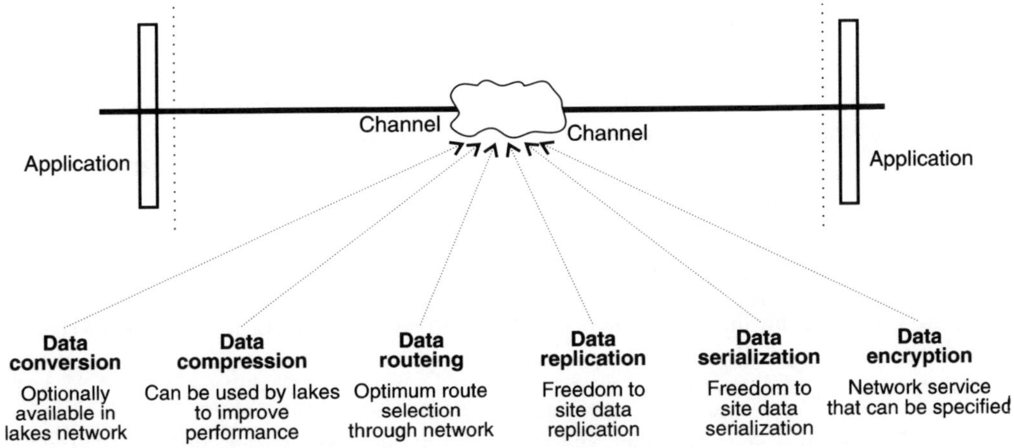

Figure 8.34 Intelligent networks

8.8 Comparison of Lakes and H.320/T.120

Support of both the T.120 and H.320 series of recommendations within the Lakes architecture is essential for interoperability. H.320 support is relatively straightforward because of its lower level and its ability to transfer data coded to private protocols. T.120 support is more complex because, not only are data covered by this standard, but the control aspects of desktop conferencing are also defined.

8.8.1 H.320 and Lakes

There are three important situations to be considered:

- An H.320 terminal, such as a video telephone, sending audio and video, where Lakes applications are unaware of the difference between that terminal and another attached Lakes node.
- An H.320, such as a video phone, sending audio and video, where Lakes applications are controlling the remote terminal directly.
- An attached Lakes node is using H.320 for communication.

The first situation, where the attached terminal is to be regarded by applications as just another Lakes node, is handled by the virtual node/virtual application concept described earlier. A call from such a terminal causes sharing with the identified local audio and video applications, just as if a call had been received from a node running those applications remotely.

The second situation requires the local Lakes application to control the remote terminal from a suitable logical device. This allows much greater control but requires specific programming to handle the situation and there is no concept of that terminal being in the call, from a call manager perspective. This approach is likely to be adopted only in special situations.

The third scenario is transparent to Lakes applications. The H.221 data partitions are used by Lakes both to send control data and to realize Lakes channels. The video and audio partitions are used by Lakes for channels with an appropriate Lakes data class. There are many H.320 compliant adapters that are incapable of supplying audio and video streams to the workstation; instead they have on-board devices that either generate or accept these streams. A Lakes application treats audio and video through logical devices and connects them to channels with suitable characteristics. Lakes detects the logical connection of the devices to the audio and video channels, and passes this information down to the LSM and ASM. In this way there is no requirement to route the data into the workstation and the application is not written in an adapter-dependent manner. Attempts to connect audio and video channels from such adapters to devices not realized on those same adapters would be rejected.

8.8.2 T.120 and Lakes

There are two important situations to be considered with respect to the ITU-T T-series of recommendations:

- A Lakes node is using the MCS component of T.120 for communication to another Lakes node.
- A T.120 terminal, such as a desktop conferencing system, is sending T.120 protocols to a Lakes node.

In the first case, Lakes can exploit the multi-point communication services of MCS in order to achieve connectivity to multiple remote nodes. There is little value in using MCS in this way for a point-to-point connection above that which would be achieved from using the LSD or HSD channels of H.320. However, in the multi-point case, where a Lakes node has access to an MCS service (e.g. through an ISDN connection to a T.120 complaint MCU within the public switched network) this could provide useful connectivity over the wide area. As far as MCS is concerned, the entire Lakes system, including applications, appears as a T-series non-standard application—MCS wrappers being used to move Lakes protocols.

The second case is the more important because it expresses the requirements for seamless inter-operability between Lakes nodes and those generating the alternative MLP streams. The needs cover the entire stack, thus providing application-to-application and including both point-to-point and multi-point configurations, with an arbitrary mix of Lakes and other T.120 complaint nodes. Necessarily, this requires that Lakes nodes must be able to accept and generate MLP streams to/from non-Lakes nodes.

Mapping between T.120 and the Lakes architecture is complex because of the different concepts employed and the multiplicity of components. A first level approximation between the two systems can be made by identifying the subsystems that offer comparable, but not identical, functions (see Table 8.2).

Table 8.2 Approximate equivalents between Lakes and MCS elements

Lakes elements	*MCS elements*
Lakes network	Collection of MCS providers
Lakes node	MCS provider
Call manager supplying high level call control services	Generic conference control
Collection of application sharing sets in a call	MCS domain
Application instances	Application instances
Application instance (may be the call manager)	MCS node controller
Channels	Channels
Tokens	Tokens

In understanding the relationship between the architectures it is easiest to begin at the MCS level. Since there are many entities and concepts which are similar but not identical, where necessary to avoid confusion, Lakes variants will be pre-fixed with L- and MCS variants with M-, e.g. L-tokens and M-tokens.

MCS domains and Lakes application sharing sets

MCS establishes a single multi-point domain over point-to-point MCS logical connections; this multi-point domain is a hierarchical structure to which application instances then attach. The result of this activity is a collection of application clients that can communicate with one another over a hierarchical set of physical connections, although these physical connections can be shared. This hierarchy of connections, however, does not imply a hierarchical relationship between the applications within the domain. The hierarchy is significant in determining where functions are implemented in MCS. For example, certain MCS function such as serialization and token management must be performed at the top provider and this may have performance consequences. The top provider, and any intermediate providers, are necessary to sustain the call. Should one or more of these go away, the call will either disappear or fragment in what will appear to users as unpredictable ways. The lack of direct addressability between providers, except up and down the hierarchy, means that information must be routed that way in order to be sent from one participant to another. In an ISDN network this is likely to coincide with the natural order and is, therefore, inconsequential; in a local area network environment, where direct connectivity is generally available between all participants, it represents considerable inefficiency.

In Lakes, there is no requirement for a hierarchical set of logical connections supporting the underlying communication between applications and there are no limits on the network topologies that can be exploited. The nearest equivalent to the MCS domain with M-application instances attached, is the Lakes application sharing sets that exist in what a user perceives as a call. In the case of MCS, application instances can only be in one such domain at a time, and only one such domain can exist over a set of connections; for Lakes, application instances can be in one or more sharing sets by the physical nature of the network.

The optional use of multiple sharing sets within a call is an important provision of Lakes because it allows the separation of the collaborating applications into groups, the members of which have directly addressability and intimate knowledge of each other. Moreover, it protects the members of one sharing set from the activities of applications in other sharing sets. Application instances in a sharing set have a relationship to each other which is generally taken advantage of in the application programming, and the introduction of an arbitrary—albeit non-participating—application into a Lakes sharing set would potentially be very disruptive.

Another significant difference between the two models is that Lakes has a sophisticated sharing process through which applications join sharing sets - involving the applications themselves and their respective call managers, thus providing considerable control over which applications instances join the sharing set. Additional flexibility arises from the support for third party shares. In MCS, any application instance can independently attach to a domain without any control mechanisms being available; there is very limited capability at the GCC level where support is provided for one application to invoke another.

M-channels and L-channels

MCS has a concept of channels for data communication. These channels are not intended for any audio or video streams, which are assumed to be catered for separately, e.g. over ISDN at the H.320 level. Although it is to be expected that in general the video and audio streams flow through the physical connections which sustain the MCS domain, they are otherwise independent of MCS. The functionality available for non-data (i.e. audio/video) traffic is, therefore, very different to that provided for data traffic and not integrated. An example of the problems that can arise is the inability to synchronize data streams with non-data streams.

M-channels are domain-wide addresses which are joined by applications in order to receive data from that channel. An application client does not need to be joined to a channel in order to send data to it. M-channels are classified as static or dynamic and identified by a numeric identifier (channel id).

Lakes channels are likewise restricted to the application sharing set, but exist between application instances; each channel joins one sending port to a receiving port. The creation mechanism is under the control of the sender of the data and needs the concurrence of the receiver. These can be used in a similar manner to MCS user id and private id channels to allow point-to-point communication or communication between a subset of the applications. Merged and serialized channel sets between all the application instances in a sharing set more closely match the static M-channels. No special provision in Lakes is needed to accomplish the MCS assigned channel id capabilities of guaranteeing an empty channel. The implicit creation of L-channels in Lakes allows them to be automatically created for an identified subset of applications in the sharing set and for particular data traffic; MCS takes a different approach by effectively having a set of static channels always available, accessible to all applications for any kind of data. There is no mechanism available in MCS for one application to control the use made of this static set by another application.

The Lakes' abilities to support synchronization between multiple channels do not exist in MCS; nor does the concept of data serialization across a channel set—this being implemented at the data packet level within a single M-channel. MCS does not support application management of communication resources, nor does it provide for any significant application involvement in quality of service negotiation.

Sending and receiving data

Two data services are provided in MCS for the actual transfer of data. MCS-send-data sends data packets on the specified channel to all clients (except the sender) joined to that channel. MCS-uniformly-sequenced-send-data parallels the send data request, but guarantees identical interleaving of data packets. The packets are serialized by being sent to the top MCS provider and from there despatched, in the same sequence, to all receiving clients —in this case, also including the sender. Data transmission in MCS is associated with a priority specification, these being used to resolve the contention issues that may arise during transmission. Associated with each priority are throughput (bandwidth) and transit delay (latency) specifications.

Lakes has two principal mechanisms for sending data, based on signals or channels. The destination of signals is controlled by the originator and is not limited to the application sharing set; one form of signal returns a reply to the originator. Signals are susceptible to all of the control and redirection possibilities also provided for application sharing and offer a simple, yet powerful, mechanism for data transmission. There is no equivalent capability in MCS. Port signalling is provided in Lakes; MCS does not support this concept.

Lakes channel data transmission sends data down the L-channel, in accordance with the quality of service properties of that channel. Data serialization in Lakes is a property of collections of channels; this allows Lakes to optimize the implementation of the function while maintaining the separation of different kinds of data. Packet-based serialization can be implemented by changing the L-channel characteristics on a packet basis, if this is appropriate. The recipients of the data across an L-channel set are determined by the remote ports attached to the sending port, established at channel creation time. There is no provision in MCS for spoiler or spoilable packets. Likewise, data compression, data encryption or data conversion capabilities are not included in the architecture and must be done by consenting applications.

MCS does not support data acknowledgements during transmission and, therefore, no information is available to the sending applications on communications progress. MCS has no equivalent of Lakes sending event ports or receiving command ports.

Tokens

MCS supports multiple tokens within a domain with the significance of the token defined by the application. Tokens may be held by one application instance at a time.

Lakes supports both global and application tokens; only global tokens are approximately paralleled in MCS. Lakes supports the concepts of both token owners and token holders; there is no MCS notion of token ownership. MCS inhibited tokens equate to Lakes shared holding of tokens. The Lakes facilities are a superset of the MCS support.

Other facilities

There is no concept of devices in MCS and, therefore, M-channel data can only be delivered to the client application. No connection or welding of ports is provided for and, as a consequence therefore, one application cannot establish connectivity on behalf of another.

MCS has no monitoring capabilities to offer applications; one application cannot be informed about the activities of another. Similarly, the absence of an audit provision means that neither a local nor a remote application can control the MCS usage of another application.

Inter-operability between MCS and Lakes

Inter-operability between applications written to the two models requires a mapping of the underlying concepts. Since Lakes offer a superset of the MCS capabilities, the solution adopted is to identify that subset of Lakes that equates to MCS and define a translation of the basic primitives involved.

There are a number of interconnection options to consider for a single T.120 style call, e.g.:

- a point-to-point call involving an MCS provider and a Lakes node
- a multi-party call involving a single MCS provider attached to a Lakes network
- a multi-party call involving a single Lakes node attached to an MCS hierarchy
- a multi-party call involving multiple nodes in a Lakes network attached to an MCS hierarchy

Assuming the application level protocols present are compatible, inter-operability requires that no changes are needed, either to any MCS applications written to the MCS T.122 API, or to any T.120 compliant MCS providers. These objectives can be met by interconnecting MCS and Lakes networks in any or all of the following ways.

- A single Lakes node directly connected to an MCS provider, and acting only for its local applications, can appear to that MCS domain as an MCS provider. It can appear as either a top provider or as a bottom provider in the MCS hierarchy. There is no limit on the number of Lakes nodes that can be so attached.

- A single Lakes node directly connected to an MCS provider, and acting only for its local applications, can appear as an MCS MCU. In this capacity it can also appear at the top or other intermediate positions in the MCS hierarchy. Again, there is no limit on the number of Lakes nodes that can be so attached. These configurations, however, are likely to be of less interest than the non-MCU case above.
- A Lakes network can be connected to an MCS network through a Lakes node acting as a bridge. In this case the Lakes network appears to MCS as a hierarchy of MCS providers; this hierarchy can form the topmost portion of the total MCS hierarchy or can appear as a complete branch elsewhere. The former is more desirable because it simplifies the implementation of functions such as data serialization, leading to improved performance. Other involved Lakes nodes can only use the services of any one Lakes bridging node; many bridging nodes can exist in a call. This restriction is introduced to avoid the creation of circular paths in the MCS hierarchy, precluded by the T.120 standard.

In all cases from an L-application perspective, an MCS network connected to a Lakes network is transparent, appearing as a uniform collection of Lakes addressable nodes. Application instances attached to an MCS domain appear as members of one or more Lakes application sharing sets, the nature of this mapping being determined by the activity at the Lakes connecting node. Likewise, from an M-application perspective, the integrity of the MCS model is preserved. A complex example of a mixed Lakes and MCS network is shown in Fig. 8.35.

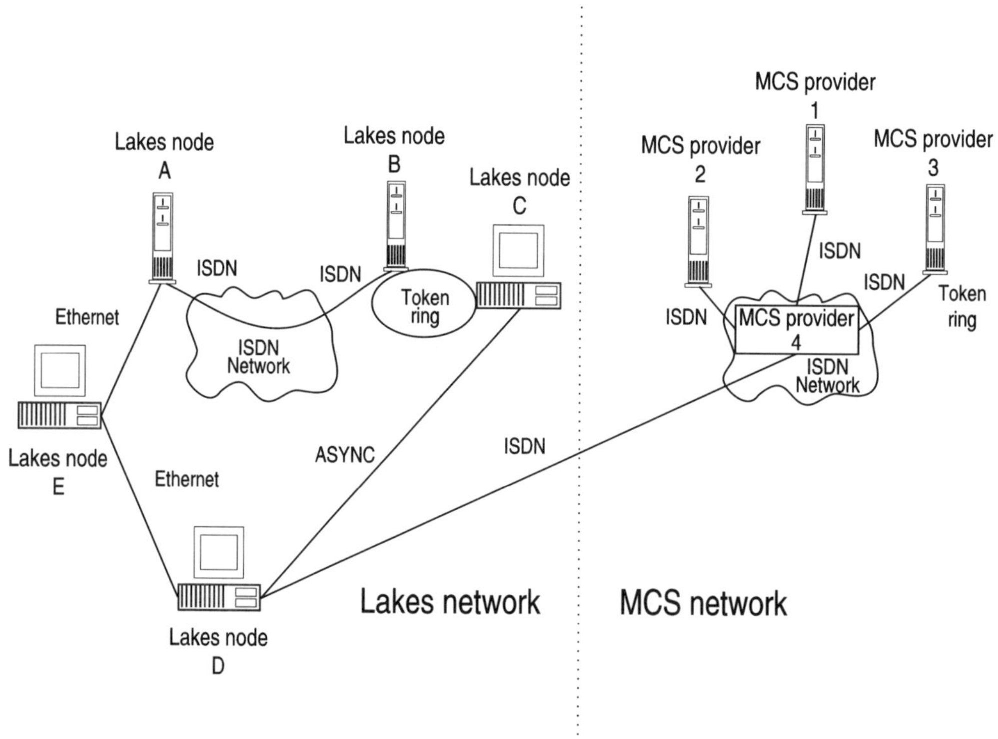

Figure 8.35 Mixed Lakes and MCS network

If it is assumed that an application exists at each node, A_A–A_E and A_1–A_4, and that all these applications are collaborating, then the MCS and Lakes views can be represented as illustrated in Fig. 8.26, assuming some allocation of applications to Lakes application sharing sets.

In the preferred MCS hierarchy, the MCS–Lakes bridge MCU becomes the top provider, with the Lakes nodes A-E appearing as directly-attached providers. The real MCS network is similarly attached. The alternative view has the Lakes nodes attached to MCS provider 4, through

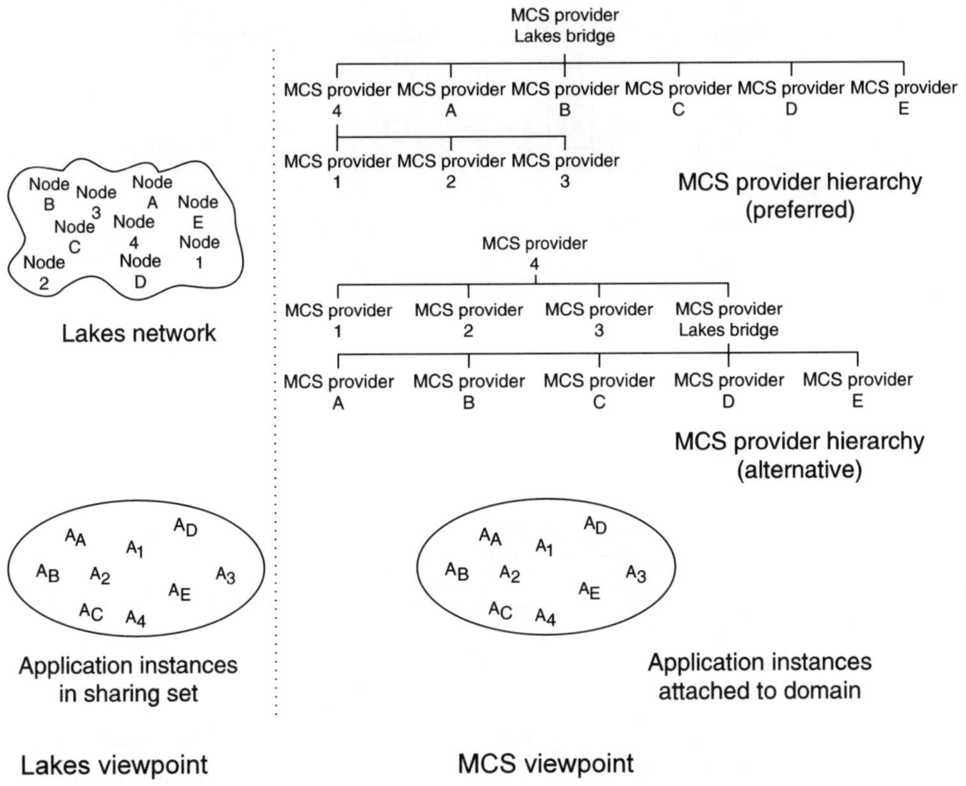

Figure 8.36 Lakes and MCS viewpoints of a mixed network

the Lakes bridge acting as an MCU. At the MCS domain level in both cases, all application instances behave as though they have attached to the domain. From the Lakes perspective, the details of the MCS connections are not visible but the MCS attached applications appear as members of the application sharing sets.

With a subset of the Lakes primitives mapped into MCS primitives, this approach means that it is possible to have full inter-operability between Lakes applications and MCS applications, assuming the applications themselves are designed to collaborate. Lakes applications implementing only this MCS compatibility subset will be designated L_M-applications to distinguish them from unrestricted L-applications. Inter-operability of L_M-applications with M-applications does not preclude other L-applications at those same nodes simultaneously exploiting the full Lakes capabilities. Furthermore, L_M-applications can freely collaborate with L-applications, subject to their application level data streams being compatible.

Implementation of inter-operability is straightforward if the protocol stream generated by a Lakes stack was a true superset of that generated by MCS. If not, then conceptually the implementation of inter-operability can be performed at the application level. Consider the following configuration involving applications A1, A2, B1 and B2 at Lakes nodes L1 and L2, and MCS providers M1 and M2. The example is illustrated in Fig. 8.37; it is assumed that all four applications are collaborating.

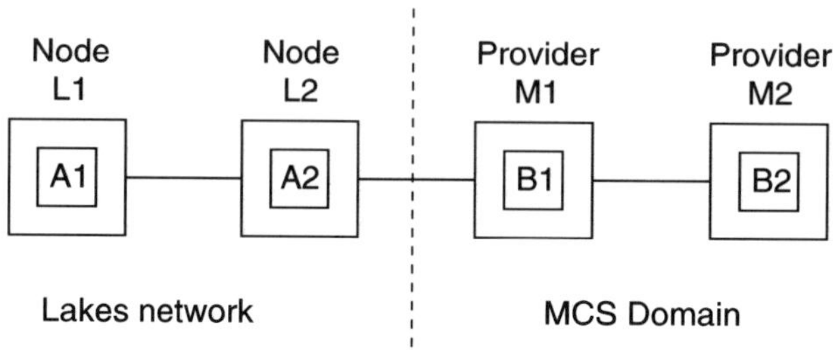

Figure 8.37 A simple mixed network

This simple mixed network can be considered logically as is illustrated in Fig. 8.38.

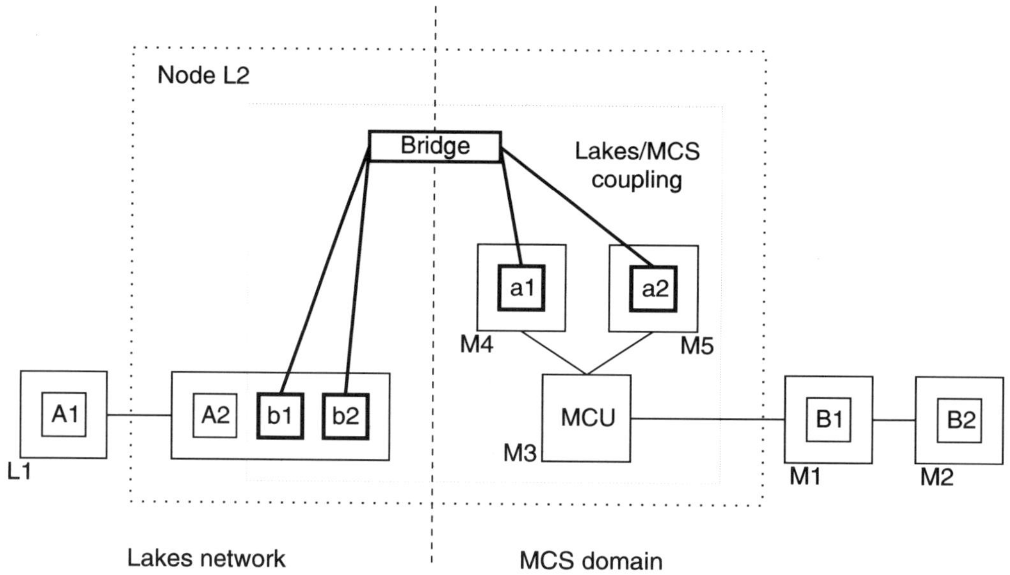

Figure 8.38 Logical view of the simple network

The Lakes network comprises two nodes, L1 and L2. At node L1, L_M-application A1 is running; at node L2 there are three L_M-applications running i.e. A2, b1 and b2. All four applications have registered with Lakes and joined a common application sharing set.

From an MCS perspective, node L2 appears as three MCS providers; M3 is an MCU and M4 and M5 are running a single application, a1 and a2 respectively, each of which have attached to that domain.

Applications a1, a2, b1 and b2 are proxies for the real applications A1, A2, B1 and B2. Thus application b1 receives the Lakes events that the real application B1 would have received if it were a Lakes application; instead b1 passes these events to the bridge code that translates them into MCS requests, where they are issued in the MCS domain via either a1 or a2, as appropriate. The converse scenario holds true when the process is viewed from an MCS perspective. The proxy applications operate only at the Lakes/MCS entity level, i.e. it is not necessary that they understand the application significance of the information that they manipulate, only that they are able to convert between MCS and Lakes primitives. The combination of function that establishes the proxies and the required MCS providers, and converts Lakes events to MCS requests and MCS indications/confirmations to Lakes requests, can be regarded as an integrated module that effectively straddles both the Lakes API and an MCS stack. Thus, for example, the Lakes application proxies may not exist but instead there could be a MCS/Lakes bridge module that registers itself as multiple Lakes applications.

CHAPTER 9

Products and practice

9.1 The marketplace

At the beginning of 1993 there were only ten vendors in the USA with products available; 18 months later that figure had more than quadrupled. Late in 1994, actual sales were still minimal but a leading USA market research company was predicting that the desktop conferencing marketplace in the USA would be worth $329 billion by 1997. A survey of a number of the principal users of video conferencing, conducted at the end of 1993, concluded that 90 per cent of those companies were interested in moving to desktop conferencing but only 40 per cent had any idea of how many systems they would buy. By late 1994, the desktop conferencing market was still in its infancy but was thought by many to be poised for explosive growth. Most of the product sold was not bought directly by users but was bundled with other components, such as modems, operating systems, personal computers and peripherals. The reason for this is that no enabled population yet exists that entices a new user to join through a direct personal purchase; instead the capability is seen by the computer industry as a value-added component to other purchasable elements. This situation will change as the market slowly takes off.

The early sales that have taken place have been mainly pilots and justified on the cost savings expected from avoided travel. Therefore the emphasis has been on video, just as for the earlier video conferencing products. Data conferencing capability is rapidly being added into the products, or is being extended from the basic capabilities already provided, and is thought to be the 'killer application' that will trigger the development of a new mass market.

Two phases of market growth are widely anticipated. Phase one, the current phase, is based on travel avoidance and is regarded by many potential users as, essentially, video conferencing at the desktop. It is necessarily a wide area phenomenon and the communications used are primarily either over ISDN or switched 56 kbits/s. lines. The state of the products available restricts the capability, with one or two notable exceptions, to a two-way call. The network operators have H.320 compliant MCUs in their networks to support multi-party calling but this does not allow any data inter-operability in a multi-way call. At the time of writing, no desktop conferencing product supports true multi-party working via an MCU, although almost all could connect to such a device—treating it as the other party to the call. This is expected to change rapidly. An essential prerequisite for a successful phase one is the development of standards that will guarantee inter-operability for audio, video and data; the ITU T.120 series is expected to satisfy most of these requirements.

Phase two will be dominated by systems that operate over LANs; it is only in this phase that sales are expected to grow rapidly. The justification for this optimism is as follows. Only in the wide area using the digital telephony networks, is isochronous communication generally available today. Moreover, switched rather than fixed links are ideal because they are used occasionally and paid for only when in use. The wide area aspect makes the travel cost avoidance argument easy to understand and at least a part of the estimated savings are probably real, certainly sufficient to justify the installation and running costs. However, this target group fails to deliver the full potential of the opportunity because: (a) most workstations are already attached to local area networks and are unlikely to be upgraded so that they are also attached directly to telephony networks, and (b) the travel cost justification is not so easily applied to the majority of workstation users. The solution depends upon the availability of a LAN/WAN gateway that will allow locally attached workstations easy access to the wide area with minimal cost, and a solution to the isochronous transmission problems over local area networks. The gateway will provide the necessary transcoding between the local and wide area protocols. Once this greater population becomes connected, desktop conferencing will not just be used for wide area communication but is also likely to become commonplace for local area communications. For closed communities within a company, it could rapidly become very important and generate considerable traffic. Moreover, for many of these users, the video element is likely to be less important than the data element. Thus, phase two should also see a rapid growth in the exploitation of data services within a desktop conferencing call.

The slow takeoff has disappointed many suppliers but is typical of the adoption of a new technology. The inhibitors present include:

1 The only benefit understood by customers today is travel cost saving. This fails to take into account improved productivity and cycle time reduction from the use of the technology. These other benefits will only become both apparent and accepted once pilot installations have demonstrated the validity of the claims.
2 Changes to working practices are required. Full exploitation of desktop conferencing calls for a re-engineering of many business processes and even the redesign of office layouts (e.g. to cater for cameras, mini-meetings at the desktop, the needs of the audio equipment).
3 There is often limited availability of ISDN and switched 56 kbits/s. lines, coupled with relatively high line charges in some countries. Similarly, there is generally poor connectivity to these networks at the desktop. Some important classes of user are totally excluded by the digital WAN emphasis, for example, the home user on an analogue telephone line, the mobile worker with a portable phone, the office worker attached to a LAN.
4 The high cost (although this is rapidly changing) of the necessary hardware upgrades to the workstation is a significant expense and often exceeds considerably the original cost of the workstation.
5 The absence of standards guaranteeing inter-operability and offering ‘future-proofing’. H.320 capability is becoming commonplace and provides inter-operability for audio and video across most manufacturers’ products. Data is still dependent upon a particular manufacturer’s equipment being present at both ends of the call. Inter-operability with room video conferencing systems is regarded as important by many purchasers.
6 Most suppliers only offer the workstation hardware and software part of the solution and leave it up to the customer to acquire and integrate the other components. Thus, typically the adapter card and software are supplied, and frequently the camera is also provided. However, installation and configuration is often difficult, especially when the target audience is the executive traveller, often unfamiliar with the plumbing aspects of a personal computer. The customer needs to acquire the line and then develop a community of other users. IBM and AT & T have realized the importance of a complete solution and have announced service offerings; other companies will undoubtedly follow. One benefit

from such an approach is that new collaborative applications and services can be provided on-line.

7 The low quality of video at 128 kbits/s. of bandwidth or less is unattractive to many people, giving a picture quality which is very fuzzy compared to a domestic television set. Effective use is limited to a talking head and excludes many applications.

8 There is a reluctance among some users to be 'on-camera'; it intrudes into personal privacy and is initially discomforting to many.

9.2 Suppliers and products

The information in this section relates to the state of the market late in 1994 and, given the pace of development, it is likely that the situation will change rapidly. The top 10 products in late 1994 selected for their sales success/visibility/usability/function and listed in alphabetical order, were:

Company	*Product name*
AT & T	Vistium
DataBeam	FarSite
Fujitsu	DTC
Future Labs	TalkShow
IBM	Person-to-Person™
InSoft	Communique!
Intel	ProShare
Northern Telecom	Visit
Nuts	Connect 918
PictureTel	PCS 100

Various elements of these and other products are common to several manufacturers. Such component sharing is normal in the industry; even some entire products were not developed by the companies that own and market them.

Measured in terms of sales in 1994, PictureTel were the market leaders, undoubtedly a consequence of the high reputation previously established by the company for video conferencing equipment, coupled with the existence of a targeted salesforce.

Measured in that intangible quantity 'public awareness', Intel were the leaders with their ProShare range. The success of Intel was due to a massive advertising campaign, a well publicized set of alliances, and a product with an arresting user interface that introduced the notebook paradigm to desktop conferencing. This delightful metaphor for collaboration uses an electronic spiral bound notebook with tabbed sections. Documents or pictures to be shared appear as sections of the notebook and are easily accessed by users. A set of aids such as highlighting pens, naturally exploits the metaphor and allows portions of the data to be identified for discussion. A ProShare printer driver allows all existing applications to print into the shared notebook instead of sending the output to the local printer; thus any document that can be produced at the workstation can also be easily shared among a group of users.

If the measurement criteria are functions and/or quality provided, then two products from the list above are of note, namely Communique! and ProShare. Communique! was released initially as a UNIX based system, with a very high quality video option using M-JPEG encoding at 24 bits/pel and 24 frames/s., integrated audio, support for a range of network types ranging from async to FDDI and T1, and featuring excellent application sharing. ProShare was announced with a fairly rich set of features, its attractive user interface and a video capability based on Intel's Indeo technology.

Cross platform capability, multiple communications protocols support and multi-party operation are a particular strength of the IBM Person-to-Person product, unequalled by any of its competitors.

The key differentiators between products are:

1 *The operating systems that are supported.* Microsoft Windows and Apple System /7 (Mac) are most commonly provided reflecting the popularity of these systems in business. UNIX variants are also available with rather less choice; OS/2 is poorly represented. Vanilla DOS is not generally regarded as a suitable opportunity for desktop conferencing products and gives suppliers implementation challenges.
2 *The range of communications protocols and link types supported.* There is tremendous diversity between the products, with many being restricted to ISDN/CSDN only. Others support a wider variety of link types and protocols but not all the function in the product is available with each protocol.
3 *The devices supported.* Desktop conferencing can exploit a wide range of devices such as:
   - system control—pens, tablets, touch screens
   - audio adapters—h/w and/or s/w codecs
   - video adapters—h/w and/or s/w codecs
   - handset support—manufacturer supplied equipment or generic interface support
   - other devices—fax, telephones, video phones
4 *Conformance to standards.* There are many standards that apply. T.120/H.320 are relevant to public switched networks. Other video and audio standards are important in other configurations. Many data standards exist for file transfer and document interchange. The goal is complete and seamless integration into the operating system. Thus, on a Windows platform, an attractive product will support DDE, OLE and a broad range of data file formats.
5 *The extent of cross-platform inter-operability.* This aspect is a consequence of the combination of other product attributes such as: operating system support, communications protocols, device support, and standards. An ideal product would inter-operate with full audio, video and data capabilities, with all other products. In practice, inter-operability tends to be poor, sometimes even between the family members from the same manufacturer.
6 *The collaborative tools provided.* These are useful utilities that integrate existing data and applications into a collaborative environment, i.e. they allow exploitation of what already exists. For example:
   - file transfer utilities
   - shared clipboard
   - window mirroring
   - desktop sharing/remote control
   - application sharing/remote control

   Within these simple tools there is scope for enormous diversity and this does not lend itself to simple analysis. The feature lists beloved of reviewers are very misleading and are no substitute for field trials.
7 *The applications provided for collaborative working.* The most common such application is the shared whiteboard and the different implementations vary widely in the fea-

tures supplied. Other less common collaborative applications are text editors, form-filling packages and games.

8 *Multi-party support and multiple concurrent call capability.* Multi-way calling capability is important and features high on surveys done on users' requirements. Typically, the need is for two to five parties to be able to simultaneously participate. Good multi-way support allows the various participants to be connected over a protocol that is appropriate to each party and does not force a common means of communication over the whole conference. Multi-way also brings with it a need for facilities to control the conference, features that are not as important in two-way operation. Multiple concurrent calls are less important, primarily because users are not normally familiar with this in everyday telephony—the nearest being to put a party on hold. As products become more equal in terms of basic features, this capability will serve to distinguish the more sophisticated offerings.

9 *The quality of the audio and video.* These factors are self-evident. Some applications demand high audio quality, e.g. music, while others are simply more comfortable with better quality. A distinguishing feature of many products is the provision and sophistication of echo suppression which can have a substantial impact on usability. Video quality is important, particularly as the default H.261 video quality over 64/128 kbits/s. from most suppliers is so poor. The majority of systems have private protocols which they use when they detect like equipment at either end and which the manufacturers' claim give better quality. Some suppliers use different algorithms depending upon the bandwidth available. Latency also differs between suppliers and high latency can make usage very tiresome, with some systems being on the border of acceptability. These factors should be evaluated in two ways: (a) with the same equipment at either end—and (b) with a reference system at one end; video quality, for example, is affected much more by the sending system than the receiving system.

10 *Ease of use characteristics.* This is a very difficult area to evaluate without a pilot installation. Many systems appear superficially attractive but can be clumsy for the specific tasks required; the converse is also true. More subtle aspects to be considered include, among many others, such things as:

- whether the system provides phone capabilities without the system unit being powered on
- ease of integration into the installation networks and data bases
- ease of installation, configuration, customization and maintenance

Performance is a major contributor to ease of use. Thus for example, some collaborative shared notebook implementations look delightful and perform well on small data volumes. However, a few of these products are exclusively image-based and become unusable when the quantity of data increases, perhaps with a long document. Other more intelligent implementations might sacrifice some fidelity (of typeface styles and layout) but, by recognizing text and using coded data streams, provide vast performance improvements over slow links. Demonstrations are a poor guide to value in this field.

11 *Technical support provided.* Given the early state of the technology and the need to integrate computers, operating systems, applications, devices and networks, it is recommended to begin with a total systems offering. As the technology matures, standards are established and the products become commodities, only then can desktop conferencing be regarded as just another application on a workstation.

12 *Price.* Hardware prices are falling dramatically and the industry is moving to software codecs as rapidly as possible. Software prices have also fallen and the tendency is to

offer multi-packs at greatly reduced prices over single systems. It is very likely that basic capabilities will be included as part of all the standard operating systems over the next few years.

13 *Product availability.* The competitive nature of the market has caused many manufacturers to commit to future support of standards, other operating systems and emerging communications protocols.

14 *Packaging options.* A trend is emerging for entry level subsets of leading products to be offered at very low prices as an incentive to users to start to exploit the technology. Typically these subsets are aimed at providing function without needing expensive hardware upgrades; thus, data sharing over asynchronous lines is usually a comon element of these starter packages. Video and ISDN support is normally available as an upgrade.

9.3 Toolkits

Besides shrink-wrapped products, there have been a number of programming toolkits either announced or shipped. The intention is to encourage the development of more collaborative applications to help to grow the market, and hence also the demand for related products such as workstations, networking infrastructure, communications capacity and value-added services. For example PictureTel have a development kit that allows new applications to be written that co-exist with the PCS 100; Apple have announced their conferencing architecture; IBM have announced Lakes; and there are others. Some of these kits enable small ancillary functions to be developed; others are designed to support the creation of global networks. Some companies have approached toolkits differently: DataBeam with their FarSite shrink-wrapped product also have an extensive range of software components that are being made available to other manufacturers rather than to users.

Ultimately, the useful elements of these toolkits will contribute to the mainstream operating systems development and become subsumed in the basic platform support for real-time multimedia communications. Remaining outside will be product-specific customization kits.

9.4 Company strategies

There are many companies involved and the reasons for their presence in the market differ widely. While they all share the common goal of creating a profitable business, some see desktop conferencing as an important element of a broader corporate strategy. The interpretations of motives which follow are necessarily subjective, but may explain some of the differences in approach.

AT & T have announced their intention of building an interactive video and data call service known as WorldWorx™ in over 22 countries. It will provide real-time and store and forward multimedia connectivity between multiple users, user equipment and applications. Two specific services are planned: (a) Global Business Video Services, providing voice and video services between two or more locations, including multi-point bridging, codec conversion, digital speed conversion, cross-network connectivity, satellite links and inverse multiplexing; and (b) Personal Conferencing Services, point-to-point and multi-point voice, video and data services at the desktop, with features such as security, conferee identification, on-line directory and standards support. The service will initially target the enrolment of large corporate customers. It is intended to provide a complete systems capability, from installation through to operation and maintenance. Other suppliers have pledged support, for example Apple, Lotus, Novell, PictureTel, Sun MicroSystems, VideoServer, HP, and Xerox, among others. Equipment will be certified as being WorldWorx compatible. AT & T's own Vistium family of personal conferencing kits is a part of the service; other manufacturers' equipment will also be supported. The real motivation is undoubtedly the network traffic expected and a desire to gain connectivity to the corporate desktop so that other services can be added later. In trying to interpret this and other similar announcements, it is common to find the same companies participating in what appear to be multiple conflicting alliances. Usually there are a small core of lead companies who create the concept and an outer circle of loosely-associated members who join, partly to distinguish themselves from the non-members, but partly also on the theory that any publicity is good publicity. In extreme cases there are examples of some (large) companies being announced as members of these groups, unbeknown to the companies themselves.

IBM has announced a not dissimilar service concept from its specially created Network Services Applications Division. The driving force is the desire to climb up the value-added chain and, instead of supplying components at what will soon become commodity prices, to offer services that are charged by the transaction with a revenue stream linked to usage.

Other telephone companies are developing products to stimulate the growth of network traffic. Thus BT, which has a successful and respected video conferencing service using its own technology, has decided to exploit this asset to encourage desktop conferencing over its underutilized ISDN network. In association with Motorola, it has cost-reduced the technology to a PC form factor card and has developed software through agreements with companies such as Olivetti and IBM. The target customer set is BT's corporate base who will be encouraged to upgrade executive telephones to desktop conferencing systems.

The leading supplier of video conferencing equipment worldwide is PictureTel. Falling costs and increased competition have persuaded PictureTel to be a leader in desktop conferencing. Inter-operability with room systems is a key consideration and the company has taken a lead in expanding the market to include local area network attached workstations through the development of a gateway capability. Exploitation of data sharing and application creativity are likely to be focus areas for companies like PictureTel, who observe that the hardware component of solutions is becoming less and less important.

The Intel Corporation has a different motivation. The 286, 386, 486, Pentium and follow-on CPU chip sets are fundamental to the PC-compatible workstation market but are under threat, particularly from the IBM, Motorola and Apple alliance with the PowerPC RISC processors. The strategy has been to embed functions within the central processor to gain efficiencies and to present a moving target to competitors. Desktop conferencing with its hardware unique components today, and a certain move to software implementations in the future, is a capability that must be well handled by the CPU. Intel also have a proprietary video format, Indeo, optimized to Intel's architectures. Having failed to persuade the market that Indeo should be the *de facto* video standard, Intel have announced their intent to also support H.261 and the rest of the H.320 and T.120 standards. Influence on future directions and protection of the CPU revenue stream is an important factor in Intel's participation.

Other smaller suppliers, such as DataBeam, are becoming technology companies. The costs of developing a technology are small compared to the costs of marketing the resulting products. New entrants find the cost of set-up for such sales and service operations prohibitive and instead, find it easier to market their technology to the industry leaders and have them incorporate it into their product line. DataBeam specializes in the software components necessary to implement H.320 and T.120 compliance and has been very successful in persuading many of the much larger players to adopt their software. As a result the presence of DataBeam technology in a product is becoming more important for inter-operability than conformance with the ITU-T standards. Assisting this trend is ambiguity in the standards themselves and the difficulty of determining cost-effective subsets to implement.

9.5 Alliances

Besides groups of companies cooperating to provide specific products or services, there exists a multitude of alliances designed to establish standards. The combinations of players in the various alliances are difficult to understand and there are many companies who appear to join several in a fairly random way, possibly only guided by a desire to emerge as a member of the winning team.

Intel have established the Personal Conferencing Workgroup (PCWG) with the intention of establishing an industry standard that defines inter-operability and compatibility for personal conferencing products. Twelve core members are responsible for writing specifications: these comprise three conferencing companies—CLI, VTel and VideoServer; three communications companies—AT & T, Ericsson and Northern Telecom; and six personal computer companies - Compaq, Intel, Lotus, Novell, SPC and Wordperfect. Three levels of specification are planned: PCS 1.0 (Jan 1995) covering ISDN and support of multi-party via MCUs; PCS 2.0 (May/June 1995) providing LAN connection, modem support, cascaded MCUs, mixed data types, and a conferencing API; and PCS 3.0 (1996).

The Multimedia Communications Community of Interest (MCCOI) was formally launched in July 1993 by BT, Northern Telecom, IBM, Deutsche Telekom, France Telecom, Telstra and Intel. The intent was to ensure that ISDN-based visual telephony could develop into full PC-based multimedia communication, and to ensure concerted and coordinated efforts by hardware and software manufacturers and telephone companies. The MCCOI was established as an open forum and by February 1994 over 40 companies had joined, with many more attending meetings. Various activity groups were established to study switched network activity, application programming interfaces, basic functions sets, LAN gateways, multi-point operation and inter-working using virtual private networks and private exchanges.

The Consortium for Audiographics Teleconferencing Standards (CATS) was incorporated in August 1993. Its purpose was to promote the creation of international standards for graphics teleconferencing and to form a critical mass of vendors and users necessary to ensure adoption. The focus of the CATS group was intended to be on voice and data standards, based on T.120. By March 1994, 25 organizations had joined, including BT, IBM, DataBeam, GPT, Sun Solutions, AT & T, MCI, Polycom, VideoServer and HP.

In September 1994 the CATS and MCCOI organizations merged to form the International Multimedia Teleconferencing Consortium (IMTC), with a total of over 70 companies as members.

There are more such arrangements and it is clear that many of these initiatives will flounder, but some may succeed. There is no doubt that the publication of open standards and testing for product compliance is essential for widespread public adoption.

APPENDIX 1

Outlook

The technology for effective desktop conferencing is available and affordable for mass market acceptance. Standards are being developed by the ITU for inter-working and these will be widely adopted within the industry. ISDN will be the basis of public access switched services and the efforts to standardize the varying ISDN implementations across countries, to increase ISDN penetration and access, will encourage further use. Such standardized facilities will provide a minimum set of functions underpinning all product offerings and will be intended for the casual user. At this level, products will be distinguished by ease of use, video quality and the extent to which they are integrated into the desktop environment. Such capabilities will slowly become a part of the standard workstation operating systems over time; similarly, a minimum level of hardware support for some degree of desktop conferencing will become the norm on personal computer systems.

Inter-operability is fundamental to market acceptance and this aspect embraces many facets. Inter-working between equipment from different suppliers is mandatory; inter-working across operating systems, networks and pervasive applications is also expected by users. Desktop conferencing is primarily a link between things that already exist—a way of communicating and sharing information on the desktop—and is thus more dependent upon integration and inter-operability than other pervasive tools, such as word processors, spreadsheets and data bases.

Just as important, and to their users more important, will be the development of high-function desktop conferencing systems for specific user groups. In large companies, with already installed networks, the prospects for ISDN-based solutions are less promising. Exploitation of existing networks and the newer technologies, such as ATM and iso-Ethernet, are likely to be the focus of desktop conferencing systems. The requirements of specific user groups in medicine, education, consultancy, industry and commerce will also drive developments that fall outside the scope of the ITU-T standards. These systems, while being able to communicate at a basic level with standards compliant implementations, will offer their users much greater costs benefits with higher levels of function. High quality audio and video, sophisticated data services, and much richer call models will distinguish these offerings from their publicly-available counterparts. The trend towards remote education, home working and the like will stimulate these developments.

As in other branches of computing, standards will be enhanced in parallel and there is already much activity directed towards improved video quality and the exploitation of higher bandwidth communication links. However, in this field, there is a sense in which the standards already lead the products in some respects and the more immediate challenge is to implement and take advantage from what has already been defined, rather than wait for new proposals from the standards community. If the gap between reality and vision increases further, there is a danger that future standards may not fully reflect customer wants and needs; the ability of technologists to predict the future without constant market testing is open to question.

Much of the industry interest in desktop conferencing does not originate from a desire to grow the equipment marketplace but, rather, anticipates the growth in network revenue and the opportunity for value-added services. Desktop conferencing will become a significant consumer of bandwidth and the desire for higher quality video than that currently on offer will drive that consumption. Audio and data services, though welcome, do not have the same potential for bandwidth utilization. Supply of raw bandwidth is not as profitable as the services that can be developed on top of desktop conferencing. Network operators will develop attractive packages including directory services, broadcast facilities, advertising, multi-point provision, answering capabilities, billing and other services on top of the basic connectivity. There is tremendous potential for a network operator if that most common piece of terminal equipment in business—the telephone—is upgraded to become a multimedia communications device.

One aspect is still unclear. Desktop conferencing, more than any other recent development, bridges the boundary between telephony and computing. The attitudes and business goals of these two industries are diametrically opposed. Telephony has a history of regulation, of monopoly supply, of control of the customer premises equipment. Almost perfect reliability and inter-operability have been the keys to phenomenal growth. The computing industry has achieved success by a very different route: through encouraging innovation, diversity, the ruthless driving down of costs coupled with tremendous competition. Reliability and inter-operability have proved to be less important than technology. The marriage of these two cultures, and the integration of the legacies of these two industries, will produce the desktop conferencing products and services of the future.

Appendix 2

Glossary

μ-law

A variant of the G.711 audio encoding used primarily in North America and Japan.

A-law

A variant of the G.711 audio encoding common outside North America and Japan.

ADPCM

Adaptive differential pulse code modulation; a technique for digitally sampling waveforms and encoding the differences between successive samples rather than encoding their actual values.

AGC

Audio graphic conferencing, i.e. a real-time interaction between multiple remote parties where audio and graphical data is exchanged. There are no video capabilities.

Analogue

Signals or data that are continuous and thus may have any value at an instant in time (as opposed to digital).

ANSI

American National Standards Institute

API

Application programming interface, an architected external interface to a set of functions generally offering services of use to an application programmer. Such interfaces often specialize in communications, data base, graphics, telephony or other capabilities.

AppleTalk

A set of specifications that define how Apple Macintosh computers, printers and other devices communicate with each other over a network. Originally it used the LocalTalk cabling system at 230.4 kbits/s. but now also supports Ethernet and token ring topologies (through EtherTalk and TokenTalk).

Application instance

An occurrence of code loaded and executing in memory when an application program has been started. Note that most applications can be launched repeatedly by a workstation user, with each launch giving rise to a separate application instance, and all of these instances running concurrently. Some operating systems use a single copy of an application code, even though it has been launched more than once by the user, but maintain separate data and other resources to represent the state of each instance.

Application program

A program, independent of the operating system, which can be launched (started) by the user to perform a task such as word processing, spreadsheet or graphics editing.

ASCII

The standard way of using numeric codes to represent characters and special symbols on personal computers. Defined in the ITU-T recommendation T.50.

Asynchronous communication

A form of communication in which each byte (or octet) is preceded by a single start bit and followed by a stop interval lasting for at least one bit time; typically used in terminal-to-terminal or terminal-to-host communications. A characteristic of this form of communication is that the timing between the bytes may vary from byte to byte. It is generally slower than synchronous communication.

ATM

Asynchronous transfer mode; a very efficient technology for transmitting data based on an assumption that the underlying network is highly reliable and uses fixed-size cells to relay data efficiently. It is typically used over optical fibre, but can be used over other media as well. Although mainly deployed in backbone networks, ATM adapters are being developed to the desktop where it is likely to provide 100–150 Mbits/s. of isochronous capability. Both time-dependent and time-independent traffic can be mixed on the same network. Broadband ISDN services can be built on top of ATM technology.

Audiographics terminal

An ITU-T expression meaning a terminal that has audio plus graphics capabilities, but no video capability.

Audiovisual terminal

An ITU-T expression meaning a terminal that has audio plus video, audio plus graphics, or audio plus graphics and video capabilities.

AVC

Audio visual conferencing, i.e. a real-time interaction between multiple remote parties where audio and video data are exchanged, optionally supplemented with graphical data.

AVI

Audio Video Interleaved. A Microsoft technology providing software synchronization and compression for audio and video signals. Competes with Quicktime from the Apple Corporation and DVI from the Intel Corporation.

B channel

An ISDN bearer service channel operating at 64 kbits/s.; able to carry audio and data.

Bandwidth

The ability of a communications link to cope with the volume of data to be transported in a fixed time, usually measured in bits/s.

BAS

The bit-rate allocation signal, a command code that is transmitted in H.221 frames and used for a wide variety of control purposes in H.320 and T.120.

Basic rate ISDN

An ISDN service comprising two B channels and one D channel.

Broadband ISDN

An ISDN service offering capacities above the primary rate.

Byte

The computing term for a group of eight bits; most computer functions operate on bytes or collections of bytes. In telephony, bytes are known as octets.

CAD/CAM

Computer aided design/computer aided manufacturing.

Call

A spontaneous collaborative real-time interaction, typically between two or more parties at different locations, in which a set of policies, or rules of behaviour, are enforced. Examples of calls include the casual telephone call, a formal conference meeting, a teacher instructing students remotely, or an announcement. Calls are typified by requiring synchronous communication.

Call manager

A program independent of the applications in a call, that controls that call through the enforcement of rules, or policies.

Call set-up

The process of establishing a group of communicating users and includes the initialization of any shared applications and other resources which the users may require to be available.

Call tear-down

The process of ending a call and freeing any resources reserved for that call.

CCIR

An international organization responsible for setting television standards.

CCITT

The International Telegraph and Telephone Consultative Committee, formerly responsible for making recommendations on standards and related matters for the ITU. Replaced by the ITU-T in March 1993.

CIF

An ITU-T standard video picture scanning format where information is stored as luminance (brightness) and two colour difference components. The luminance is held at 352 pels/line and 288 lines/picture; the colour differences are held at 176 pels/line and 144 lines/picture.

Circuit switched network

A type of public data network which requires a physical communication to be established between the end-points before the data are transmitted, for example ISDN. Normally suited for isochronous transmission. The alternative scheme is a packet switched network.

Codec

A coder/decoder, typically used to convert analogue signals (typically audio and video) into digital, and vice versa. May also be used to compress and decompress the digital data.

Collaborative application

An application designed to operate in a shared multi-user environment where the interactions of one user may have an immediate impact upon the interactions of another.

CSCW

Computer supported collaborative work.

CSDN

Circuit switched digital network.

D channel

An ISDN signalling channel, to carry user to network data; can also be used to carry packet mode user data. Operates at 16 kbits/s. in basic rate ISDN; 64 kbits/s. in primary rate ISDN.

DDE

Dynamic data exchange, an architected *de facto* standard for program-to-program communication commonly used between personal computers.

Desktop conferencing

An ability to use a suitably configured personal computer for spontaneous audio, data and, optionally, video real-time exchanges.

Digital

Signals or data that can only take on discrete values (typically binary), as opposed to analogue.

DVI

Digital Video Interactive. An Intel technology providing proprietary hardware synchronization and compression for audio and video signals. Competes with Quicktime from the Apple Corporation and AVI from the Microsoft Corporation.

E-mail

Electronic mail, a form of electronic message where, if replies are required, there is no requirement that the communicating parties are simultaneously connected to the electronic mail system.

Ethernet

Also known as IEEE 802.3, is an ISO standard for a physical layer networking scheme. It normally runs at 10 Mbits/s. with a linear bus topology. Any workstation can share the network cable but only one can use it at a time. The access method that permits this is known as carrier sense multiple access with collision detection or CSMA/CD. Variants of Ethernet are defined to run at speeds from 1 Mbit/s. to 100 Mbits/s., with distances between workstations ranging from 100 metres to 4 kilometres, using a variety of cables including twisted pair, coax and optical fibre.

FAS

A frame alignment signal—a special sequence of bits placed in a fixed position in the frame in order that frames can be identified.

FDDI

A networking standard also known as IEEE 802.3 normally offering 10 Mbits/s. throughput and using a carrier sensing access method in which only one workstation can use the cable at a time. Attempts at multiple concurrent access are known as collisions, and an algorithm is used to back-off the colliding parties and determine when each should re-try. Various forms of Ethernet have been standardized over different kinds of cable (such as coax, twisted pair and fibre) and are known as 10Base-5, 10Base-2, 10Base-T, etc., where the type of cable used affects the distance supported. A 1 Mbits/s. version exists, as do 100 Mbits/s. variants. For desktop conferencing, an interesting development of the standard is Iso-Ethernet.

FDDI

A fibre-optic cable networking standard operating at 100 Mbits/s. and capable of supporting up to 500 network nodes over a distance of 100 kilometres. A copper variant of the standard also exists. A derivative, known as FDDI-II, offers isochronous communication services.

FDDI-II

A development of FDDI that uses multiplexing techniques to provide multiple isochronous circuits suited to multimedia traffic.

Frame

A unit information for transmission at the physical layer; in H.221, frames are 80 octets in size and identified by special bit patterns known as the FAS.

G.711

An ITU-T recommendation for the digital representation of speech producing a 64 kbits/s. data stream. This is the most common form of audio representation in telephony networks. Two variants exist: A-law and μ-law.

G.721

An ITU-T recommendation for the digital representation of audio producing a 32 kbits/s. data stream with the same audio quality as G.711.

G.722

An ITU-T recommendation for the digital representation of audio producing a 64 kbits/s. data stream with a much higher audio quality than G.711.

G.728

An ITU-T international audio encoding recommendation producing a 16 kbits/s. data stream.

GCC

Generic conference call—a set of conference services described in the ITU-T T.124 recommendation.

Graphics

A data representation, typically used for line art or simple visual representations such as graphs, where the elements of the picture are stored as objects such as lines, circles, arcs and other shapes.

H channel

An ISDN bearer service channel operating at higher rates than 64 kbits/s.; able to carry audio and data. H_0 has a bandwidth of 384 kbits/s.; H_{11} 1.536 Mbits/s.; H_{12} 1.920 Mbits/s.

H series

Sometimes used as a shorthand for the set of recommendations described in ITU-T H.320.

H.261

An ITU-T international video encoding recommendation which is used in both H.320 and T.120. It is also referred to as px64 because the picture is carried in a communications pipe defined in multiples of 64 kbits/s.

H.320

An ITU-T international recommendation for audio and video conferencing, targeted particularly at ISDN networks. It also forms the basis for T.120 which standardizes conference control and data conferencing.

HDLC

High-level data link control, an ISO standard link level protocol used for wide area communication over synchronous networks and supporting full duplex transmission.

IEC

The International Electrotechnical Commission.

Image

A data representation, typically used for natural pictures or photographs, where each individual regular rectangular element of the picture is separately stored.

IPX

Internetwork packet exchange, a peer-to-peer networking protocol used in Novell's Netware network operating systems products, providing a connectionless capability.

ISDN

An integrated services digital network, able to provide a wide variety of services, including audio and data. Basic rate ISDN is normally able to use the PSTN local wiring from the telephone exchange but requires specialized equipment to be installed in place of the conventional phone.

ISO

The International Organization for Standardization.

Isochronous communication

A form of communication between computers where there is a smooth guaranteed flow of data, that is data does not get delayed during transmission such that it emerges in bursts. Audio and video require isochronous communication; file transfer or messaging do not.

Iso-Ethernet

An evolution of the Ethernet standard to support isochronous communication. Each workstation is connected to a hub and has a dedicated 10 Mbits/s. data connectivity to other attached workstations, using the existing Ethernet communications protocols. Additionally, isochronous channels are provided based on the 64 kbits/s. ISDN B channels and can, therefore, be used in parallel for audio, video and data and are switched by the hub.

ITU

The International Telecommunications Union—an agency of the United Nations.

ITU-T

The ITU's telecommunications standardization sector, a permanent organ that is responsible for studying technical and other issues for telecommunications standardization. Replaced the CCITT in March 1993. Works under the auspices of WTSC.

JBIG

Progressive bi-level image compression—a standard optimized for lossless encoding of text, half-tone and line art images. Specified as an ISO/IEC international standard by the Joint Bi-level Image Group.

Jitter

A measure of the consistency of the latency parameter for a communication link; represents the instantaneous variation in latency, or the statistical distribution of the data packet communication delays.

JPEG

A compression standard optimized for continuous tone images. Specified as an ISO/IEC international standard by the Joint Photographic Expert Group.

LAN

See local area network.

LapD

Link access procedure for the data link layer, an ITU-T recommendation for the link level protocol for the D channel of an ISDN connection. Also known as Q.921.

LapF

Link access procedure for frame mode beaver services, an ITU-T recommendation for the link level protocol for the B channel for an ISDN connection. Also known as Q.922.

Latency

The delay imposed by a communications network. The time taken for the first bit of data to be carried from the point of entry to the point of departure. Latency is a critical factor in characterizing transmission links and low latency is particularly important for person-to-person interaction.

Local area network

LAN, a communications network typically interconnecting devices and workstations in a relatively small geographic area. Characterized by high speed, i.e. >1 Mbits/s. fixed connections (i.e. not switched) and a small number of attachments (≈ 100–200). LANs may be bridged together to form wide area networks. Originally designed for data traffic, not audio or video.

MCS

Multi-point communications services—the data services that underpin the T.120 recommendation.

MCU

See multi-point control unit.

Messaging

The asynchronous exchange of messages between users. See also E-mail.

MIDI

The Musical Instrument Digital Interface, a standard way of connecting musical instruments together so that they play in unison.

MLP

See multi-layer protocol.

MMC

The Multimedia Marketing Council, owners of the MPC trademark.

MPC

The trade-marked abbreviation for the Multimedia Personal Computer or multimedia PC, owned by the MMC, and used for certifying multimedia equipment.

MPEG

A compression standard optimized for motion video. Specified as an ISO/IEC international standard by the Motion Picture Expert Group.

Multi-layer protocol

Or MLP—refers to the data protocol generated by MCS and is transmitted on partitions established by the H.221 recommendation of the H.320 series.

Multimedia

A vague term which literally means the full range of data types including numeric, text, image, graphics, audio and video data. More usually used to mean the inclusion of the more exotic computer data types such as audio and video.

Multi-point control unit

Or MCU, a device generally installed inside the ISDN or PSTN that enables multiple users' equipment to inter-communicate by implementing an agreed set of rules controlling the flows of data between the users' equipment.

NDIS

The network driver interface specification, developed by Microsoft, to allow multiple communication protocol stacks to be concurrently loaded and active through a single network adapter.

NetBIOS

Network basic input output system, an application programming interface for computers on the same local area network that provides session layer communication services.

NTSC

A standard for television broadcasting established by the National Television Standards Committee. Used in North America, Japan and some other countries. See PAL and SECAM.

Octet

The telephony term for a group of eight bits; in computing the term bytes is used instead.

OLE

Object linking and embedding—an architected Microsoft *de facto* standard for program-to-program communication and object exchange/update.

PABX

Private automatic branch exchange or private switch—an internal telephone exchange that provides internal extensions and generally also allows access to the PSTN.

Packet

An assembled collection of data, combined with routeing and/or delivery information.

Packet switched network

A type of public data network in which packets of data are routed from users to their destinations, e.g. X.25. Packet switched networks are not normally suitable for isochronous transmission. A connection-less service, in that a dedicated communications channel from source to destination is not established prior to transmission. The alternative scheme is a circuit switched network.

PAL

A standard for television broadcasting used in Western Europe (except France which uses NTSC). See NTSC and SECAM.

Palette

A finite set of colours, each one being defined by the contribution of at least three independent primary colours—typically red, green and blue. Palettes provide a way of specifying a subset of all the possible colours and are used because they reduce the amount of memory needed to describe a picture. Palettes can be changed and the colour contents chosen to suit the pictures to be displayed; thus a palette suitable for flesh tones would not be good for grey scale images such as black and white photographs.

PCM

Pulse code modulation—a technique used for the digital sampling of sounds.

PCMCIA

Personal computer memory card international association, a body which agrees standards for a wide range of credit card sized adapters that plug into personal computers and provide networking, storage and other capabilities. Standard software support known as card services and sockets services, recognizes the nature of the card and configures the machine appropriately. Plug-and-play technology, based on these services, allows PCMCIA cards, and indeed other devices, to be added or removed without the computer needing to be restarted.

Pel

Picture element—the smallest addressable unit on a visual display unit. Each pel can be set to a colour to make up the picture on the display; this colour is usually an index into a palette.

Phone book

Sometimes referred to as an address book, a computer representation of user names and related ancillary information that also includes the details of the network connections and addresses such that contact can be established with the computer associated with that user.

Primary rate ISDN

An ISDN service comprising either 23 B channels and one D channel, 24 B channels, or 30 B channels and one D channel.

Priority token ring

See Token ring.

Protocol

The set of rules that govern the interchange of information between devices that allow them to inter-communicate.

PSDN

Packet switched digital network.

PSTN

The public switched telephone network.

PX64

See H.320.

QCIF

An ITU-T standard video picture scanning format where information is stored as luminance (brightness) and two colour difference components. The luminance is held at 176 pels/line and 144 lines/picture; the colour differences are held at 88 pels/line and 72 lines/picture.

QuickTime

An Apple technology for digital imaging and audio multimedia. Competes with DVI from the Intel Corporation and AVI from the Microsoft Corporation.

Q.921

See LapD.

Q.922

See LapF.

RGB

A method of specifying a colour by using numbers to designate the intensities of the red, green and blue components.

RLE

Run length encoding—a simple way of compressing a bit string in which occurrences of consecutive '0' or '1' bits are replaced by one such bit and a count field of the number originally present. Although not the most efficient form of compression for all images, it is fast to code and decode, and particularly suited to certain images such as scanned documents where there are large areas of white space.

RTV

Real time video, a video format which is part of Intel's DVI suite of proprietary encoding.

SDLC

Synchronous data link control, a link level protocol developed by IBM for the control of communications over a wide area synchronous network. It supports point-to-point, multi-point and loop configurations.

SECAM

A standard for television broadcasting used in Eastern Europe, France and certain African countries. See NTSC and PAL.

Skew

The difference in presentation times between two related objects; for example, lip movements should be synchronized with the corresponding sounds and the extent to which they are out of sync represents the skew.

SPX

Sequenced packet exchange, a peer-to-peer networking protocol used in Novell's NetWare network operating systems products, providing a connection-orientated service. SPX uses IPX.

SVGA

Super VGA—denotes a type of display adapter in the personal computer responsible for displaying the picture on the monitor. SVGA is very common and usually has a resolution of 800 x 600 or 1024 x 768 pixels. The pixels are square in shape and can be selected from a colour palette of varying sizes depending upon the adapter.

Synchronous communication

A form of communication in which the two end-points are kept in step during data transmission through a common timing signal. It is generally faster than the alternative asynchronous communication.

T series

See T.120.

T.120

An ITU-T set of recommendations for audiovisual and audiographic conferencing. The key element of T.120 is the provision of conference control and data conferencing. It is built on top of the H.320 series of recommendations.

T.122

See T.MCS.

T.124

See T.GCC.

T.126

See T.SI.

T.127

See T.MBFT.

T.AVC

An ITU-T recommendation, forming part of the T.120 series, that describes the data protocols of a standardized application used to control the audio and video capabilities present in a desktop or video conference. This standard extends the capabilities offered by H.320.

TCP

See TCP/IP.

TCP/IP

Transmission control protocol/internet protocol, a suite of protocols designed to provide interconnecting between a variety of host systems. Orignally developed by the US Defense Advanced Projects Agency in the mid-1970s but now in widespread use commercially and becoming increasingly important. IP is connectionless; TCP is connection-oriented and uses IP. The internet network is based on the TCP/IP protocol suite.

TDM

Time division multiplexing, a transmission technology for combining multiple data streams by allocating each fixed positions in a stream of frames. The frames are transmitted at regular intervals and thus each stream receives its designated fraction of the total bandwidth at all times, irrespective of any other traffic.

Text

A data representation, typically used for documents, where the individual characters are stored as coded representations with appropriate formatting codes to represent font and layout information.

T.GCC

An ITU-T recommendation, forming part of the T.120 series, that describes the generic conference control, or call management services used in a desktop or video conference. T.GCC is also known as GCC or T.124.

T.MBFT

An ITU-T recommendation, forming part of the T.120 series, that describes the data protocols of a standardized file transfer application (multi-point binary file transfer). T.MBFT is also known as T.127.

T.MCS

An ITU-T recommendation, forming part of the T.120 series, that describes the multi-point communication services, used by data applications (such as T.SI and T.MBFT) and call management (T.GCC) in a desktop or video conference. T.MCS is also known as MCS or T.122.

Token ring

A networking standard also known as IEEE 802.5 normally offering 4 or 16 Mbits/s. throughput and using a token-passing ring network that can be configured in a star topology. Normally unsuited for isochronous traffic, but with bandwidth management software at each workstation and exploiting its priority mechanism to distinguish traffic types, it is possible to use it in this way. This has been proposed as 'priority token ring' but is not yet commercially important.

Transaction processing

Transactions are units of work, such as extracting data from a file or calculating an item of information. On-line transaction processing operates in real-time to collect and process transaction-related data and to post changes. Of particular importance is guaranteeing the security of transactions and being able to roll-back a transaction that was not completed.

T.SI

An ITU-T recommendation, forming part of the T.120 series, that describes the data protocols of a standardized still image application. This has the functionality of the shared whiteboard present in most desktop conferencing systems. T.SI is also known as T.126.

UDP

User datagram protocol, part of the TCP/IP suite and provides applications with access to the connectionless features of IP.

VGA

Denotes a type of display adapter in the personal computer responsible for displaying the picture on the monitor. VGA is very common and represents the lowest resolution now commonly available, 640x 480 square pixels.

Video conferencing

Real-time audio and video interactions between groups of people, normally in specially equipped rooms and using high bandwidth communications.

WAN

See wide area network.

Whiteboard

Also known as a chalkboard, an electronic representation of a shared drawing area upon which all the parties in a call can sketch and have the drawing displayed on each workstation.

Wide area network

WAN, a communications network formed by interconnecting LANs over a wide geographic area through bridges and routers.

Windowing system

A computer operating system that supports a graphical user interface, normally presenting the output of applications in one or more rectangular windows on the visual display screen. Common examples are IBM's OS/2 and Microsoft's Windows.

WTSC

The World Telecommunications Standardization Conference which meets every four years to agree topics for the ITU-T to study, it also approves their recommendations.

YUV

An encoding method used in digital video applications. Y represents the luminance of the image, and U and V define the hue and saturation.

X.25

An ITU-T protocol designed for packet switched services. It is based on temporary or permanent logical circuits being established.

Bibliography

Audio and video

Jennings, Roger (1994) *Windows 3.1 Multimedia*, Que Corporation, ISBN 1-56529-060-7.

Buford, John F. Koegel (1994) *Multimedia Systems*, ACM Press, ISBN 0-201-53258-1.

Computer communications

Aldred, B. K., Bonsall, G. W., Lambert, H. S. and Mitchell,H. D. (1995). 'Multimedia Communication Services for Realtime Collaboration', *IBM Systems Journal*, (to be published Autumn 1995).

Griffiths, John M. (1990). *ISDN Explained,* J. F. Wiley & Sons Ltd., ISBN 0-471-92675-2.

IBM Lakes Collaborative Working: Architecture and Programmer's Guide (1994). International Business Machines Inc.

Kessler, Gary C. (1990). *ISDN Concepts, Facilities and Services,* McGraw-Hill Inc., ISBN 0-07-0342-42-3.

Sheldon, Tom (1994). *Lan Times Encyclopaedia of Networking,* McGraw-Hill Inc., ISBN 0-07-8819-65-2.

CCIR standards

601-2, Encoding parameters for digital television, (1990) Dusseldorf.

Computer supported cooperative work

Baecker, R. (1992), *Readings in Groupware and CSCW,* Morgan Kaufmann, ISBN 1-5586-0241-0.

Communications of the ACM, 'User agents', July 1994.

Ellis C.A., Gibbs S.J., Rein G.L.; 'Groupware—Some issues and experiences', *Communications of the ACM,* Vol 24, No 1, January 1991.

Hopper, A., Harter, A. and Blackie, T. (1993). *The active badge system,* INTERCHI '93; Conference Proceedings, pp. 533–4, ACM Press.

Human Factors in Computing Systems: Sponsored by the ACM SIGCHI; INTERCHI '93 Amsterdam 1993; CHI '94 Boston; ACM Press.

IEEE COMSOC International Workshop on Multimedia Communications: Multimedia '92, 4th. Workshop, Monterey April 1992; Multimedia '94, 5th. Workshop, Kyoto May 1994.

Marco, D. and Bock, G. (1992).*Groupware: Software for CSCW,* IEEE Press, ISBN 0-8186-2637-2.

Proceedings of the Conference on Computer-Supported Cooperative Work: Sponsored by the ACM SIGCHI and SIGOIS; CSCW'86 Austin, Oct 1986; CSCW'88 Portland, Oct 1988; CSCW'90, Los Angeles, Oct 1990; CSCW'92 Toronto, Nov 1992; CSCW'94 Raleigh, Oct 1994; ACM Press.

Proceedings of the European Conference on Computer-Supported Cooperative Work: 2nd ESCW Amsterdam, Sept 1991, Kluwer; 3rd ESCW Milan 1993.

ISO/IEC standards

9660, CD-ROM table of content and directory structure.

10149, CD-ROM data track format.

10918, Digital compression and coding of continuous-tone images, 1993. Also ITU-T recommendation T.81. (JPEG)

11544, Coded representation of picture and audio information - progressive bi-level image compression. Also ITU-T recommendation T.82. (JBIG)

11172, Coding of moving pictures and associated audio for digital storage media at up to about 1.5 Mbits/s., 1993.

ITU-T recommendations

Prior to March 1993, the International Telegraph and Telephone Consultative Committee (CCITT) was the permanent organ of the International Telecommunication Union (ITU) responsible for studying technical, operating and tariff questions and issuing recommendations on them with a view to standardizing telecommunications on a worldwide basis. The CCITT was replaced on 1 March 1993 by the ITU-Telecommunications Standardization Sector (ITU-T). The World Telecommunication Standardization Conference (WTSC), which meets every four years, establishes the topics for study by the ITU-T study groups, which, in their turn, produce recommendations. These are subsequently submitted for approval to the WTSC and, if approved, become approved recommendations (i.e. standards).

In this section, all standards and recommendations will be attributed to the ITU-T, even though they may have originated under the auspices of the CCITT. Similarly, no distinction will be made between approved and proposed recommendations, in part because proposals are generally implemented by operators and suppliers before they gain final approval.

The numbering process for ITU-T standards is complex; the following may be of use:

Approved recommendations are published every four years, following WTSC approval. They are published in a set of books which are known by the colour of their covers:

1976	orange
1980	yellow
1984	red
1988	blue

The blue book is now, to a large extent, superseded by the new white recommendations which appear in separate booklets.

The recommendations are grouped in several series, each containing related topics. The more relevant of these series are:

G series	telecommunication transmission systems
H series	visual telephony
I series	general ISDN
Q series	signalling systems

T series	terminal equipment and protocols for telematic services
V series	data communications over the switched telephone n/w
X series	dedicated data communications networks

Complexity arises from the multiple designation of certain recommendations, i.e. Q.931 is also I.451. Additionally audiovisual topics have an AV designation illustrating their place in the audiovisual framework; recommendations here may be known by their AV number or their series number, i.e. G.711 is AV.251; H.261 is AV.261. The H.200 recommendation relates the AV series numbers to the topic series numbers.

The selection given has been chosen to allow a technical understanding of the principles behind videoconferencing and desktop conferencing systems. Many more standards exist; H.200 is a useful starting point, others are referenced from the ones listed below.

G.711	Pulse code modulation (PCM) of audio frequencies
G.722	7 kHz audio-coding within 64 kbits/s.
G.725	System aspects for the use of the 7 kHz audio codec within 64 kbits/s.
G.728	Coding of speech at 16 kbits/s. using low-delay excited linear projection
H.200	Framework for recommendations for audiovisual services
H.221	Frame structure for a 64 to 1920 kbits/s. channel in audiovisual teleservices
H.230	Frame-synchronous control and indication signals for audiovisual systems
H.231	Multi-point control units for audiovisual systems using digital channels up to 2 Mbits/s.
H.242	System for establishing communication between audiovisual terminals using digital channels up to 2 Mbits/s.
H.243	Procedures for establishing communication between three or more audiovisual terminals using digital channels up to 2 Mbits/s.
H.261	Video codec for audiovisual services at *p* x 64 kbits/s.
H.320	Visual telephone systems and equipment
I.430	ISDN basic user network interface—link layer specification
Q.921	ISDN user-network interface—data link layer specification
Q.922	ISDN data link layer specification for frame mode bearer services
Q.931	ISDN user-network interface layer 3. Specification for basic call control
T.120	Overview of AGC recommendations
T.121	Audiographic conferencing
T.122	Multi-point communications services for audiographics and audiovisual conferencing—service definition
T.123	Protocol stacks for audiographic and audiovisual teleconferencing applications
T.124	Generic conference control for audiovisual and audiographic terminals and multi-point control units
T.125	Multi-point communication service for audiographic and audiovisual conferencing—protocol specification
T.AVC	High level audio and video control
T.MBFT	Multipoint binary file transfer
T.SI	Still image conferencing application
X.200	Reference model of open systems interconnection for CCITT applications
X.224	Transport protocol specification for open systems interconnection for CCITT applications
X.225	Session protocol specification for open systems interconnection for CCITT applications
X.226	Presentation protocol specification for open systems interconnection for CCITT applications
X.227	Association control protocol specification for open systems interconnection for CCITT applications

Index